Support in Times of No Support

Wolfgang Frindte • Ina Frindte

Support in Times of No Support

A Social Psychological Search for Traces

 Springer

Wolfgang Frindte
Institut of Communication Research
Friedrich-Schiller-University Jena
Jena, Germany

Ina Frindte
Jena, Germany

ISBN 978-3-658-38636-8   ISBN 978-3-658-38637-5   (eBook)
https://doi.org/10.1007/978-3-658-38637-5

This Springer imprint is published by the registered company Springer Fachmedien Wiesbaden GmbH, part of Springer Nature.
The registered company address is: Abraham-Lincoln-Str. 46, 65189 Wiesbaden, Germany

Preface

Only if one has a sense of the direction of history [...] can one love earthly reality and believe – with charity – that there is still room for hope (Eco, in Martini & Eco 1999, p. 28).

It is this hope that has driven us in writing this book, the hope for and interest in a future worth living, for ourselves, our children and our grandchildren.

We thank our daughters, sons-in-law and grandchildren for the patience they had to muster when we were not with them in real life or even just in our thoughts now and then, but with our texts.

We thank the Italian part of the family for their help with Italian.

We also do not want to omit the names of two friends and colleagues who helped us to put the text down on paper in a comprehensible way and to whom we owe many a suggestion for further writing. Matthias John has once again proven himself to be an excellent connoisseur of philosophy and history and has critically scrutinized each of our arguments for fit and comprehensibility. Many thanks. Daniel Geschke did the same and provided us with new social science sources and ideas. We also thank him from the bottom of our hearts.

We found inspiration for our social psychological search for fixed points in moving times in Umberto Eco. And so it is also an homage à Eco.

Of course, we are solely liable for what we have written.

We have had a good working relationship with the Springer-Verlag publishing house for a long time now. This time, too, the alliance has proven its worth. Our special thanks therefore go to Ms. Eva Brechtel-Wahl, Dr. Astrid Horlacher, Mr. Kent Muller, Mr. Shubham Khare and Mr. Manigandan Jayabalan for their help in completing the final manuscript.

Note in August 2022: The first German edition of the book was published before the Corona pandemic and before Russia's war of aggression on Ukraine. In the years 2020 to 2022, the times have become even more unstable and the search for support has become greater.

Jena, Germany   Ina Frindte
in August 2019   Wolfgang Frindte

Contents

About the Authors

Ina Frindte is a graduate physicist (Friedrich Schiller University of Jena 1977); 1977–1981 scientific assistant in the field of medical device development at the research center of Carl Zeiss Jena; 1981–1991 project manager for hospital and ophthalmic optics (Carl Zeiss Jena); and 1991–2018 senior manager for medical technology (Analytik Jena AG). She is involved in planning and realization of projects in Germany, Russia, India, United Arab Emirates, Qatar, Greece and Egypt, among others.

Wolfgang Frindte Prof. i. R. Dr. phil. habil., graduate psychologist (Friedrich Schiller University Jena 1974), 1981 doctorate and 1986 habilitation. From 2008 to March 2017, he was head of the Department of Communication Psychology at the Institute of Communication Science at Friedrich Schiller University Jena; 1998–2005 visiting professor for Communication and Media Psychology or Applied Social Psychology at the Institute of Psychology at Leopold Franzens University Innsbruck; and February to April 2004 fellow at the Bucerius Institute of the University of Haifa (Israel). Since 2007, he is member of the academic board of the Human Communication Program at Dresden International University. His research interests are macro-social stress and terrorism research, xenophobia, anti-Semitism, right-wing extremism, digital media and violence.

List of Figures

List of Tables

1

Introduction: The Foucault Pendulum and the Search for the Fixed Point

There at last I saw the pendulum. The ball, free-floating at the end of a long metallic thread fixed high in the arch of the choir, described its wide constant oscillations with majestic isochrony (Eco, 1990, p. 9).[1]

Thus begins the novel *Foucault's Pendulum* by *Umberto Eco*. The title of the book refers to the pendulum designed by the French physicist *Léon Foucault* to demonstrate the rotation of the earth. *Léon Foucault,* born in Paris in 1819 and died there in 1868, based his design on experiments by *Vincenzo Viviani,* a student of *Galileo Galilei.* As early as 1661, Viviani observed that pendulums begin to turn clockwise when they are heavy enough and suspended from a long rope. Viviani could not explain this effect conclusively. It was not until Léon Foucault that he succeeded. He experimented with ropes of different lengths and various pendulums. In March 1851, he presented a pendulum to the Parisian public in the Panthéon – consisting of a 28 kg ball suspended from a 67 m long rope. The pendulum swung and rotated. Gravity could not be the cause, because it acts vertically and pulls the pendulum downwards. According to Foucault's interpretation, it could only be the ground, the earth, that was moving. Foucault was also able to prove his experiment mathematically. According to this, the pendulum turns in the opposite direction to the earth's rotation, most clearly observable at the north pole (there it turns clockwise) and at the south pole (here counterclockwise); at the equator, such a pendulum would swing, but would not perform any rotational movement.

---

[1] All quotes from Umberto Eco that we use in this book were not taken from original Italian publications, but from German translations of Eco's works.

W. Frindte, I. Frindte, *Support in Times of No Support,*
https://doi.org/10.1007/978-3-658-38637-5_1

Today, Foucault pendulums can be found in many church buildings, museums and public buildings, including the San Petronio Basilica in Bologna, the German Museum in Munich, the United Nations Headquarters. The world's heaviest Foucault pendulum hung from 1931 to 1986 in St. Isaac's Cathedral in Leningrad, now St. Petersburg. One of the latest installations of the pendulum hangs in the Dominican Church in Münster and was designed by *Gerhard Richter,* one of Germany's most famous painters. In 2017, the church, which until then had been used primarily by the Catholic university community, was profaned by the auxiliary bishop of the Münster diocese, i.e. officially deconsecrated as a place of worship. In the run-up to Richter's installation, there were critical voices, namely from the ranks of theologians at Münster University, who feared a disrespect for the place of worship despite the fact that it had already been profaned. At the presentation of his project, Richter had spoken, among other things, of a "small victory of natural science over the church" (Rauterberg, 2018). Now this did not suit some theologians at all. They even speculated that Richter was trying to inherit religion with his art. Although the Catholic Church rehabilitated *Galileo Galilei* in November 1992 and thus also recognized the heliocentric world view – at least formally.

After all, since the installation was opened to the public in June 2018, visitors have flocked to the church to marvel at Richter's pendulum.

It does move, the earth. The Foucault pendulum illustrates this impressively. In this respect, the pendulum is not only a pendulum, but also a symbol for the correctness of the heliocentric world view.

For *Umberto Eco,* however, the Foucault pendulum is more than just an illustration of the victory of the natural sciences over the traditional church belief that the earth is the center of the universe. Eco uses the pendulum as a powerful metaphor. At the beginning of the novel, Eco transports his protagonist Casaubon to the Parisian abbey church of Saint-Martin-des-Champs, now part of the Musée des Arts et Métiers. There, Casaubon looks at the pendulum, moved, and realizes:

> I knew that the earth rotated, and I with it, and Saint-Martin-des-Champs, and all Paris with me; we all rotated together under the pendulum, which in reality never changed its plane of oscillation, for up there, from where it hung down, and along the ideal extension of the thread, endlessly up to the farthest galaxies, up there stood, motionless for all eternity, the Fixed Point …(Eco, 1990, p. 11).

The Fixed Point: Aren't people constantly striving to find the fixed, fixed points in life? And doesn't life only appear to be meaningful and significant, worth living, and shapeable, when we have found it, the fixed point. Although everything moves and flows, we do not give up our search.

But where and how can the fixed points be found? Can they be found in the ideologies, which anyway only reflect "false consciousness" – as Friedrich Engels wrote in a letter to *Franz Mehring* on 14 July 1893? (Engels 1968, p. 97, original: Engels, 1893). Or are the fixed points to be found in religions, whose object is to "preserve the memory of a time …long past" – according to *Maurice Halbwachs* (the French sociologist who was murdered in the Buchenwald concentration camp on March 16, 1945; 1985, p. 261)? Or do the media, namely social media, even provide the fixed points? Is social media, is the digital the new substitute for religion (Cachelin, 2017)? And what about the political parties? *Peer Steinbrück,* the former German finance minister and later SPD candidate for chancellor, opined in an interview with the *Süddeutsche Zeitung* in October 2018:

> What we need are firm positions that are clearly stated. Citizens expect parties to stand for something, to explain it and not to exhaust themselves in self-centredness (Gammelin, 2018).

There are many sides and facets to people's pursuit of the fixed points – on both a large and small scale: We locate ourselves in a more or less imaginary political spectrum that still maps the seating arrangements of democratic parliaments. Now and then we think that believing in God makes us blessed.

However, if one takes a closer look at the results of relevant social science studies, one cannot help but notice: Satisfied people are mostly those with a job, good health, a spouse and trusting friends (Grunewald, 2017).

People strive for fulfillment in their work, for harmony in their social relationships. People desire health. They like to orient themselves to friends and close people. But they also appreciate the synchronization of things, the favorite restaurant, the favorite pub, the favorite sweater, the baker on the corner. They try to make the fixed points of their lives fixed and visible through symbols, deeds, cars, wedding rings. The fixed points are also supposed to become engrained in thinking and feeling as inner schemes, structures, categories with which people think they can cope with everyday chaos. They construct reality for themselves in order to find a foothold.

Psychology, namely social psychology, has enough findings and insights to point to the individual and communal search for stability and fixed points. In Innsbruck, *Tatjana* Schnell (2016) deals with the meaning of life from a psychological perspective. For her, reason, morality, love, community, care, but also religion, spirituality and self-knowledge are important sources of meaning. *Yuval Noah Harari,* an Israeli historian whose books have stormed the bestseller lists in recent years, thinks relatively little of all these ways of developing a sense of the meaning of life. Rather than searching for the meaning of life, we humans should be asking how we might end suffering (Harari, 2018, p. 401). Harari thus refers to a topic that has preoccupied Buddhism for more than 2000 years.

Happiness research (yes, it really does exist) comes to similar conclusions. In two relatively small longitudinal studies, the Grant Study and the *Glueck Study,* researchers[2] at Harvard University in Boston studied US Americans for 75 years and asked them what makes people happy. The answer: it is the good and close relationships with people close to us that make us happier and healthier (Study of Adult Development, 2019).

Now, as we know, a happy life and a meaningful life do not have to be one and the same, but having good and close relationships can make a life happy and meaningful, as a 2017 survey in the US shows. In a representative survey, the Washington-based polling institute *Pew Research Center* asked almost 5000 US Americans to describe in their own words what gives them support, meaning and security in their lives. Almost 70% named family, 34% work and career, 23% money and 20% referred to their faith (Reserarch, 2018).

According to a 2017 EU survey, an astonishing 94% of Germans are happy with their family life. The very happiest with their family life are the Danes with 99% and the least happy are the Bulgarians with 74%. 95% of Germans are happy with their life in Germany. Even happier with their country are again the Danes with 99%. The greatest differences between the EU countries are to be found in the answers to the question about happiness in one's job or current occupation. Here the Irish lead with 84%. Among Germans, 69% are happy in their job or occupation and the Greeks (37%) and the Bulgarians, Cypriots and French feel the least happy in their job or occupation, with 49% agreement in each case (Eurobarometer, 2017).

One could therefore conclude that for Germans and many other Europeans, happiness with one's family, one's job and the country in which one lives seem to be part of a meaningful life and one of the fixed points in life that provide stability. However, national differences in the perception of happiness and the meaningfulness of different areas of life cannot be overlooked. While, for example, 71% of Irish people, 69% of Austrians and Luxembourgers or 60% of Germans believe that every citizen in their own country has the chance to be successful and happy, only 28% in Portugal and Spain see this. Younger

---

[2] As a rule, we try to use gender-conscious language in this book. This does not always succeed and does not fit in some places. We ask for your understanding for this.

people, industrial workers and the unemployed in these countries in particular are very pessimistic about their chances of becoming successful and happy in their own country. Greeks (31%) and Bulgarians (29%) also think that the chances of success are not particularly evenly distributed in their country.

Where then, it must be asked, do people in economically weak countries find support and meaning in life?

Researchers *Shigehiro Oishi* and *Ed Diener* (2014) proposed an interesting and understandable hypothesis: They hypothesized that people of poor nations – despite worse conditions – feel more meaning in their lives than people from wealthier nations. The authors attribute this to the role that religiosity plays, especially in the populations of poor nations. Religion gives people of faith answers to the "biggest" questions in life and offers them support in everyday life. In a study conducted in 132 countries, the authors tested and confirmed their assumption. People in poorer nations (as measured by gross domestic product) were more religious and felt more meaning in their lives than people in richer nations. The different levels of religiosity in poorer and richer nations were shown to be the deciding factor for support in life, compared to other conditions such as education level or birth rate.

Not uninteresting in this context is the well-known cultural theory by *Geert Hofstede* (2001). The aim of his research was to identify similarities and differences between the various nations of the world in order to better understand why certain ideas or business practices work better in some countries than in others. The basic idea behind his approach is that cultures shape the values of their members and their behavior. To investigate this, Hofstede analyzed internal surveys of work-related values with 1,16,000 IBM employees in more than 40 countries in the 1960s and 1970s. As a result, Hofstede formulated six cultural dimensions that can be used to characterize work-related value systems in different countries: *Power Distance, Uncertainty Avoidance, Individualism versus Collectivism, Masculinity versus Femininty, Long-Term versus Short-Term Orientation,* and *Indulgence versus Restraint* .

The cultural dimension that is exciting in our context is *uncertainty avoidance.* This refers to the degree to which members of a culture feel threatened by uncertain or unknown situations and seek support and security. Almost all cultures have developed rules and security systems to protect themselves from uncertainty and risk. For example, technologies are developed and used to protect against natural risks; legal systems serve to provide protection against behavior by third parties that endangers the norm; religions are intended to provide support and security when all other protective mechanisms fail.

People look for fixed points in their realities in order to find a foothold. But which fixed points are we actually talking about? Is it about avoiding insecurity, not losing control over one's own life, finding the meaning of life, being happy? Or is it even about the fixed point from which, with a long lever, the earth could be unhinged? "Give me a point where I can step and I will move the earth," is the surviving statement of *Archimedes of Syracuse* (probably 287 BC to 212 BC). While *René Descartes* rigorously moved the said point into human thought, *Hannah Arendt* supposes the point "probably much further from the earth" (Arendt, 2002, p. 335, original 1958).

But perhaps we humans, in our search for fixed points, simply want to find ways to be able to face the large and small threats in our lives? It seems to be common knowledge that people, when they feel threatened, look for stability and security in order to avoid the threats or to be able to deal with them in one way or another.

A few years ago, the second author of this book and physicist explained to the first author, husband and psychologist, a formula that can be used to describe the movement of the Foucault pendulum and that can be expressed in words something like this: The period of oscillation of a thread pendulum (the pendulum of a clock or, indeed, the Foucault pendulum) depends on the length of the pendulum and on the place where the pendulum is located. The mass of the pendulum has no influence on the period of oscillation. The number and the acceleration due to gravity of an object at a given location also play an important role in said formula. Admittedly, the first author found it difficult to understand. But the Foucault pendulum has haunted his work ever since. Then, in the summer of 2018, the authors stood in the Musée des Arts et Métiers in Paris. The pendulum swung on a long rope under the dome of the former convent church of Saint-Martin-des-Champs. And we now felt like Casaubon in Umberto Eco's book *Foucault's Pendulum*. We wondered what could be at the ideal end of the thread pendulum. The fixed point that could give us support and security in an uncertain world and difficult times? What uncertainties, what times or even what threats are we actually talking about? Where can we find the fixed points, the safe spaces of our lives? This book deals with these and other questions. We found motivation and inspiration for the book in *Umberto Eco*. And so it is also a homage to Eco.

We grew up in the GDR and still live in the east of Germany. Place, time and especially the last 30 years have shaped our view of the world. Some of the arguments and memories shared in this book, e.g. of the time before and after 1989, are also shaped by this world view. In addition, in a tried and tested manner, we have also drawn on our own reflections that have been published elsewhere (e.g. Frindte, 1998, 2013; Frindte & Dietrich, 2017). We have referred to the relevant passages in the text. Then it is easier for the critics to compare.

In the first part of the book, we recall, among other things, the loss of fixed points after the end of the GDR and the threats to democracy posed by right-wing populist and extreme right-wing movements or by terrorism. New threats, e.g. through fake news, climate change, and the apparent clash of civilizations and its staging in the media, are the focus of the second part. In the third part of the book, we deal with the question of whom the major and minor narratives about the "end of history", about national foundations, anti-Semitic conspiracies and Islamist fundamentalisms promise support and security. We concretize our social-psychological search for the fixed points, the possibilities of finding hold, in the fourth part. In our search for visions and utopian islands, we come across innovative, optimistic minorities in the fifth part, which encourage us to assert that the times of the great real utopias of a humane and peaceful future are not over, but are just beginning. Real utopias are feasible and successful if they go beyond the limits of what has been done so far, start from the free spaces of the present, formulate alternatives for a better future and are put into perspective by innovative minorities. A virtual conversation with *Umberto Eco* concludes our social-psychological search for traces, which is not free of subjective perspectives. One can accept, share or even criticize them. We rely entirely on an open-minded readership.

References

Arendt, H. (2002). *Vita activa. München: Piper. Original: The Human Condition* (p. 1958). Chicago: Chicago Press.

Cachelin, J. L. (2017). *Internetgott – Die Religion des Silicon Valley*. Bern: Stämpfli.

Eco, U. (1990). *Das Foucaultsche Pendel*. Berlin: Verlag Volk und Welt.

Engels, F. (1968, Original: 1893). Brief Engels an Franz Mehring vom 14. Juli 1893. *Marx-Engels Werke, Bd. 39*. Berlin: Dietz.

Eurobarometer. (2017). Future of Europe. https://www.politico.eu/wp-content/uploads/2017/11/ebs_467_social_issues_en.pdf. Accessed: 17. Marz 2019.

Frindte, W. (1998). *Soziale Konstruktionen*. Wiesbaden: Westdeutscher Verlag.

Frindte, W. (2013). *Der Islam und der Westen. Sozialpsychologische Aspekte einer Inszenierung*. Wiesbaden: Springer VS.

Frindte, W., & Dietrich, N. (Hrsg.). (2017). *Muslime, Flüchtlinge und Pegida. Sozialpsychologische und kommunikationswissenschaftliche Studien in Zeiten globaler Bedrohungen*. Wiesbaden: Springer VS.

Gammelin, C. (2018). Steinbrück: Bankenrettung mitschuld an Krise der Volksparteien. *Süddeutsche Zeitung*. https://www.sueddeutsche.de/wirtschaft/peer-steinbrueck-spd-1.4192241. Accessed: 21. Nov. 2018.

Grunewald, M. (2017). Kirchentag 2017 – Steigert Religiosität das Glücksempfinden? http://blog.iw-akademie.de/2017/05/29/kirchentag-2017-was-die-religiositaet-mit-der-lebenszufriedenheit-zu-tun-hat/. Accessed: 21. Nov. 2018.

Harari, Y. N. (2018). *21 Lektionen für das 21. Jahrhundert*. München: Beck. English Version: 21 Lessons for the 21st Century. London: Random House.

Hofstede, G. (2001). *Lokales Denken, globales Handeln: Interkulturelle Zusammenarbeit und globales Management*. München: Beck. English Version: Think locally, act globally: Cultural constraints in personnel management. Management and international review, 1998. *38*, 7–26).

Oishi, S., & Diener, E. (2014). Residents of poor nations have a greater sense of meaning in life than residents of wealthy nations. *Psychological Science, 25*(2), 422–430.

Rauterberg, H. (2018). Gott raus, Kunst rein. In Münster hängt Gerhard Richter ein Foucaultsches Pendel in eine leere Kirche. *Taugt das als Religionsersatz? DIE ZEIT, Nr. 26*.

Pew Reserarch. (2018). Where Americans find meaning in life. http://www.pewforum.org/2018/11/20/where-americans-find-meaning-in-life/#measuring-meaning. Accessed: 5. Jan. 2019.

Schnell, T. (2016). *Psychologie des Lebenssinns*. Berlin: Springer-Verlag.

Study of Adult Development. (2019). https://www.adultdevelopmentstudy.org/grantandglueckstudy. Accessed: 13. Jan. 2019.

Part I

Of Threats Great and Small – Memories

2

The End of Cosiness

To paraphrase a quotation from *Christa Wolf,* one could say: we can know when the end begins, but what signs point to the coming end even before the end? If there were rules, they would have to be passed on. In clay, in stone, handed down. What would it say? It would say, among other things, "Do not be deceived by those who are your own."[1]

Long before the supposed end of an epoch, its end times had already been announced. *Umberto Eco's* book "Foucault's Pendulum" appeared in the original Italian edition in 1988. A few years earlier, West German intellectuals had stated a fundamental structural crisis of modernity. In 1985, *Jürgen Habermas* diagnosed a "new lack of clarity" in the January issue of the magazine "Merkur". "The future," Habermas wrote in the article, "has negative connotations; on the threshold of the 21st century, the horror panorama looms. At the threshold of the 21st century, the horror panorama of the worldwide endangerment of general interests of life is emerging: the spiral of the arms race, the uncontrolled proliferation of nuclear weapons, the structural impoverishment of the developing countries, unemployment and growing social imbalances in the developed countries, problems of environmental pollution, large-scale technologies operating close to catastrophe are the keywords that have penetrated the public consciousness via mass media" Habermas, 1985, p. 1 f.).

---

[1] The original quote is: "You can know when war begins, but when does the pre-war begin? If there were rules, they'd have to be passed on. In clay, in stone, handed down. What would it say? There would be, among other phrases: Do not be deceived by those who are your own" (Christa Wolf, Kassandra 1984, p. 268).

© The Author(s), under exclusive license to Springer Fachmedien Wiesbaden GmbH, part of Springer Nature 2022
W. Frindte, I. Frindte, *Support in Times of No Support,*
https://doi.org/10.1007/978-3-658-38637-5_2

A year later, *Ulrich Beck* created the succinct and catchy concept of the *risk society*. Social production of wealth, Beck (1986) argues, cannot be had without risks. In contrast to social production in the industrial society of the 19th century, these risks in the industrial societies of the late 20th century are not only collectively and medially reflected, but consciously produced. In other words, today we know whether the risks we produce through production in particular and in the way we live our lives in general. We know and reflect on the risks of globalized mass production, hunger in the Third World, the increasing ecological collapse in the regions of the rainforest or at the poles, the patchwork of civil wars, the new or revived old fundamentalisms, the worldwide migration movements, and so on. And we argue about whether these and the many other risks are man-made or just illusions of left-utopian cranks.

Reflecting on the risks in the industrial societies of the late 20th century, however, was not only an obsession of thoughtful people in the West. In the late 1970s, small but quite effective social movements also formed in the East, namely in the GDR, whose supporters were critically concerned not only with the mass destruction of the environment by social production. Environmental, peace and human rights problems formed the core of the confrontation with the rulers in the SED state. It was primarily in the churches in the GDR that the places of origin and organization of these social movements developed. The intellectual centers of the independent peace and environmental movement included the Kirchliches Forschungsheim in Wittenberg, the Environmental Library in East Berlin's Zionskirche and later in other locations, the green-ecological network "Arche" with regional groups in Berlin, Erfurt, Halle, in Greifswald, Dresden and Leipzig, but also various local groups of the International Association of Physicians for the Prevention of Nuclear War (IPPNW). Psychologists founded a committee "GDR Psychologists for Peace" in the mid-1980s; not only to work for world peace, but to critically examine the economic, ecological and political problems in their own country.

The fact that such activities, centers and the independent peace and environmental movement were not only eyed critically by the state security in the GDR, but that peace and environmental activists were persecuted and criminalized, should not be forgotten. For example, on the night of November 24–25, 1987, the Stasi raided the environmental library of Berlin's Zion Church. Seven people, including a 14-year-old, were arrested and later released. Western media reported on the raid and the Environmental Library, which became known overnight in East and West and became a symbol of GDR opposition.

And then came the turning point. At first, there was no more talk of the risks of modernity and their reflection. After "Marx's ghosts" (Derrida, 1995)[2] apparently left the world stage in defeat, the global race of systems seemed to have been settled.

The systemic contradiction between capitalism and communism, because one of the opposites, namely communism, had dropped out of the contest, had lost the form in which it could operate.[3]

And for a short time, with the "end of history" from 1989, the further course of world political events seemed clear. At the end of the 20th century, "liberal democracy" had prevailed over its authoritarian competitors (fascism and communism) as the sole and "final human form of government" and thus the "end of history" had been reached. At least this is how the US-American political scientist *Francis Fukuyama* argued in the summer of 1989 in an essay that became famous with the title "The End of History?" and in the book "The End of History and the Last Man" published three years later, which was simultaneously translated into 14 languages (Fukuyama, 1992). Under the impression of the terrorist attacks of September 11, 2001, however, Fukuyama became more skeptical about the final triumph of the Western liberal world order (Fukuyama, 2004). Today he is concerned about its decline (Fukuyama, 2018).

> But the worst diagnosticians of any era are always the contemporaries. My giants have taught me that there are transit zones where the coordinates are missing and one does not see very well into the future, which is why one does not yet understand the lists of reason and the imperceptible plots of the zeitgeist (Eco, 2019, p. 32; emphasis in the original).

But did it not seem as if an epochal turning point had been reached in 1989? Under *Mikhail Gorbachev*, the Soviet Union had relinquished its supremacy in Eastern Europe; in Poland, Hungary and Czechoslovakia,

---

[2] *Jacques Derrida's* book "Specters of Marx: The State of the Debt, the Work of Mourning and the New International" was published in the original French in 1993. Derrida, like, for example, Louis Althusser, Roland Barthes, Jean Baudrillard, Gilles Deleuze, Michel Foucault, Jean-Francois Lyotard and others, is one of the great philosophers, all of whom – somehow also inspired by Karl Marx and Marxism – have, not infrequently with steep theses, sharply criticized the prevailing social relations. Derrida believed that the ghosts that Marx and Engels made the subject of the "Communist Manifesto" are far from dead. Marx had to be appropriated anew in order to be able to adequately criticize and (perhaps) change today's world.

[3] This formulation is a reference to Karl Marx, who occasionally noted that the method by which real contradictions are resolved is by creating a form in which they can move (Marx 1977; Das Kapital, vol. 1, MEW, vol. 23, p. 118, original: Marx, 1867).

reform movements were growing into decisive political and system-changing forces; the economies of the former socialist countries were no match for the West; the reunification of East and West Germany could no longer be halted.

In November 1990, 32 European countries as well as the USA and Canada declared the Cold War over in Paris. This marked the end of the "age of extremes" (Hobsbawm, 1994) and also of the grand narratives, the system-stabilizing grand myths and the social utopias containing ideas about a harmonious, rationally organized coexistence of people in a well-structured community.

The year 1989 is thus not only the year in which the GDR collapsed and East and West Germans celebrated their honeymoon, which, however, was over very quickly and had to give way to a harsh married life, but also marks the keystone of that epoch in which the two great world systems stood in fundamental and cold opposition to each other.

> The year 1989 marked the beginning of the new era in which real or perceived local, national and global threats multiplied and the grand narratives were publicly adopted.

Not only did the "grand narratives" of socialist utopia seem to have come to an end with the collapse of "real existing socialism", but also the ideas about the constantly prospering capitalist society began to falter in view of the risks produced by highly developed industrial societies worldwide.

References

Beck, U. (1986). *Risikogesellschaft Auf dem Weg in eine andere Moderne*. Frankfurt a. M.: Suhrkamp.

Derrida, J. (1995). *Marx' Gespenster*. Frankfurt a. M.: Fischer.

Eco, U. (2019). *Auf den Schultern von Riesen*. München: Hanser.

Fukuyama, F. (1992). *Das Ende der Geschichte*. München: Kindler. English Version: The End of History and the last Man. Florence, MA: Free Press.

Fukuyama, F. (2004). *State-building: Governance and world order in the 21st century*. Ithaca: Cornell University Press.

Fukuyama, F. (2018). *Identity: Contemporary identity politics and the struggle for recognition*. London: Profile Books Ltd.

Habermas, J. (1985). Die Neue Unübersichtlichkeit Die Krise des Wohlfahrtsstaates und die Erschöpfung utopischer Energien. *Merkur, 39*(431), 1–14.

Hobsbawm, E. (1994). *The age of extremes: The short twentieth century, 1914–1991*. London: Michael Joseph.

Marx, K. (1977, Original: 1867). Das Kapital, Bd. 1. *Marx-Engels Werke, Band 23*. Berlin: Dietz.

Wolf, C. (1984). *Kassandra. Vier Vorlesungen. Eine Erzählung*. Berlin: Aufbau-Verlag.

3

Insecurities: From the End of the GDR

Until the mid-1980s, everything still seemed clear to many: The world was threatening but manageable. The West, with the United States of America at its head, faced the so-called Eastern Bloc, the socialist states led by the Soviet Union, in a harsh conflict called the Cold War. Both systems came close several times to a nuclear war that would have destroyed humanity.

However, there was hardly any great uncertainty within the leaderships of the respective systems as to who was to bear the responsibility for the dangers and threats. For the politicians in the Eastern bloc, the imperialist West and especially the "imperialist warmongers" in the FRG and the USA were the bad guys and responsible for the Cold War. They threatened the socialist states and world peace. And only socialism and the socialist states could secure peace on a world scale.

This idea was an essential part of the communist state ideology. This ideology with its pillars – anti-imperialism, anti-fascism and planned economy – was the fixed point to which not only the functionary elites in the socialist countries oriented themselves in order to find a *foothold*. Thus, the broad majority of the population in the GDR parroted the political-ideological empty formulas of imperialism threatening peace not only in order not to endanger their own individual position and possible social advancement, as the historian *Günther* Heydemann (2002) suspects. Even in anonymous surveys, it was not uncommon for a majority to agree with these ideological empty formulas.

© The Author(s), under exclusive license to Springer Fachmedien Wiesbaden GmbH, part of Springer Nature 2022
W. Frindte, I. Frindte, *Support in Times of No Support*,
https://doi.org/10.1007/978-3-658-38637-5_3

As an example: Between May and June 1986, the then Central Institute for Youth Research in Leipzig conducted such an anonymous survey with 3.910 GDR adults aged up to 50.

- 82.6 % of the respondents said they were completely convinced of the statement "The stronger socialism is, the more secure peace is"; 15.3% said they were only partially convinced.
- Of the statement "Imperialism and war belong directly together" 57.9% were completely convinced and 31.5% only partly convinced.
- "The Bundeswehr is an army with aggressive aims towards the socialist states" was considered true by 55.1%.

(Central Archive for Empirical Social Research Cologne, n.d.).

Certainly, doubts about such results are always appropriate. But the assumption that the state ideology of socialism was also part of the everyday consciousness of many GDR citizens cannot be completely dismissed.[1]

A not insignificant part of the GDR citizens was convinced of the feasibility of the socialist idea. The well-read people could refer to the famous sentence in the "Manifesto of the Communist Party" from 1848, according to which bourgeois society is lawfully followed by an association, "... in which the free development of each is the condition for the free development of all..." (Marx-Engels Works, Vol. 4, p. 482, original: 1848).

Such a conception of socialism places the autonomy and emancipation of the individual as a *conditio sine qua non* (as a necessary condition) for the humanistic development of society; not vice versa!

The practice, however, was different.

In the course of its development, the social system in the GDR structured itself more and more on the basis of administrative centralism. The facts are well known. The economy, culture, science, and everyday life came under the encroachment of the political system, whose claim to order developed into an end in itself. An everyday philosophy, which can also be described as a *control myth,* functioned as an implicit instruction for action with which the political actors attempted to legitimize their claim to political control.

This myth of the plannable, orderly and ultimately closed society was based primarily on the following postulates:

---

[1] In the following we fall back on considerations which we already presented some years ago (Frindte, 1994). This is therefore a self-quotation.

- A social system does not order itself; order must first be created and then strictly controlled.
- This order and control must be based on a unified ideology and universally shared values.
- Everything must be subordinated to the ideology. Everything that does not correspond to the given ideology must be tabooed.
- Order and control in the system must be hierarchically structured and secured. The top of the hierarchy makes the system-relevant decisions.

Society and its subsystems (economy, politics, education, jurisprudence, science, culture, etc.) developed highly hierarchical structures of management, administration and control, in which administrative influence "from above" was largely guaranteed, but the individual's scope for action and his or her degrees of freedom in dealing with society were increasingly reduced.

And this had consequences: The officially invoked centralism actually functioned as administrative authoritarianism. In this way, especially the "guardians" of power at the various points of social order and control alienated themselves from the humanist ideals of socialism. The exercise of political power by means of factually unjustified authority became the end in itself of their actions. The officially proclaimed consensus of interests between society and the individual was in fact realized as hierarchically secured conformism. The practical implementation of the *control myth* led to "GDR-specific" deformations of individual ways of thinking and acting. The compulsion to say something different from what one thinks and to do something different from what one believes to be right became a matter of course for many. For inter-individually very different reasons, the majority of the population – following this compulsion – largely conformed to the social demands. The individual reasons for social conformism may be very different. In his forms of public expression, the average GDR citizen was a conformist citizen. Only a few had the courage and strength to take on the role of oppositional, independent thinkers and actors.

Our behavior (we use the plural deliberately) was satirized very aptly by *Matthias Biskupek* in the "Weltbühne" shortly after the de facto end of the GDR:

We have always expressed our displeasure. Or at least murmured the displeasure out of us almost very clearly. We were brave fellow murrers. Although we formed the prescribed trellis when a high-ranking management visit was announced, it was actually a human chain even back then. When we were given flags to wave, we nevertheless held the flags bravely against the wind, so that they fluttered properly. Even in those days our shouts were so loud and impudent that they must have rung in the ears of the powerful. We did criticize the supply of vegetables, even the lack of it, and also the thousand little things. We denounced private land that did not belong to us. We almost returned the unjustly paid premiums – and the play, which contained such things, we watched frankly, regardless of all reprisals. On the first of May we deliberately held the banner at an angle, on which the unbreakable role and the glorious office were written in block letters (block! – letters). Everyone could see it… We were not afraid to call sleepyheads by name. We even reported on this or that sleepiness that could have harmed us out of sheer lack of vigilance… (Biskupek, 1990, p. 74).

The officially proclaimed proletarian internationalism was in fact realized in the GDR in permanent self-idealizations and Outgroup-stigmatizations. Such processes of idealization and stigmatization were activated above all in dealings with people who thought differently politically, but also in everyday social intercourse with foreigners: Foreigners in GDR times appeared – at least in most official pronouncements – mostly as the abstract others, as strangers who either needed help in solidarity or were representatives or sympathizers of the "class enemy." Concrete dealings with foreigners were usually limited to restricted holiday opportunities in the "friend's country" or to minimal and state-controlled work contacts. It is obvious that in this way only very undifferentiated political-ethnic stereotypes about other peoples could develop. The current problems of xenophobia and nationalism in East Germany also have their roots here.

The supposedly convinced anti-fascism in broad circles of the population was in fact a state-imposed anti-fascism, as *Ralph Giordano* noted.

Because it is a state and party anti-fascism, a summarily decreed one, and this under rape of easily verifiable history. The state and population of the GDR have been officially declared by the leadership there to be fellow victors, posthumously, so to speak, part of the anti-Hitler coalition, and this, of course, side by side with the Soviet Union. An adventurous lie! This transformation of fellow losers into triumphants did not … come from the people, but was regarded by the SED leadership as a necessary prerequisite for the new, socialist man, and his new, socialist morals and way of life, and was therefore decreed (Giordano, 1987, p. 219).

Those who began to found a new, humanistic society in East Germany in 1945 were convinced anti-fascists. They had to pay for their convictions during National Socialism with stays in concentration camps, fascist penitentiary or being forced into exile. Compared to the majority of the German people in the Soviet occupation zone at that time, the real anti-fascists of the first hours with their anti-fascism were clearly in the minority. However, they made their anti-fascist conviction – qua party and state policy – the measure and the official reference system for the majority of the population. By virtue of official anti-fascist policy, the silent, complicit followers of the Third Reich were denied the "grace of repentance" (Weiß, 1990, p. 15).

Some of the founding fathers and mothers of the GDR, however, found themselves on the grindstone of political dogma quite soon after its founding. Above all, those who came to the Soviet-occupied zone from English, Swedish, Mexican, or U.S. exile, such as *Anna Seghers, Walter Janka, Alfred Kantorowicz, Jürgen Kuczynski,* or *Paul Merker,* were suspected of being agents of U.S. imperialism, followers of Trotskyism, or simply cosmopolitans. They either left the GDR (according to Alfred Kantorowicz), were sentenced to long prison terms (Paul Merker), or officially conformed to the SED ideology (extensively Leo, 2018).

However, it should not be forgotten that there were certainly artists, writers, scientists, young and old people in the GDR who took responsibility for the crimes of National Socialism and tried to deal with its consequences. Often in clear contrast to the predefined anti-fascist ideology of the superiors. *Christa Wolf,* for example, breaks with a taboo in the GDR in her book *Kindheitsmuster (Patterns of Childhood), which* was also praised in the old Federal Republic, and deals with the flight and expulsion of Germans from Poland (Wolf, 1977). In 1969 *Jurek Becker* published the novel *Jakob der Lügner (Jacob the Liar),* which describes life in a ghetto during Nazi rule. *Franz Fühmann,* a member of the Reiter-SA during National Socialism and later a soldier in the Wehrmacht, dealt with National Socialist ideology and its consequences in his works and also increasingly recognized parallels between National Socialism and Stalinism.

In feature films, too, homage was paid not only to the anti-fascism of GDR citizens. One's own fellow traveler status in the times of National Socialism was certainly thematized, for example in the films "Naked Among Wolves" based on a novel by Bruno Apitz, "The Adventures of Werner Holt" (based on a novel by Dieter Noll), "The Murderers Are Among Us" (directed and written by Wolfgang Staudte) or "Professor Mamlock" (directed by Konrad Wolf, based on a play by Friedrich Wolf).

Under the protection of the Protestant Church, an independent branch of the *Aktion Sühnezeichen* initiative developed in the GDR from 1961 onwards. Young people from the GDR met in summer camps, undertook pilgrimages to Poland and the CSSR, and visited the Auschwitz death camp.

Certainly, anti-fascist ideology dominated the culture of remembrance and the way National Socialism was dealt with in the GDR. After Auschwitz, the GDR also took on a difficult legacy. It did not master it[2].

But, as is usually the case in history, critical minorities have also successfully resisted this ideological dominance.

Every systemically educated person knows that innovative developmental thrusts within a social system are usually to be expected from those subsystems that form the "edge" of the system and thus occupy minority positions. Whether a social system is capable of development therefore depends not insignificantly on how efficiently this system is able to deal with deviating subsystems, with minorities.

Thus, even in the GDR, individual groups and communities repeatedly evaded or resisted the social system's precepts. In this way, the *control myth* within administrative socialism was also dampened and redirected in various ways.

In subcultural and ecological niches, some tried to evade the political demands for order and control and to find a *foothold in small things*. In the former GDR, for example, the allotment garden clubs and aquarists in the "Kulturbund" had subcultural structures in a typically German way. For artist groups and various youth groups, such as punks, goths, or skinheads, "refusal" and "getting out" were important motives for action. Opposition and opposition to the GDR state played the driving role in small neo-Nazi milieus. A working group of the GDR Ministry of the Interior counted more than 15,000 people moving in these milieus at the end of the 1980s (Heitzer, 2018, p. 17), which included youthful skinheads, fascists, and violent football fans as well as latent anti-Semites and right-wing extremists of various ages. At the latest when right-wing extremist skinheads attacked a punk concert in East Berlin's Zion Church in October 1987, beating up concertgoers and shouting "Sieg Heil" and "Jew pigs", these milieus also became known to the public. However, the Ministry for State Security (MfS) had been collecting reports of such incidents since the late 1970s. As early as 1978 and 1979, the MfS recorded "188 cases of 'written agitation with a fascist character' such as the graffiti on a Soviet memorial. It was aware of incidents such as the use of the 'Hitler salute', 'birthday celebrations on 20 April, swastika graffiti, shouting Nazi slogans and occasionally also attacks on foreigners who could be seen to be of non-European origin'" (Süß, 1993, p. 17 f.).

---

[2] For further reading, we recommend the book "Nach Auschwitz: Schwieriges Erbe DDR" (Heitzer et al., Heitzer, 2018). The editors and authors argue for a paradigm shift in GDR contemporary history research.

Meanwhile, members of various oppositional groups resisted the state's claims to order and control in order to create new visions for a humanistic democracy (e.g., church and non-church peace and eco-movements). The oppositional groups were guided by the idea that social change was possible through consistent and stable influence of social minorities.

The official ways in which political power dealt with subcultures and oppositional movements were quite different. The existence of so-called subcultures was usually subject to a reinterpretation of reality. Thus, at the latest since the mid-1970s, official party and state documents interpreted those subcultural leisure activities with which large sections of the population attempted to escape from official policy prescriptions in a largely "silent" manner (e.g. through involvement in allotment garden movements) as specific forms of the "socialist way of life". Such subcultural leisure activities could be sure of state support. Those subcultures, on the other hand, that tried to publicly represent ideas of norms and values that did not fit the "socialist" pattern (e.g. "rebellious" young punks or right-wing extremist skinheads) were stigmatized or – like the right-wing extremist skinheads – punished as "hooligans" with sometimes severe prison sentences (Quent, 2016).

In dealing with opposition groups, the political power apparatus also developed various coping mechanisms.. Political oppositions existed in the GDR from the beginning of its founding. They first appeared on the public scene before and after 1953 (e.g. the groups around *Walter Janka* and *Wolfgang Harich*). In the 1960s, a politically and culturally very influential opposition came together around *Robert Havemann* and *Wolfgang Biermann*. With the expatriation of Wolf Biermann in 1976, this group transcended its primarily intellectual circle of thought and action and reached the broad GDR public (Jander, 2018).

In the 1980s, new opposition groups were formed within the church and non-church peace and environmental movements. In all cases, the official political rulers reacted to the political opposition with occupational bans, repression, exclusion, arrest or expulsion from the country.

However, the dimmer the prospects for political change in the GDR became, the more the ability to persevere diminished, especially among those sections of the population who had hitherto passively hoped for change. The majority of those who wanted to leave the country, and thousands of whom did so in the summer of 1989, were recruited primarily from those sections of the population that had in the past sought to escape the central claims to control in various social niches and subcultures.

On the occasion of the presentation of a new semiconductor chip, the 32-bit chip, at the Erfurt microelectronics plant on August 14, 1989, *Erich*

Honecker, General Secretary of the Central Committee of the Socialist Unity Party of Germany (SED) and Chairman of the Council of State, opined, "Neither ox nor donkey stops socialism in its tracks" (Evangelisch.de, 2014).

At this time, however, several thousand GDR citizens were ready to run or willing to run away, and between August and October they used the open border between Hungary and Austria to flee to the West.

Others stayed and took to the streets or churches in Leipzig, Berlin, Erfurt, Dresden, Jena and elsewhere to demand democratic reforms and to make it clear to those in power who the people were. On Monday demonstrations, those who stayed chanted "Freedom, Equality, Fraternity", "We stay here", "Gorbi, Gorbi", "Allow new forum".

The fact that the social upheaval in the GDR actually took place in the autumn was due above all to the oppositional and innovative citizens' movements (the "Neues Forum", "Demokratie Jetzt", the newly founded East German SPD, the various left-wing alternative groups):

- With their political conceptions, they were able to offer real alternatives to the prevailing dogmas for social change.
- They represented alternative points of view (as a critique of the prevailing conditions) in a stable manner over time.
- They remained largely consistent in their political appearance (as relatively closed social movements) and were only intimidated to a limited extent by state repression.

Overview

The majority of the GDR population remained "…behind the curtain and waited until the autumn of 1989. It is a 'fairy tale' to claim that the East German revolution was a matter for a majority. No revolution is a majority event, because then it would not be needed at all" (Kowalczuk, 2019).

For the rest, it will probably be left to subsequent generations of historians (following a modified Marxian phrase according to which the anatomy of a present society is the key to understanding the past one) to examine how the historical "footnote"[3] GDR was actually erased and whether today's explanations can still prove useful for later purposes.

---

[3] The metaphor of the GDR as a "footnote of history" is used by the historian *Ulrich* Wehler (2008) in the fifth volume of his Monumental History. The copyright for the use of the metaphor, however, probably belongs more to *Stefan Heym,* who on the evening of 18 March 1990 commented on the result of the first free Volkskammer election with the words that of the GDR "nothing will be but a footnote of world history" (Heym, 1990).

On 18 October 1989 Erich Honecker resigns. The demonstrations increase. Now there are already hundreds of thousands demonstrating in Berlin, Chemnitz, Erfurt, Gera, Leipzig, Dresden, Jena, Halle, Magdeburg, Plauen, Rostock, Schwerin, Stralsund, Zwickau and elsewhere for reforms, democracy, freedom of travel, free elections.

On November 4, up to 500,000 people stand on Berlin's Alexanderplatz, listen to speeches by prominent artists and civil rights activists, and demand the resignation of the SED leadership. *Stefan Heym,* the great writer, calls out to the masses: "It is as if someone has thrown open the windows after all the years of stagnation, of intellectual, economic, political, the years of dullness and fustiness and bureaucratic arbitrariness, of official blindness and deafness" (Heym, 1989).

Then, on the night of November 9–10, the border to the West opens, first in Berlin, then throughout the country. East and West Germans lie in each other's arms and weep with joy. *Erich Follath* writes in *Stern Extra* on 16 November: "The celebration of joy at the Brandenburg Gate, the tears of reunion after the opening of the borders carried television cameras into living rooms in France, the USA and Scandinavia. And everyone could see it: All of Berlin was a (Trabbi) cloud. No one will forget the moving hours..." (Follath, 1989, p. 4).

It is still feared that the Soviet troops in the GDR might move out of their barracks to put the brakes on the course of history. But things turn out differently; the Soviet forces stay out of the events, as do the American, British and French. Meanwhile, the GDR citizens travel to the West to receive their visitor's money.

The Monday demonstrations also continue. Instead of "We are *the* people", one now occasionally hears "We are *one* people". In Bonn, meanwhile, the government under Chancellor *Helmut Kohl* is discussing a ten-point plan aimed at unifying East and West Germany. In the GDR, men and women of the civil movement were working at the time on a program for a reformed socialism, which was also to be directed against the appropriation of the GDR by the West (appeal "For our country", 26 November 1989).

By this time, the SED's leadership role had effectively come to an end. Arrest warrants are issued for Erich Honecker and other leading SED officials. A central "Round Table" is organized in Berlin to prepare for new elections and a new constitution. The central "Round Table" referred to the rounds of talks attended by representatives of the GDR government and members of various opposition movements between December 1989 and March 1990.

At the beginning of December 1989, the district administrations of the Ministry for State Security in Erfurt, Leipzig and Suhl are occupied. On 15

January 1990, the central administration in Berlin was also stormed. Some time later it became clear that the State Security had not only about 91,000 permanent employees, but that about 1,89,000 people were also working for the State Security as unofficial employees, supplying information and spying on people (BF informs, 1993).

At this time, civil movements still hoped that it would be possible to preserve the sovereignty of the GDR and to guarantee democratic development in eastern Germany via the two-state status of Germany. Ideas of a future military neutrality of both German states were discussed by the civil movements ("For our country" appeal, 26 November 1989; Aufruf "Für unser Land", 1989). An annexation of the GDR to the Federal Republic – in the sense of Article 23 in the West German Basic Law – was rejected by the central "Round Table" in Berlin. This article provided that a unification of the two German states should take place on the basis of the laws of the Federal Republic. The alternative, which was preferred by the civil movements in the GDR, was the drafting of a new common German constitution. This was to enshrine a right to work, to housing and education, a right for women to self-determine pregnancy, a basic right for children, a general ban on discrimination and the protection of the environment.

Psychologists in the GDR also set out and in a declaration of 9 December 1989 demanded, among other things, democratic elections, a radical reorientation of psychology and an interdisciplinary environmental conference (Psychologen im Aufbruch, 1990).

However, the people in the GDR and the political authorities in the Federal Republic had already made a different decision at this time. Especially in the south of the GDR, the call for "Germany united fatherland" could not be ignored at the weekly demonstrations. In Eichsfeld, on 21 January 1990, around 50,000 people gathered for a symbolic departure. They crossed the border from Worbis to Duderstadt with suitcases and posters that read, among other things, "If the SED comes back to power, we will leave the same night" to demonstrate for German unity. In the evening they return home (NDR 21.01., 2015).

In Bonn, work is already underway on a monetary and economic union. In Moscow, *Michael Gorbachev*, General Secretary of the Communist Party and President of the Soviet Union, and *Helmut Kohl*, Chancellor of the Federal Republic of Germany, agree to achieve German unity as quickly as possible.

On 18 March 1990, the GDR held its last Volkskammer elections. They were also the only free and democratic elections in the history of the GDR. The "Alliance for Germany", a conservative electoral alliance of the CDU, Demokratischer Aufbruch (DA) and Deutscher Sozialer Union (DSU) achieved a total of 48%, followed by the SPD with 21.9% and the PDS (the Party of Democratic Socialism, which had emerged from the SED) with 16.4%. The Bund Freier Demokraten, which would later join the West German FDP, scored 5.3%. The environmentally and peace-oriented parties, such as Bündnis 90 or the Neue Forum (which were founded in the autumn of 1989), received just 2.9% of the voters. The then West German Green politician and later SPD interior minister Otto Schily held a banana up to the television cameras on election night, and the SPD candidate for chancellor at the time, Oskar Lafontaine, smugly remarked that many GDR citizens had thought that "if we vote for Kohl, the money will flow".

> "Nach Golde drängt, am Golde hängt doch alles" (Goethe, Faust. Der Tragödie erster Teil, 1973 [1808], p. 238). For many East Germans, Mammon seemed to guarantee a new stability in times of uncertainty. In most cases, however, it was the others who had gold and money.

In April 1990 the People's Chamber of the GDR rejected the draft for a new, independent constitution of the GDR prepared by the Round Table, and in August 1990 the People's Chamber decided to accede to the Federal Republic in accordance with Article 23 of the Federal German Basic Law.

The freely elected GDR government of CDU, SPD and Liberals remained in office for a good six months, until 3 October 1990, the future day of unity. The first all-German federal elections took place on 2 December 1990. The CDU became the strongest force in the Bundestag with 41.8% and formed a black-yellow government with the FDP. With 11.1%, the PDS also entered the German Bundestag, as did Bündnis 90/Die Grünen (6.2%).

With the fall of communism in 1989, not only did the GDR disappear, a state that is sometimes described as a dictatorship, sometimes as a state of injustice, which was in any case a closed society, but in which there was also a right life in the wrong one. "There is no right life in the wrong one" is a sentence from *Theodor W. Adorno's* writing "Minima Moralia" (Adorno, 2003, p. 43). Shortly after the fall of the Berlin Wall, politicians, writers and academics argued about this sentence. Some, mostly from West Germany, thought that it was impossible to lead a good, humane life in a state of injustice like the GDR. Those who did not leave the GDR had adapted and thus supported the unjust state. Others, who had stayed in the country not only out of fear and adaptation, countered that it had not all been bad. Not only the green arrow or the sandman, but also the love of one's own children or the reliability and trust of close friends had been *firm points* in difficult times.

Richard Schröder, philosopher, theologian, member of the People's Chamber of the GDR, freely elected in 1990, and later judge at the Constitutional Court of the State of Brandenburg, as well as Professor of Philosophy and Systematic Theology at the Humboldt University in Berlin, wrote in 2006: "Of course there were also fulfilled lives and happy days in the GDR, but not because of, but in spite of the dictatorship. Anyone who claims that there is no right life in the wrong one has not experienced dictatorship" (Zeit Online, 2006).

On 1 July 1990, the day on which the State Treaty on the Monetary, Economic and Social Union of East and West Germany came into force, the then Chancellor Helmut Kohl promised in a televised speech that it would soon be possible to "transform Mecklenburg-Western Pomerania and Saxony-Anhalt, Brandenburg, Saxony and Thuringia into flourishing landscapes again, where it is worth living and working" (Kohl, 1990). From 1 July 1990, the East Germans were able to enjoy the West German money, which was now also their money, and buy the bananas they had long longed for. However, the East Germans initially paid for the freedom they had won for themselves with the massive loss of jobs, the demolition of businesses, and the loss of economic and social stability.

The Treuhandanstalt, an institution still decided by the first freely elected government of the GDR in June 1990, was to privatize the GDR's nationally owned enterprises, but also to ensure their efficiency and competitiveness. This was provided for in the Law on the Privatization and Reorganization of the People's Owned Assets (the Treuhand Law). The original draft for the law was submitted to the Central Round Table by the opposition group *Democracy Now* in February 1990, before the last Volkskammer election. On 1 July 1990, the Treuhand owned around 45,000 GDR businesses employing some four million people. Between 1990 and 1993, numerous companies in the East were privatized, wound up or closed down. Many West German companies took advantage of the closure of plants in the East to get rid of possible competitors or to acquire the operational facilities and lucrative real estate cheaply. Not only serious business consultants and company owners visited the Treuhandanstalt to acquire possible GDR companies; fraudsters, soldiers of fortune and conmen also roamed the East German lands to enrich themselves.

On March 29, 1993, Der Spiegel reported under the headline "Krimi im Krause-Land" (Spiegel, 1993) that the then Minister of Transport *Günther Krause* was also one of the promoters and winners of West German gambling. Krause was Parliamentary State Secretary in the last democratically elected government of the GDR from April to October 1990. In this capacity, he negotiated the German-German Unification Treaty together with *Wolfgang*

Schäuble on the side of the old Federal Republic. After the German-German unification Krause became Federal Minister for Special Tasks and in 1991 Federal Minister for Transport. In 1993 he resigned as Minister of Transport because of several affairs (e.g. the illegal sale of the East German motorway service stations), became a private citizen, bought a real estate company, became co-owner of a bank, went bankrupt, had to take an oath of disclosure and was convicted of bankruptcy, embezzlement, fraud and tax evasion.

A particularly characteristic and painful example is the winding up of the plants of the VEB Kalibetrieb Südharz, especially the "Thomas Müntzer" potash plant in Bischofferode in the Eichsfeld region of Thuringia. It was at the nearby Volkenroda potash plant that the first author learned to use combination pliers and electric cable in the late 1960s. He also learned that the potash salt in the tunnels in the southern Harz was particularly rich in content. And so it was in many respects. About 1800 people worked at the Bischofferode plant. They extracted the salt from a depth of more than 1000 meters. The region lived from salt, for generations already. The plant was highly profitable in GDR times and a stable source of foreign currency.

In 1992, the Treuhand decided to hand over the Bischofferode potash plant and the other operations of the Südharzer Kalikombinat to the potash group K + S, based in Kassel. The group decided to close the plants, thus eliminating an unwelcome competitor.

The potash miners fought back and with them many like-minded people. They occupied the plant and kept production going. They organized a protest march to Berlin to the Treuhand. Twelve miners entered the hunger strike. The miners turned desperately, but unsuccessfully, to *Bernhard Vogel,* then prime minister of Thuringia. He promised support, but it remained only with words. On 22 December the miners in Bischofferode worked their last shift. The promise made by the politicians to create 700 replacement jobs after the mine closed was never realized. Twenty men are still employed in the shaft today to safeguard the mine; just 100 people found work in a new industrial estate.

"Bischofferode is everywhere" was the slogan of the Bischofferode miners in 1992/1993. *Volker Braun,* the great writer, playwright and dissident, in 2000 he received the Büchner Prize, describes in "Die hellen Haufen" an uprising of the potash miners that never took place. An uprising that, "if it has its truth, it is not because it would have been, but because it is conceivable" (Braun, 2011, p. 9). After all, Bischofferode was everywhere in eastern Germany in 1992 and 1993. The other potash mines in Thuringia were also closed. And not only these. From 1989 to 1997, employment in eastern Germany as a whole fell by a third, and in some regions by almost 50%.

In 1989, for example, the Carl Zeiss combine with its headquarters in Jena employed around 30,000 people and paid them well. Here, optical high technology was developed that was competitive and in demand worldwide. Two years later, 20,000 people were laid off. In 1990, the unemployment rate in the Jena employment office district was less than 5%. In 1992 it increased to more than 13%. In the East, the rate at that time was just under 15% overall.

For Jena, the savior came from the West. *Lothar Späth,* former Minister President of Baden-Württemberg, became the chief redeveloper in Jena and the Carl Zeiss combine was divided. One part, the optical core business, was taken over by Carl Zeiss GmbH. The other part, with the future name Jenoptik AG, was led back into the black by *Lothar Späth,* first as a state-owned company and later as a stock corporation. But, to quote *Bertolt Brecht* (1989, original: 1936): "Who built the seven-gated Thebes? In the books are the names of kings. Did the kings haul the boulders?"

The Zeissians remembered their own abilities and founded a number of new high-tech companies in and around Jena, which are also active on the world market today. Jena thus established itself as a symbol for the promised flourishing landscapes in the East.

Overview

The *Spiegel* of 11 March 1991 read: "Many unemployed people from Jena in Thuringia spend their time under palm trees". The exotic plants, set up in the consulting room of psychologist Christine Löhle, 43, are supposed to loosen up the visitors and make it easier for them to talk. The green stuff works. In hour-long sessions, the unemployed expose their innermost feelings to Christine Löhle. They reveal a "feeling of total helplessness", "my fear of the future" and the "shame of talking about it". For Ms. Löhle, who has worked as a company psychologist at the Carl Zeiss factories for 20 years, the findings are shockingly clear: "There is naked existential fear here." The doctor is hardly better off than her patients. The company polyclinic is to be closed. "We are all," she says in a low voice, "being decimated by the West in human terms."

While the economy in the West is intoxicated by record sales and rising returns, the citizens of the East are plagued by a hangover after the jubilation of reunification. Their economy, once at the forefront of the Eastern bloc, is now threatened with expulsion from the world markets. The companies are firing their workforces at such a rapid pace, as if it were a matter of achieving the planned target of zero. Ludwig Erhard's concept of the social market economy is now only insulted in the German East as "brutal market economy" … Regine Hildebrand, labor minister in Brandenburg, predicted the downturn in sentiment – first disillusionment, then frustration – early on. "Now it stinks to high heaven", says the minister, "that you can no longer smell it" (Spiegel, 1991, p. 139).

The economic, political and cultural upheaval in the East is a historically unique process. "Probably never in economic history has there been such a massive collapse in peacetime," writes historian *Stefan Wolle*, scientific director of the *GDR Museum* in Berlin, in *Die Zeit* of 23 September, 2010.

It was not only in Bischofferode that workers defended themselves against liquidation and plant closures. There were also protests in Rostock, Suhl, Stralsund, Wolgast and Zwickau. However, *Jana Hensel* (Engler and Hensel 2018) also notes that such resistance remained unsuccessful on the one hand and was hardly anchored in the collective memory on the other.

It may be, but it doesn't have to be. At least the great admonishers remember and express that.

Volker Braun, for example: "The blessing of the last Volkskammer (of the GDR, WF/IF) was the Enabling Act for capital. It meant the greatest redistribution of property since the Thirty Years War. Practical disenfranchisement. […] The dismissal of almost the entire working class with its technical skills was tantamount to the depravation of the defeated peasants in the German Peasant War. From this the East has not recovered – and I have to discuss obscuration, re-entry, xenophobia" (Braun, 2019, p. 297). One can doubt it, true remains the feeling.

In 1992, 83% of West Germans said that their own economic situation would remain the same or improve in the future; 88% of East Germans were also of this opinion. Only 17% in the West and 12% in the East thought their economic situation would deteriorate in the future (Social Report for the Federal Republic of Germany, 2016, p. 425). In 1996, 66% of East Germans and 50% of West Germans were still happy about German unification (Institut für Demoskopie, 2014).

In other words, after 1989 many East Germans seemed to share the West Germans' conviction that the new visions of the future not only promised the good, but also provided the means for the good to come.

References

Adorno, T. W. (2003). *Minima Moralia. Reflexionen aus dem beschädigten Leben.* Frankfurt a. M.: Suhrkamp Taschenbuch. Original 1951.

Aufruf "Für unser Land". (1989). http://www.chronik-der-mauer.de/material/178900/aufruf-fuer-unser-land-neues-deutschland-26-november-1989. Zugegriffen: 13. März. 2019.

BF informiert. (1993). *IM-Statistik 1985–1989 (3).* Der Bundesbeauftragte für die Unterlagen des Staatssicherheitsdienstes.

Biskupek, M. (1990). Wir Widerstandskämpfer. *Weltbühne*, Nr. 3, 16. Januar 1990.

Braun, V. (2011). *Die hellen Haufen*. Berlin: Suhrkamp.

Braun, V. (2019). *Die Verlagerung des geheimen Punkts*. Berlin: Suhrkamp Verlag.

Brecht, B. (1989). Große kommentierte Berliner und Frankfurter Ausgabe. In W. Hecht, J. Knopf, W. Mittenzwei, & K.-D. Müller (Hrsg.), *Bd. 12: Gedichte 2. Sammlungen 1938–1956*. Suhrkamp: Frankfurt a. M. Original: 1936.

Engler, W., & Hensel, J. (2018). *Wer wir sind: Die Erfahrung, ostdeutsch zu sein*. Aufbau Verlag.

Evangelisch.de. (2014). „Weder Ochs noch Esel" – Erich Honeckers Realitätsverlust. https://www.evangelisch.de/inhalte/108899/14-08-2014/weder-ochs-noch-esel-erich-honeckers-realitaetsverlust. Zugegriffen: 21. Juni. 2019.

Follath, E. (1989). Als die Vopos lächeln lernten. *Stern Extra*, 16. November 1989.

Frindte, W. (1994). Vertrauen ist gut, Kontrolle ist besser…: Ein sozialpsychologischer Erklärungsversuch zum gesellschaftlichen Umbruch in der DDR. In W. Frindte & H. Pätzolt (Hrsg.), *Mythen der Deutschen*. Leske + Budrich: Leverkusen.

Giordano, R. (1987). *Die zweite Schuld oder von der Last, Deutscher zu sein*. Hamburg: Rasch und Röhring.

Heitzer, E. (2018). DDR-Systemgegnerschaft von rechts. In E. Heitzer, M. Jander, A. Kahane, & P. G. Poutrus (Hrsg.), *Nach Auschwitz: Schwieriges Erbe DDR*. Frankfurt a. M.: Wochenschau.

Heydemann, G. (2002). Gesellschaft und Alltag in der DDR. *Bundeszentrale für Politische Bildung.*. http://www.bpb.de/izpb/9766/gesellschaft-und-alltag-in-der-ddr?p=all

Heym, S. (1989). Rede am 4. November 1989 in Berlin. https://www.dhm.de/archiv/ausstellungen/4november1989/heym.html. Zugegriffen: 8. Mai 2019.

Heym, S. (1990). Kommentar im Fernsehen am 18.3.1990. http://www.doku-archiv.com/literatur/heym.htm. Zugegriffen: 6. Sept. 2019.

Institut für Demoskopie Allensbach. (2014). *Das Ende der "Mauer in den Köpfen". Eine Dokumentation des Beitrags von Dr. Thomas Petersen in der Frankfurter Allgemeinen Zeitung Nr. 269 vom 19. November 2014*. Institut für Demoskopie Allensbach. https://www.ifd-allensbach.de/uploads/tx_reportsndocs/FAZ_November_Mauer.pdf. Zugegriffen: 21. Okt. 2017.

Jander, M. (2018). Antifaschismus ohne Juden Der Kollaps der DDR und die linke DDR-Opposition. In E. Heitzer, M. Jander, A. Kahane, & P. G. Poutrus (Eds.), *Nach Auschwitz: Schwieriges Erbe DDR*. Frankfurt a. M.: Wochenschau.

Kohl, H. (1990). Fernsehansprache von Bundeskanzler Kohl anlässlich des Inkrafttretens der Währungs-, Wirtschafts- und Sozialunion. https://www.helmut-kohl.de/index.php?msg=555. Zugegriffen: 16. Nov. 2018.

Kowalczuk, I.-S. (2019). Eine Minderheit bahnte den Weg. https://www.faz.net/aktuell/feuilleton/debatten/zu-aktuellen-versuchen-die-ostdeutsche-revolution-umzudeuten-16284484.html?GEPC=s2&premium=0x9e12d6e096dd278a07a

8a7a6b8d43a39&fbclid=IwAR2H6uhC62tzMSFO_zN2zbBK-Ul7c–PR3XBbd HmEx6HPqqRIs-8TRIJm5A. Zugegriffen: 15. Juli. 2019.

Leo, A. (2018). Die Falle der Loyalität. In E. Heitzer, M. Jander, A. Kahane, & P. G. Poutrus (Eds.), *Nach Auschwitz: Schwieriges Erbe DDR.* Frankfurt a. M.: Wochenschau.

NDR. 21.01.2015. Vor 25 Jahren: Kofferdemo im Grenzgebiet. https://www.ndr.de/ kultur/geschichte/chronologie/Vor-25-Jahren-Kofferdemo-im-Grenzgebiet,kofferdemo102.html. Zugegriffen: 13. März 2019.

Psychologen im Aufbruch. (1990). *Stellungnahme von PsychologInnen aus der DDR.,* Bewußt-Sein für den Frieden Marburg: Rundbrief der Friedensinitiative Psychologie – Psychosoziale Berufe e.V.

Quent, M. (2016). Sonderfall Ost – Normalfall West? In W. Frindte, D. Geschke, N. Haußecker, & F. Schmidtke (Eds.), *Rechtsextremismus und "nationalsozialistischer Untergrund".* Wiesbaden: Springer VS.

Sozialbericht für die Bundesrepublik. (2016). Bonn: Bundeszentrale für politische Bildung. https://www.destatis.de/DE/Publikationen/Datenreport/Downloads/ Datenreport2016.pdf?__blob=publicationFile. Zugegriffen: 4. März. 2019.

Spiegel, D. (1991). Dann fahr' ich gegen den Baum. *Heft, 11,* 139–146.

Spiegel, D. (1993). Krimi im Krause-Land. *Heft, 13,* 26–30.

Süß, W. (1993). *Zu Wahrnehmung und Interpretation des Rechtsextremismus in der DDR durch das MfS.* Berlin: Der Bundesbeauftragte für die Unterlagen des Staatssicherheitsdienstes der Ehemaligen Deutschen Demokratischen Republik: Reihe B, Analysen und Berichte.

Wehler, U. (2008). *Deutsche Gesellschaftsgeschichte* (Bd. 5). München: C. Beck.

Weiß, K. (1990). Die neue alte Gefahr. Junge Faschisten in der DDR. *Elternhaus und Schule, 1,* 14–17.

Wolf, C. (1977). *Kindheitsmuster.* Berlin: Aufbau-Verlag.

Wolle, S. (2010). Damals war's so viel besser! https://www.zeit.de/2010/39/ Wiedervereinigung. Zugegriffen: 23. Juni. 2019

Zeit Online. (2006). Auch wir hatten glückliche Tage. https://www.zeit.de/2006/27/ DDR-neu. Zugegriffen: 23. Apr. 2019.

4

German Angst: After the Honeymoon

Transformation became a scientific term in the 1990s to describe and name the means for a good end. On the one hand, transformation meant a transfer of institutions, elites, finances and legal structures from West to East; on the other hand, more than one million people migrated from East Germany to West Germany between 1989 and 2012. In Saxony-Anhalt, the population fell by 20% between 1991 and 2012, in Thuringia and Mecklenburg-Western Pomerania by 15% each, in Saxony by 13%, and in Brandenburg by almost 4% (Bundesministerium für Wirtschaft und Energie, 2018). From West Germany came the political, economic and scientific advisors and consultants who tried to show and tell the East Germans where and how to use the above-mentioned means for the good end.

> A joke made the rounds in East Germany at the time: the West rooster rolled a huge ostrich egg into the East henhouse and stood up in front of the hens: "Ladies, I don't want to complain, but I wanted to show you how we work!"

But the good end did not come. Unemployment increased rapidly in Germany (and also in the post-socialist countries of Eastern Europe) after 1990. While in 1991 around 2.6 million people were unemployed in Germany, in 1997 – *according to official figures – the* number rose to 4.4 million (with an unemployment rate of 11.4%) and peaked at 4.9 million in 2005. In eastern Germany the absolute number of unemployed and the unemployment rate climbed rapidly: from 1991 to 2005 the number of unemployed rose from one million to 1.6 million; the unemployment rate grew to almost 19% (see

Fig. 4.1). In parts of Saxony-Anhalt and Mecklenburg-Western Pomerania, the unemployment rate even exceeded the 27% mark in 2005.

The situation at the East German universities also became precarious. As early as the turn of the year 1990 to 1991, academic institutes that were considered close to the system (such as philosophy, history, sociology) were closed and their staff dismissed. Thus, as *Peter Pasternack* rightly points out, membership in an academic institution that was considered politically problematic or factually superfluous, i.e. a collective characteristic, decided one's further "…individual professional existence, without the individual having any realistic chance of escaping collective condemnation" (Pasternack, 2004, p. 131).

Approximately 60% of the scientists at the GDR universities and more than 80% of the scientists in industrial research lost their jobs by 1992. A smaller proportion were dismissed because they were informal collaborators of the state security or were considered to be too close to the system. By far the greater part were terminated – as it was so unpleasantly called – because of a lack of professional competence. The criteria for these professional evaluation processes were set by academic representatives of West German disciplines, who as a rule also undertook the academic evaluation of the East German academics. It is reasonable to assume that, for professional reasons,

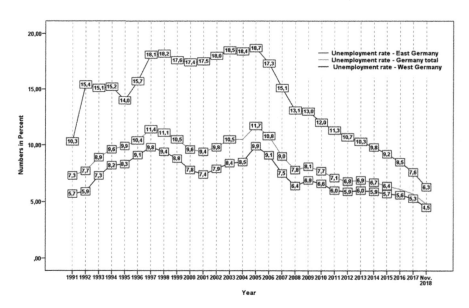

Fig. 4.1 Development of the unemployment rate over time from 1991 to November 2018. (Source: Federal Employment Agency – Statistics 2019; own representation)

the process also had the effect of creating academic living space for the second and third garniture of West German science.

The upper curve in Fig. 4.1 illustrates the rapid development of unemployment in eastern Germany up to its peak in 2005. From 2006/2007 onwards, things went downhill again – in a positive sense. In 2018, the unemployment rate in the eastern German states ranged from 5.8% in Thuringia to 8.4% in Mecklenburg-Western Pomerania.

Incidentally, fear of one's own unemployment followed a similar time course in Germany as the development of the unemployment rate. In 1991, R + V Versicherung began its annual representative surveys of Germans according to their greatest fears. In these surveys, around 2400 people aged 14 and over are asked each year about their personal fears and worries they have about society, the economy, politics and their own life situation (R + V Versicherung, 2018).

Fear of one's own unemployment was and is apparently also one of the major problems Germans are afraid of. The following figure (Fig. 4.2) illustrates the development of fear of one's own unemployment over the last decades: In 1991, 30% of Germans nationwide express fear of their own unemployment. In 1996, the figure is over 50%. In 2005, the year in which

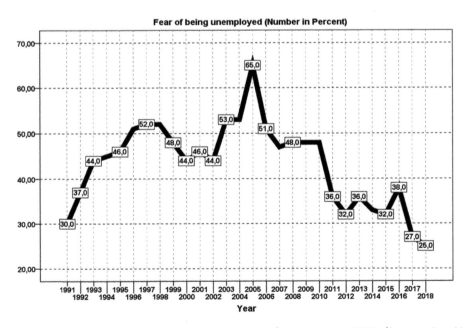

Fig. 4.2 Fear of own unemployment over time from 1991 to 2018. (Source: R + V Versicherung; own representation)

the unemployment rate in eastern Germany is just under 19%, 65% of Germans are afraid of their own unemployment. A year later, the figure is "only" 51%, but with clear differences between eastern and western Germany (67% versus 47%).

For many East Germans, however, the economic upturn that began to emerge in the second half of the 2010s came too late; not to mention the depressing experience of being made unemployed through no fault of their own.

A large proportion of those who became unemployed in eastern Germany in the 1990s either retired in the 2010s or had turned their backs on the east in the meantime in order to find a *foothold* and work in western German regions. Between 1990 and 2006, around 1.2 million citizens left the eastern German states for the west. Young, well-educated people in particular sought their salvation in the old federal states. Until 2008, more women than men migrated from the new to the old federal states, which led to a strong surplus of men in some eastern German regions, at least until 2014. Only since 2016 does this structural change seem to be slowing down (Welt.de, 2017).

However, there are other sides to the structural change in eastern Germany: Wages in the east are still more than 15% to 20% below those in the west. For example, average gross earnings in the new federal states in 2017 were around EUR 2600, while in the west they were around EUR 3300. And it is still predominantly West German managers who call the shots in (East) German institutions and companies. East Germans occupy about 1.6% of management positions in the German economy as a whole, and 33% in eastern Germany. In administration and justice, the East German share is about 5% nationwide; in East Germany it is 13%. In the new federal states, only about 13% of judges have an East German socialization (Hannoversche Allgemeine, 2019).

"Even if at first glance things look different with Angela Merkel as chancellor and former German president Joachim Gauck: On the ground, the dominance of West Germans in the elites is still experienced as cultural colonialism... There are simply different experiences and cultural practices colliding. You have to talk a lot...", said the former East German civil rights activist and current president of the Federal Agency for Civic Education, *Thomas Krüger,* in an interview with the Berliner Zeitung on 31.10.2017.

In his argumentation, Krüger falls back on the concept of "cultural hegemony", a concept introduced by the Italian philosopher and communist *Antonio Gramsci* in the 1930s. Gramsci wanted to draw attention to the fact that – in the time of fascism – it is not only a matter of fighting against the economic power of capital, but also of opposing the *structural* hegemony, i.e. the power of capitalism and fascism, with the new *culture of* a civil society.

Be that as it may: Krüger's critique of the hegemony of West German elites quite soon challenged the opposition of (West) German intellectuals. The social scientist *Samuel Salzborn of* the Center for Research on Anti-Semitism at the Technical University of Berlin, for example, criticized Krüger's hasty choice of the term "cultural hegemony" as only reinforcing "an East German victim myth" in which one could "settle comfortably into a permanent lamentation at a distance from the political system of the Federal Republic" (Gensing, 2017). Moreover, the term is also playing into the hands of the "New Rights", who have instrumentalized Gramsci's concept to justify their hostility to elites and to proclaim a cultural revolution from the "right".

Now, neither *Antonio Gramsci* nor *Thomas Krüger* can be held responsible for the new-right instrumentalizations. Gramsci would probably turn in his grave in view of this. More annoying is Salzborn's formulation of the East German victim myth and the indirect reproach to the whining Ossis. As Krüger put it, since different experiences and cultural practices clash, one would have to talk a lot. Certainly also with each other.

But that's what the Easterners and Westerners actually wanted shortly after the fall of the Wall. But they didn't do it, or didn't do it enough, or only one-sidedly, or they talked past each other.

Ossi: "We are the people". Wessi: "We too".

In an Emnid survey conducted in September 2018, 60% of East Germans said that the relationship between people in East and West Germany had not improved since reunification. Only 33% of East Germans think that people from West and East have become closer. West Germans have the opposite opinion. Here, 60% believe that East and West Germany have become closer. Moreover, 56% of East Germans accuse West Germans of arrogance (Zeit Online, 2018).

Thirty years after the political and economic turnaround in East Germany, West German politicians are now also saying that something might have gone wrong. *Die Zeit* has collected and published some of these statements, unfortunately only on the page "Zeit im Osten" (Die Zeit, 2019), which is published in the East. Here is an annotated selection:

Herbert Grönemeyer (on November 11, 2018): "Merkel is not to blame for the strengthening of the right. But one of her failings was that she never brought us closer to the mentality of the people in the East … It has never been talked about what dramatic differences there are in the East and West German cultures." Dear Mr. Grönemeyer, we are big fans of her songs, but aren't you grown up and capable enough to have discovered these differences – if they should exist – yourself in the last 30 years?

Robert Habeck (on January 20, 2019): "I also feel it personally a mistake that I was not particularly interested in German unity in the 90s ". Well, what should you do, continue to vote GREEN anyway?

Dunja Hayali (December 6, 2018): "This transformation experience is just stark. We should all have been more interested in this in the West. I understand that the East Germans are angry about it". Dear Ms. Hayali, thank you for your understanding, but why didn't you in the West take an interest in what was happening there in the East?

Wolfgang Schäuble (February 2, 2019): "These injuries – we did not suspect that this could happen". Now that is a blatant statement, Wolfgang Schäuble was the one who negotiated the Unification Treaty on the West German side. He really should have known what he was doing.

References

Bundesministerium für Wirtschaft und Energie. (2018). Demografische Situation in den ostdeutschen Ländern. https://www.beauftragter-neue-laender.de/BNL/Navigation/DE/Themen/Gleichwertige_Lebensverhaeltnisse_schaffen/Demografie/Demografische_Situation/demografische_situation.html. Accessed: 19. Nov. 2018.

Die Zeit. (2019). Das muss mal gesagt werden. Ausgabe vom 14. Juni 2019, S. 10–11.

Federal Employment Agency – Statistics. (2019). https://statistik.arbeitsagentur.de. Accessed: 7. März 2019.

Gensing, P. (2017). Was ist kulturelle Hegemonie? ARD-Faktenfinder. https://faktenfinder.tagesschau.de/inland/kulturelle-hegemonie-101.html. Accessed: 8. März. 2019.

Hannoversche Allgemeine. (2019). Ostdeutsche in den Eliten unterrepräsentiert. http://www.haz.de/Nachrichten/Politik/Deutschland-Welt/Ostdeutsche-in-den-Eliten-unterrepraesentiert. Accessed: 7. März 2019.

Pasternack, P. (2004). Die wissenschaftlichen Eliten der DDR nach 1989. In H.-J. Veen (Hrsg.), Alte Eliten in jungen Demokratien. Böhlau: Köln.

R + V Versicherung. (2018). *Die Ängste der Deutschen.* https://www.ruv.de/presse/aengste-der-deutschen. Accessed: 1. Febr. 2019.

Welt.de. (2017). Abwanderung von Ost nach West auf niedrigstem Niveau seit Wiedervereinigung. https://www.welt.de/newsticker. Accessed: 28. Febr. 2019.

Zeit Online. (2018). Ostdeutsche kritisieren Uneinigkeit von Deutschland. https://www.zeit.de/politik/ausland/2018-10/umfrage-deutsche-einheit-ostdeutsche-westdeutsche. Accessed: 06.2019.

5

"The Boys Are Back in Town": Threat to Democracy

In 2015, millions of people fled from Syria and Iraq to Europe. More than one million refugees came to Germany. The German government opened the borders and Chancellor *Angela Merkel* proclaimed "We can do it". Yes, why shouldn't we actually be able to handle the "onslaught" of refugees? Germany is the richest country in Europe, its democratic constitution is stable and the majority of German natives seem to be quite hospitable.

However, the Chancellor had not agreed her "bill" or her creative optimism with all German "hosts". On August 26, 2015, the Chancellor visited a refugee home in Heidenau, Saxony, and was called a "traitor to the people" and a "whore" by locals. A few days later, at Budapest train station, Syrians, Albanians and Iraqis shout "Germany, Germany" and "Merkel, Merkel"; they want to go to Germany. There they are initially greeted by a wave of hospitality, but also by scepticism, rejection and open hostility from parts of the German population.

Violence against refugees has also increased dramatically since then. The attacks on refugee shelters have been and continue to be fueled in particular by right-wing populist movements, which have been demonstrating on the streets since autumn 2014 under the name of "Patriotic Europeans against the Islamisation of the Occident" (PEGIDA), among others. On the posters carried by Pegida supporters, there is not only agitation against "Islam" and against a failed immigration and asylum policy. People are supposed to take to the streets because – as one could read on the Facebook pages of PEGIDA and PEGIDA offshoots (e.g. SÜGIDA in southern Thuringia, LEGIDA in Leipzig) – they are "fed up with the lies and the established parties". On the

© The Author(s), under exclusive license to Springer Fachmedien Wiesbaden GmbH, part of Springer Nature 2022
W. Frindte, I. Frindte, *Support in Times of No Support*,
https://doi.org/10.1007/978-3-658-38637-5_5

Facebook pages of the PEGIDA movements, there was also talk of "lying press", "lying propaganda" or of top German politicians who despise their own people.

In early November 2014, PEGIDA mobilized more than 1000 people in Dresden for the first time. On December 8, more than 10,000 and on December 22, 2014, more than 17,000 people followed the call to demonstrate (Durchgezählt, 2016).

Starting in Dresden, offshoots of the movement formed in numerous German cities, as well as in other European countries and North America. In addition to the visible protests in the form of *evening walks* and rallies, the Facebook page of the Dresden PEGIDA movement reached more fans than any political party in the Federal Republic of Germany, with over 200,000 likes in some places (Dietrich et al., 2017; Süddeutsche.de, 2016).

Around the same time as PEGIDA in Saxony, another political movement entered the political stage as a party – the *Alternative for Germany* (AfD). Founded in 2013 as a party critical of Europe, it shed its skin several times and, after a few power struggles at its top, emerged after 2015 in its current right-wing populist and nationalist "top form". In the election program for the 2017 Bundestag elections, the focus was primarily on issues of internal security, immigration, foreigner criminality, and the alleged Islamization of Germany.

PEGIDA and AfD played and still play with the fears of the population of "Überfremdung", "headscarf girls" and "alimented knife men", who seem to threaten the "millennial future" of Germany.

In the following months, the fear of a supposed Islamisation of the "Occident" developed into anger and hatred towards migrants, politicians and the media.

At the end of August 2018, Daniel K. dies of five knife wounds at a city festival in Chemnitz. The suspects are refugees from Iraq and Syria. In the afternoon of the same day, the Chemnitz AfD calls for a funeral rally. Around 800 people march through the city and chant "We are the people". Hooligans also take part in the march and in attacks against foreigners. The demonstrations continue over the next few days. Less than a week later, PEGIDA founder *Lutz Bachmann* and the AfD state chairmen *Jörg Urban* from Saxony, *Björn Höcke* from Thuringia and *Andreas Kalbitz* from Brandenburg march through Chemnitz together with members of the right-wing alliance "Pro Chemnitz" and 8000 supporters. Approximately 3000 people opposed the march. Several people were injured in the clashes between right-wing demonstrators, counter-demonstrators and police, including a cameraman from Mitteldeutscher Rundfunk.

But is that so new?

Shortly after the fall of communism in 1989, right-wing extremist and xenophobic crimes in Germany took on alarming proportions: in 1990, the Office for the Protection of the Constitution reported 1.848 right-wing extremist crimes and other crimes in the area of "politically motivated crime – right-wing"; in 1997, the figure was as high as 11,719, and for the year 2000, 15,951 right-wing extremist crimes were reported. *Figure* 5.1 illustrates that this development over the years – and especially in the twenty-first century – can still be increased.

In retrospect, *Andreas Klärner* (2008, p. 26 ff.) points out, among other things, that party-based right-wing extremism lost considerable relevance in the 1990s. Instead, it was primarily youth-cultural right-wing extremist tendencies that gained in importance: "From East Germany, a wave of xenophobic violence spread throughout Germany, and the perpetrators came primarily from these new youth cultures".

In this context, it is worth remembering the pogrom-like riots against refugee and contract worker accommodation in Hoyerswerda in September 1991, in Rostock-Lichtenhagen in August 1992, as well as against the homes of Germans of Lebanese and Turkish origin in Hünxe in October 1991, in Mölln in November 1992 and in Solingen in May 1993. *The Spiegel* of 30 September 1991 refers to the riots in Hoyerswerda with a cover picture showing young men in front of the slogan "Gewalt gegen Fremde – HASS" (Violence against

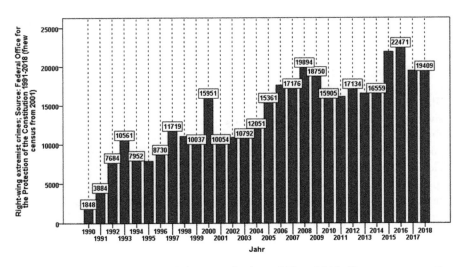

Fig. 5.1 Right-wing extremist violence and crime 1990 to 2018. (Own representation, based on data from the Federal Office for the Protection of the Constitution, 1991–2018)

foreigners – HATE), saluting with raised hands and extended middle fingers (Der Spiegel, 1991a). In the same issue there is an article with the title "Lieber sterben als nach Sachsen" (Better to die than to go to Saxony); it quotes from a nationwide Emnid survey according to which 21% of East Germans and 38% of West Germans express "understanding" for "right-wing radical tendencies" (Der Spiegel, 1991b).

Despite all this: In the 1990s, right-wing extremism did gain in breadth, diversity and violence. However, xenophobia and right-wing extremism still seemed to be phenomena on the fringes of the majority society during these years. And the latter reacted to the xenophobic and right-wing extremist developments, for example, through mass demonstrations and chains of lights in the transition from 1992 to 1993. Thus, between November 1992 and February 1993, more than 30,00,000 people took to the streets against xenophobia, anti-Semitism and right-wing extremist violence. The democratic community thus still seemed to be functioning and to be at peace with its basic values and optimistic ideas about the future.

However, numerous studies conducted in the 1990s provided sufficient evidence that xenophobia, anti-Semitism and right-wing extremist violence pose a threat to the democratic polity in Germany (e.g. Heitmeyer et al., 1992; Ohlemacher, 1999; Otto & Merten, 1993). The studies showed, among other things, that xenophobic attitudes (without violence) are in a ratio of 2:1 to right-wing extremist attitudes (with violence) (approx. 30% xenophobes are opposed by 15% xenophobes with violent affirmation).

In the 1999 report on the protection of the constitution, one could read, among other things:

> Since the beginning of the 1990s, right-wing extremist skinheads and their entourage have formed the largest group of those prepared to resort to violence. They repeatedly appear through spontaneous acts of violence and their aggressive right-wing extremist, partly inciting music. Due to the high fluctuation in the violent scenes and the small number of structures, the proportion of right-wing extremist skinheads among those prepared to use violence cannot be clearly quantified, but it is probably around 85%. The potential is particularly high in the eastern German Länder. With a population share of about 21%, more than half of the right-wing extremist skinheads live in the east. Larger, supra-regionally active scenes can be found in southern and eastern Thuringia, western Saxony and southern Brandenburg, among others. There are numerous groups distributed throughout the country and mostly active only locally or regionally in smaller communities in all eastern German Länder (Bundesamt für Verfassungsschutz 1999, p. 25).

In public discourse in the 1990s, very different patterns of explanation for the loud and violent xenophobes, especially in East Germany, were rampant:

- "The East is browner than many politicians want to admit" (*Die Zeit*, September 10, 1998).
- "The main cause is the authoritarian upbringing in the crèches, kindergartens, schools and youth organizations of the GDR" (Christian Pfeiffer, then Justice Minister of Lower Saxony; *Der* Spiegel, 1999).
- "The West Germans have democratically won convictions that are generally accepted. In any case, anyone who contradicts the consensus of values must expect disapproval or even exclusion. In the West, political correctness alone forbids open xenophobia. In East Germany, on the other hand, tolerance is not a value in itself" (*Die Zeit*, 8 April 1999).
- Xenophobia and right-wing extremism in East Germany are the consequences of deprivation and serious structural crises (Deutsche Shell, 13th Shell Youth Study 2000).

These somewhat woodcut-like descriptions only changed in the course of the 2000s. Increasingly, a distinction was made – at least in academic discourse – between the right-wing extremist perpetrators of violence (the actors in the foreground), persons with right-wing extremist attitudes acting as ideologues in the background, the right-wing extremist and xenophobic parties and organizations (DVU, the NPD, the former "Junge Nationaldemokraten (JN)" or Thüringer Heimatschutz),[1] persons or groups with xenophobic attitudes without a right-wing extremist worldview and people with nationalist or authoritarian attitudes without a distinct political orientation.

Above all, the studies on group-related hostility towards people (Heitmeyer, 2002–2012) and the so-called "center studies" by *Oliver Decker* and colleagues (e.g. Decker et al., 2012) revealed serious differences, but also commonalities, between the brutal right-wing extremists and the majority population. Group-focused enmity, such as hostility towards immigrants, anti-Semitism, Islamophobia, racism, devaluation of the disabled, gays and lesbians, are – according to the core findings – not exclusively widespread phenomena among right-wing extremists. Rather, they have meanwhile arrived in the middle of society.

In autumn/winter 2008, *Andreas* Zick et al. (2010) investigated facets of group-focused enmity in eight European countries (approximately 1000 adults were surveyed in Great Britain, Germany, France, Italy, the Netherlands,

---

[1] With the exception of the NPD, these organizations have since been dissolved or banned.

Portugal, Poland and Hungary). It became clear that prejudices against "others" are not only present in Germany, but also in other countries of the European Community. In Germany, for example, 50% agree with negative attitudes towards immigrants (in the EU as a whole, the figure is 50.4%, with peaks in Great Britain at 62.2%, Italy at 62.5% and Portugal at 59.6%). Anti-Semitic statements are endorsed by 48.9% in Germany, 41.2% in the EU, 68.1% in Hungary and 72.2% in Poland. Traditionally racist statements (e.g. that there is a natural hierarchy between "black" and "white" peoples) are agreed with by 30.5% of Germans, 45.1% of Portuguese, 41.6% of Poles and 41.8% of Hungarians.

Overview

At this point, we take the liberty of making a methodological criticism that should be remembered even when we present our own research results in later sections of this book: As researchers, we know that population surveys also have their pitfalls. Frequently in such cases, questionnaires are used that are usually standardized, that is, they consist of a fixed set of questions or statements. Respondents are supposed to answer these questions or rate the statements. Standardized answer formats, so-called answer scales, are also available for the answers or evaluations. When respondents answer the questions or rate the statements on these scales, researchers must decide whether the answers or ratings now actually reflect the attitudes of the respondents or whether the respondents have merely reacted in a socially desirable way to the restrictive situational conditions of the survey. Researchers are thus confronted with a decision-making dilemma that is almost impossible to resolve. Unless, that is, they dispense with all standardization and leave it to the respondents to express themselves as they wish. But even then, the dilemma is not solved. Indeed, researchers must again ask themselves what the motivations are for those who freely express what they express. In other words, opinion or attitude researchers are usually observers of something that is fuzzy and idiosyncratic.

And then this: In November 2011, the right-wing terrorist group *National Socialist Underground* (NSU) was uncovered. Uwe Mundlos, Uwe Böhnhardt and Beate Zschäpe had been in hiding for almost 14 years. Prior to that, the three had been active in the far-right Jena youth scene and in the far-right "Thuringian Homeland Security", taking part in far-right demonstrations in Jena, Dresden and elsewhere, and building bombs. During the time security authorities were searching for the trio, the three murdered eight people of Turkish origin and a Greek small business owner, as well as a German police-woman. On June 7, 2014, *Der Spiegel* writes that since the NSU murders became known, around 700 homicides have been examined by the investigating authorities for a right-wing extremist motive and asks in this context:

"Were there other murder gangs along the lines of the NSU? Or are there possibly more acts to be blamed on the right-wing extremists Uwe Mundlos, Uwe Böhnhardt and Beate Zschäpe?" (Baumgärtner et al., 2014, p. 34).

According to the research of the victims' fund CURA of the Amadeu Antonio Foundation, 178 people died between 1990 and 2013 as a result of inhuman violence. The search mishaps that became known after November 2011, the destruction of files at the police and the Office for the Protection of the Constitution, the possible right-wing extremist supporters of the terror trio and their contacts to the Office for the Protection of the Constitution are still occupying committees of inquiry at the state and federal level. And so it is not surprising that the murders of the NSU, its networking with domestic and foreign right-wing extremist movements and its contacts with the Office for the Protection of the Constitution can ultimately still irritate, disturb, make helpless and angry.

On September 29, 2017, the red-red-green coalition in the Thuringian state parliament decided on a compensation fund for the surviving dependents of the victims of the NSU terror and the establishment of a "Site of Remembrance and Remembrance for the Victims of the National Socialist Underground". The CDU and the AfD voted against the motion of the governing coalition, i.e. against such a fund and against a memorial site. CDU and AfD justified their rejection with different arguments. The CDU parliamentarians said that first the courts would have to decide whether the Thuringian security authorities were at all responsible for NSU murders. Members of the AfD faction accused the governing coalition of instrumentalizing the victims of the NSU in order to turn Thuringians into devout anti-fascists. Ultimately, the compensation fund and the memorial were just another instrument of the red-red-green coalition to establish a left-green state of mind (Landtag, 2017).

What the AfD members of the Thuringian state parliament expressed on this 29th of September, however, is not a democratic alternative, but a perfidious attempt to use the NSU murders, the victims and the bereaved families to attack democracy.

Incidentally, the AfD was elected to the Bundestag with 12.6% after the 2017 federal election. In eastern Germany it achieved 21.9%, in the Free State of Saxony even 27.0% and thus ended up even ahead of the state CDU (26.9%). The AfD is now represented in almost all state parliaments.

On election night, September 24, 2017, *Alexander Gauland, the* AfD's top politician and one of two leaders of the party's parliamentary group in the German Bundestag until 2019, said:

It can warm up this federal government. We will hunt them down. We will hunt down Frau Merkel or whoever and take back our country and our people (Zeit Online, 2017).

So they are back, the right-wing populists, their supporters and the very special agitators from the far-right corner, not only on the streets but also in parliaments. They are attacking democracy and are supported by fellow right-wingers in East and West, but also by those who still call themselves democrats.

Racism is also part of everyday life, in Germany and in some other countries. Racism has become a material violence, in Saxony, in Saxony-Anhalt and in Thuringia, but not only there and *not only* as a pattern of interpretation and action of screaming and angry male baldies. Racism marks the argumentation strategies of politicians in the Bundestag, in the East and West German state parliaments, in talk shows and feuilletons. Racism marks the language in many an everyday argument. Racism is neither a consequence of persistent fears in the face of the influx of migrants nor the expression of a lack of intelligence or economic disadvantage and marginalization.

In September 2018, the authors treated themselves to a holiday in France. On a beautiful late summer day, she and he are sitting on the terrace of a café somewhere on the French Atlantic coast, drinking a petit café and reading together a well-known German weekly newspaper whose front page reads, among other things: "Uprising from the right? Were there riots in Chemnitz?". An elderly couple is sitting at the next table. The somewhat obese man turns to the first author after a while: "Excuse me, sir, are you German?". The author: "Yes, on holiday". The obese gentleman: "I just looked at your newspaper. I'm not spending any more money on that sausage rag. They're all liars. No journalist tells the truth. Seehofer is right. Migration is the mother of all problems. It's just not in the papers." The author: "Really all the problems? The diesel scandal too? Is that also related to migration?". The gentleman from the next table: "Sure, that one. By the way, my name is R. M. My wife and I have our holiday home near here. We live here almost the whole year. At home we are in B. in Westphalia." Author: "Pleased to meet you. My name is WF. We spend our holidays here. But seriously, what does the diesel scandal have to do with migration?" Neighbor: "The billions spent on asylum seekers should be spent on retrofitting diesel cars. But no, it's all being blown up the refugees' asses. There's a shortage of police officers and teachers. There's no money for that either, which is now going into the pockets of the refugees. All of this scares us. Germany is going down the drain. Everywhere only refugees, asylum seekers and migrants." The author: "But actually, here in France you are also foreigners". "No, no, it's something completely different. The French are part of our culture", says the neighbor, wishes a "good day" and a pleasant holiday and leaves. The Authors are left speechless.

References

Baumgärtner, M., Röbel, S., & Winter, S. (2014). Fundstück im Pappkarton. *Der Spiegel, 24*, 34–36. http://magazin.spiegel.de/EpubDelivery/spiegel/pdf/127396 609. Accessed: 7. Dez. 2016.

Bundesamt für Verfassungsschutz. (1991–2018). *Verfassungsschutzberichte*. Bonn: Bundesministerium des Innern.

Decker, O., Kiess, J., & Brähler, E. (2012). *Die Mitte im Umbruch: Rechtsextreme Einstellungen in Deutschland 2012*. Bonn: Dietz.

Dietrich, N., Gersin, E., & Herweg, A. (2017). Analysemöglichkeiten der Online-Kommunikation auf Social Network Sites am Beispiel PEGIDA und Facebook. In W. Frindte & N. Dietrich (Eds.), *Muslime, Flüchtlinge und Pegida* (pp. 235–266). Wiesbaden: Springer VS.

Durchgezählt. (2016). *Statistik zu Pegida in Dresden*. https://durchgezaehlt.org/pegida-dresden-statistik/M. Accessed: 4. Aug. 2016.

Heitmeyer, W. (2002–2012). *Deutsche Zustände. Folge 1 bis 10*. Frankfurt a. M.: Suhrkamp.

Heitmeyer, W., et al. (1992). *Die Bielefelder Rechtsextremismus-Studie*. Weinheim: Juventa.

Klärner, A. (2008). *Zwischen Militanz und Bürgerlichkeit. Selbstverständnis und Praxis der extremen Rechten*. Hamburg: Hamburger Edition.

Thüringer Landtag. (2017). 96. Plenarsitzung. http://www.parldok.thueringen.de/ParlDok/dokument/64284/96_plenarsitzung.pdf. Accessed 12. Juli 2019.

Ohlemacher, T. (1999). Fremdenfeindlichkeit und Rechtsextremismus. Mediale Berichterstattung, öffentliche Meinung und deren Wirkungen. In F. Dünkel (Ed.), *Rechtsextremismus und Fremdenfeindlichkeit – Bestandsaufnahmen und Interventionsstrategien*. Mönchengladbach: Forum Verlag Godesberg.

Zeit Online. (2017). "Wir werden sie jagen". https://www.zeit.de/politik/deutschland/2017-09/reaktionen-bundestagswahl-cdu-spd-afd. Accessed: 10. März 2019.

Otto, H.-U., & Merten, R. (Eds.). (1993). *Rechtsradikale Gewalt im vereinigten Deutschland. Jugend im gesellschaftlichen Umbruch*. Opladen: Leske + Budrich.

Deutsche Shell (2000). *Jugend 2000. 13. Shell Jugendstudie*. Opladen: Leske + Budrich.

Der Spiegel. (1991a). Gewalt gegen Fremde – HASS. *Der Spiegel, 40.* Quelle: http://www.spiegel.de/spiegel/print/index-1991-40.html. Accessed: 6. Dez. 2016.

Der Spiegel (1991b). Lieber sterben als nach Sachsen. *Der Spiegel, 40*, 30–38. http://magazin.spiegel.de/EpubDelivery/spiegel/pdf/13492514. Accessed: 6. Dez. 2016.

Der Spiegel. (1999). Anleitung zum Hass. Der Spiegel, 12, 60–66. http://www.spiegel.de/spiegel/print/d-10245923.html. Accessed: 10. März 2019.

Süddeutsche.de. (2016). *Unbekannte übernehmen Pegida-Facebookseite.* https://www.sueddeutsche.de/news/politik/extremismus-unbekannte-uebernehmen-pegida-facebookseite-dpa.urn-newsml-dpa-com-20090101-160722-99-787067. Accessed: 17. Aug. 2016.

Zick, A., Küpper, B., & Wolf, H. (2010). *Wie feindselig ist Europa?* In Wilhelm Heitmeyer (Hrsg.), Deutsche Zustände, Folge 9. Frankfurt a. M.: Suhrkamp.

6

Changing Times – "…The Times They Are a Changing" (Bob Dylan, 1964)

In Eastern and Southern Europe, above all in the former Yugoslavia, but also in the Middle East, national and transnational contexts disintegrated at the beginning of the 1990s, were worn down in civil wars or – as in the Second Gulf War – became embroiled in the most serious war since the Second World War. The Bundeswehr participated in the Second Gulf War with naval mine countermeasures forces and also in the Balkan wars with Operation *Adria* as part of NATO deployments. But all this seemed to take place from the German perspective "…far behind, far, in Turkey" (Goethe, 1973, p. 176, original: 1808).

When the events of upheaval and crisis in Eastern and Southeastern Europe led to a serious change in asylum immigration, these international events of war and crisis also came into the focus of German attention.

In 1990, about 190,000 people sought asylum in Germany; by 1992, there were already 440,000 refugees, most of whom came to Germany from Eastern and Southern Europe (above all from the former Yugoslavia). Not least as a result of spectacular deportations, the number of refugees (mainly from Bosnia and Herzegovina) fell to around 245,000 in 1997 (Bade & Jochen, 2005). In 1999, the situation in the former Yugoslavia came to a head again. In the so-called Kosovo conflict, Serbian security forces and Kosovo Albanian troops slaughtered each other; massacres of the non-Serbian population were reported in the media; hundreds of thousands of Kosovo inhabitants were on the run. NATO bombed Serb targets, including civilian infrastructure and cultural monuments. Russian paratroopers also fought on the side of the Serbs (Der Spiegel, 2008).

© The Author(s), under exclusive license to Springer Fachmedien Wiesbaden GmbH, part of Springer Nature 2022
W. Frindte, I. Frindte, *Support in Times of No Support*,
https://doi.org/10.1007/978-3-658-38637-5_6

As a result of the war, the UN Security Council adopted *Resolution 1244* in mid-1999, according to which a UN administration was to be established in Kosovo, but the region was still to be administered by the then Yugoslav government. There is no wording in this resolution about the actual legal status of Kosovo, so that the actual political problems have not been solved even today. About 55,000 Kosovars fled to Germany shortly after the Kosovo war. In the meantime, despite serious economic problems, the German government has classified this region as a safe area of origin (Bundesregierung, 2015).

Another consequence or side effect of the civil wars in the former Yugoslavia, however, hardly played a special role in the public and political perception: Between 1992 and 1995, more than 7000 Jihad fighters were smuggled into Bosnia and Herzegovina by *Al-Qaeda* (Hirschmann, 2006) to fight on the side of Muslim units against the Serbs. After the above-mentioned UN resolution, many Jihad fighters left the region again, but a not insignificant number remained in Kosovo.

The terrorist attacks perpetrated worldwide by national and transnational terrorist organizations in the 1990s were also initially hardly reflected in the perception and interpretation of the Germans.

Some examples: On February 26, 1993, the first bombing occurred at the World Trade Center in New York City; on June 25, 1996, members of Saudi Hezbollah carried out a terrorist attack on a housing complex in al-Chubar, Saudi Arabia, that housed U.S. Armed Forces soldiers; on November 12, 1997, employees of a U.S. oil company were murdered in Pakistan; on August 7, 1998, U.S. embassies in Kenya and Tanzania were destroyed by bombings, with more than 200 people killed. And in the days following 31 August 1999, Chechen separatists carried out several explosive attacks in Russia.

For *Ulrich Schneckener* (2006), these and other terrorist attacks fall into a phase in which *Al-Qaeda* developed into the prototype of transnational terrorism and the "Western world", above all the USA, came even more strongly into the terrorists' field of vision. The Al-Qaeda network, whose precursor had already been founded in Afghanistan and Pakistan in the 1980s with the help of the CIA, declared "holy war" on the USA and its allies in the second half of the 1990s ("Declaration of War Against the Americans Occupying the Land of the Two Holy Places" of 23 August 1996 and "Jihad Against Jews and Crusaders" of 23 February 1998; cf. Schneckener, 2006, p. 55).

For Germans, especially West Germans, the memory of the terrorism of the *Red Army Faction has* not yet faded in the 1990s – after all, on April 1, 1991, the then Treuhand chairman, *Detlef Karsten Rohwedder,* was murdered by a sniper. However, the danger posed by transnational terrorism is hardly perceived as a threat.

From 1996 onwards, the annual surveys of Germans by *R + V Versicherung* also ask about fear of terrorism: in 1996, 30% of Germans nationwide say they are afraid of terrorism; 51% are afraid of their own unemployment in Germany. In 1998 and 1999, fear of unemployment again tops the list of German fears. One could also say that at this time, i.e. at the end of the 1990s, the fear of threats in the personal vicinity is greater among Germans than the fear of threats from afar.

And yet, increasing uncertainties are developing about the course of events and the insight into the unpredictability of social development. Initially, it was media makers and scientists who drew attention to these uncertainties. Again it was *Der Spiegel,* which already in 1992 in its issue 31 with the "Onslaught from the Balkans" addressed the increasing number of refugees (Der Spiegel, 1992). And on November 23, 1998, *Der Spiegel* appeared with the title "Too many foreigners?" (Der Spiegel, 1998).

Honegger and Rychner (1998) diagnose an "end of coziness" in this period, and *Richard Sennett* (1998) sees the "end of organized capitalism" coming.

However, it was not yet that far. First, the step into the twenty-first century had to be mastered.

At the turn of the millennium, first the followers of end-time sects celebrate the coming end of the world with their fantasies. Scientists also get infected by the talk about the apocalypse, if you look at the scientific publications that appeared on this topic in the year 2000. Examples may suffice: *Tanja* Busse (2000) presents a book worth reading, "Weltuntergang als Erlebnis" (Apocalypse as an Experience). *Jacques Derrida* (2000) publishes a German translation of his work "Apokalypse" (original: 1984). And the chairman of the First German Fantasy Club, *Gustav* Gaisbauer (2000), makes readers happy with his book "Weltendämmerungen: Endzeitvisionen und Apokalypsevorstellungen in der Literatur" (Twilights of the World: Visions of the End of Time and Conceptions of the Apocalypse in Literature).

A more factual threat is also publicized in the media during 1999 with the label "Y2K problem". It was a computer problem diagnosed in connection with the two-digit indication of years in computer systems. The storage and functioning of most operating systems, user programs, and data files pro-grammed to date relied exclusively on the year and decade when specifying years. The digits referring to the century were generally not used. This means that with the transition to the year 2000, operating systems etc. programmed in this way could have crashed. Banks, the economy, power plants, and national defense systems were all at risk of being crippled.

The computer problems that actually occurred were ultimately limited, not least thanks to extensive international investigations of the globally networked computer systems. However, this did not seem to have been cheap (Schulz & Sempert, 2013). The actual and virtual end of the world did not take place in the transition to the new millennium either.

On the other hand, a speculative bubble burst in March 2000, which mainly affected the high-tech and IT companies of the New Economy and led to huge asset losses and insolvencies in the western industrialized countries. The accelerated development in the IT, Internet and mobile phone sectors had led to high profit expectations and rising share prices. The highly or over-valued IT companies could not meet the profit expectations. The virtual houses of cards collapsed and the "new" capitalism got a damper.

The fact that three months earlier, on 31 December 1999, Russian President *Boris Yeltsin* resigned and *Vladimir Putin* took the helm, however, probably had little to do with it. At the beginning of the new millennium, Russia and the other countries of the former Soviet Union are the focus of a different international or transnational development.

It is true that the Russian economy was on the upswing in the transition to the new millennium (Götz, 2006). Power struggles and independence aspirations in republics of the *Commonwealth of Independent States* (CIS), such as Chechnya, Yakutia and the North Caucasus, were perceived by the government as a threat and fought partly with military means. Above all, however, Russia – like the "West" – found itself in the crosshairs of terrorism. In 1997, the Taliban advanced from Afghanistan towards the Tajik border. Cross-border crime, drug trafficking and terrorist groups threatened Russia's internal security. As early as 1996, Russia, together with China, Kazakhstan, Kyrgyzstan and Tajikistan, had concluded an agreement in Shanghai on confidence-building measures, in which the fight against international and transnational terrorism also played a role.[1] The military operations in Chechnya from autumn 1999 to spring 2000 were – from Moscow's point of view – primarily designed as anti-terrorist measures.

Terrorism and anti-terrorism[2] became the hallmarks of a "dark threat" in the 2000s, which took on reality on September 11, 2001. For *Giovanna Borradori* (2006, p. 9), September 11, 2001 is the "apocalypse", for Hoffmann and Schoeller (2001) the "turning point", and *Ulrich Schneckener* (2006, p. 12) calls it a "superlative without precedent". For *Andreas* Bock (2009), too, it was an "act of unprecedented symbolic power", and for *Jean Baudrillard* (2003) the attack on the World Trade Center is even the "mother of all events".

---

[1] The so-called Shanghai Five, which later became the Shanghai Cooperation Organization.

[2] Anti-terrorism refers to the manifold instruments of counter-terrorism, which are supposed to guarantee more security at the expense of freedom.

Baudrillard published his views on the terrorist attacks of 11 September 2001 in *Le Monde* on 30 November 2001, and the reactions were fierce. This was probably also due to the fact that Baudrillard saw in the attacks a reaction to the imperial stance of the USA, which since the collapse of communism has been trying to assert its position of world power without restraint. No question, for Baudrillard terrorism is immoral, but globalization is also immoral. What is globalized, according to Baudrillard, is not human rights, freedom, culture, and democracy; what is globalized is the capitalist market and the "continued flow of money" (Baudrillard 2003, p. 51). Terrorism has by no means appropriated everything from modernity and globalization ("the information and space technologies, money and stock market speculation") in order to universalize its own values, but solely so that "the system, in response to the multiple challenges of death and suicide, kills itself" (p. 60). In this sense, terrorism is the "final stage of globalization" (p. 63). One might counter that Baudrillard's diagnosis can neither be verified nor falsified because the intentions of the assassins defy scientific analysis. However, Baudrillard's basic idea that the "fight against terrorism" is *ultimately* directed against the "system" that tries to wage this fight should be understood as a warning with the highest priority.

On the evening of September 11, 2001, then US President *George W. Bush* famously announced the "war on terrorism" and German Chancellor *Gerhard Schröder* wrote to Bush assuring him of Germany's "unlimited solidarity". On September 12, 2001, the day after the attacks, NATO decides for the first time in its history to declare an alliance emergency: "An armed attack against one ally is considered an attack against all," declares Secretary General *George Robertson*. The United Nations Security Council, in its resolutions 1368 and 1373, also considered the attacks of 11 September as acts that bring the right of self-defense to bear.

Thus the USA, NATO and possibly the "Western world" redefined the global friend-enemy contradiction: on the one side, the friend side, stands the civilized West, which on the other side is threatened by the main enemy No. 1, global terrorism, and is forced to go to war. That such statements reduce the world political situation to a simple friend-foe relationship is obvious. Criticism of the war speeches of *George W. Bush* and his Secretary of Defense *Donald Rumsfeld* consequently developed vehemently not only in Germany after September 11, 2001.

But there is no question that the world has changed dramatically since that day: Since 9/11, the US, and perhaps the Western world as well, has been in a "war on terrorism".

The increase in terrorist attacks after 2004, which can be seen in Fig. 6.1, is mainly due to terrorist incidents in South Asia and the Middle East or North Africa.

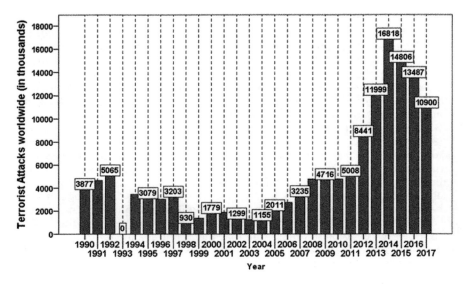

Fig. 6.1 Quantitative trends in terrorist attacks worldwide from 1990 to 2017, own illustration based on data from the Global Terrorism Database (2017). The Global Terrorism Database (GTD) is an open-access resource maintained by the National Consortium for the Study of Terrorism and Responses to Terrorism (an agency of the US Department of Homeland Security) and based at the University of Maryland. The information on which GTD's data on international terrorism is based comes from freely available sources, such as Internet news, digital archives, books, newspapers, and other public documents); no data is available for 1993

Since the beginning of the new millennium, terrorism and counter-terrorism have had the highest news values in media reporting. *Daniel Schmidthäussler* (2006), for example, shows in an analysis of 2744 *Tagesschau*[3] news reports from 1968 to 2006 that the presence of terrorism in ARD's main news has increased dramatically since September 11, 2001. The coverage of terrorism-related topics doubled in the years between 2001 and 2006 compared to the time before 2001, and in the meantime was even three times the average of the previous 30 years. In this context, the finding that an impressive increase in the presence of anti-terrorism measures can be observed in the reports after 2001 is also noteworthy (Frindte & Haußecker, 2010). Especially since September 11, 2001, terrorists have thus succeeded in receiving a high level of attention in media coverage. They have spread a diffuse atmosphere of insecurity and fear and have continuously maintained it through further media-generated attacks. On the one hand, the dissemination media can hardly be blamed or held responsible for the terrorist attacks of recent years.

---

[3] The news program of the public broadcaster ARD.

On the other hand, the dissemination media create the conditions for local terrorist events to achieve global effects and find a global audience. From this point of view, too, 9/11 represents a turning point.

> To put it bluntly and admittedly provocatively: Since 9/11 at the latest, the dissemination media have entered into an unwanted, but for media users tragic symbiosis with terrorism (cf. also Glaab, 2007).

This did not remain without consequences on the side of the recipients: In the aforementioned annual representative survey of German adults by R + V Versicherung, 21% of respondents expressed fear of terrorism in the month before 9/11. A year later, 36% said they were afraid of terrorism, and in 2003 the figure was 58%. Incidentally, Germans' fear of terrorism reached its highest level in 2016 (at 73%).

National and international findings after 2001 also show close links between negative or hostile attitudes towards Muslims, the increase in so-called ingroup favoritism (ethnocentrism, nationalism and patriotism) and attitudes towards terrorism in general and fear of terrorist attacks in particular (e.g. Bonanno & Jost, 2006; Cheung-Blunden & Blunden, 2008; Kam & Kinder, 2007).

These correlations were also confirmed in our own studies (Frindte & Dietrich, 2017). In a non-representative study, 950 German adolescents and adults aged between 15 and 85 were surveyed. In an online survey, respondents were presented with, among other things, various scales to capture attitudes toward Islam (e.g., "Islam is a dangerous religion."), toward Muslims (e.g., "Muslims should be prohibited from immigrating to Germany."), fear of Muslims and Islam (e.g., "The many Muslims in Germany scare me."), and associations of Islam or Muslims and terrorism (e.g., "The majority of Muslims support terrorism."). At the same time, the proportion of migrants in the regions could be taken into account via the postcode of the town in which the respondents live.

The following Fig. 6.2 illustrates an excerpt from the findings. Prejudice against Islam and Muslims, fear of Islam or Muslims, and associations of Islam/Muslims with terrorism are not only significantly related,[4] but are also highest among those respondents who live in regions with a relatively low proportion of migrants. This is indicated by the expressions on the attitudes

---

[4] Correlation coefficients were calculated as statistical measures that indicate the degree of association between two characteristics, and can take values between −1.00 and + 1.00. In this case, the correlation coefficients are between 0.76 and 0.85 and are highly significant.

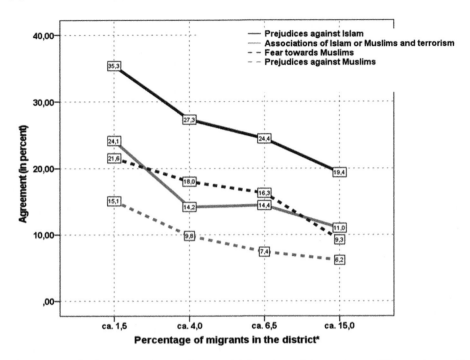

Fig. 6.2 Attitudes towards Muslims and Islam by migrant share. (*Percentage of migrants in the district or independent city in which the respondents spent the longest period of their lives, (collected via postcode). Data source: Destatis (2015), own presentation)

recorded in the regions with a proportion of migrants of around 1.5%. The differences between respondents from regions with different proportions of migrants are also significant.

Talking and reporting about "the West," "Islam," and the "clash of civilizations" has apparently condensed into a new meta-narrative that is certainly not quite as grand as the one whose swan song *Jean-François Lyotard* (1986) reports, but is no less powerful. Meta-narratives or socially relevant grand narratives are social constructions about the past, present and future (see more in Chap. 13).

The economic dislocations and financial crises observable in numerous European countries in the new millennium are also echoed in new meta-narratives. The financial crisis that began in 2007 and was linked to a euro crisis from 2009 onwards led not only to financial losses, insolvencies and rising unemployment worldwide, but also to a new skepticism about capitalism's chances of survival. The *Occupy movement,* which organized itself in the fall of 2011, first in the USA and later worldwide, is sometimes dismissed as a left-wing protest movement, but it claimed to represent 99% of the population against the 1% of the super-rich (Baecker , 2011).[5]

In the annual survey conducted by R + V Versicherung in 2016, which has already been mentioned several times, 68% of West Germans and 66% of East Germans said they were afraid of extremism (R + V Versicherung, 2016). One can assume that the fear of left-wing extremist threats is lower than that related to right-wing extremist threats, because the real attack on democracy in Germany and Europe comes primarily from right-wing extremism and right-wing populist currents.

However, Western democracy and Western culture are under attack also from another direction: on 28 June 2014, the terrorist organization "Islamic State" (IS, formerly ISIS) proclaimed in a video message a new "Islamic Caliphate" based on the model of the Prophet Mohammed for Iraq and Syria and declared "holy war" on all "non-believers". The violent expansion with which the so-called Islamic State swept the Middle East from 2014 onwards, murdering Yazidis, Christians, but also Muslims, raping women and girls, and beheading and mutilating prisoners on camera, seemed to defy conclusive explanations. On September 27, 2014, 126 senior Sunni Islamic scholars addressed an open letter to the self-proclaimed caliph *Abu Bakr al-Baghdadi* and to the fighters and supporters of the so-called Islamic State. In this letter, the scholars attempted to justify why the extremist fundamentalist views of the IS contradict the teachings of the Prophet Muhammad (Letter to Baghdadi, 2014). However, the IS fighters were hardly impressed by the religious arguments.

In total – according to estimates in 2015 – the IS terrorist group in Syria and Iraq now has around 50,000 fighters.[6] Of these, about 20,000 came from abroad, especially from the Arab region and Europe (Merkur.de, 2015). By 2018, more than 1000 Islamists had left Germany to join the IS. Among them were predominantly young people between the ages of 18 and 30, approximately 20% were women. The majority of those who left were born in Germany and came from German municipalities with social hotspots and ghetto-like neighborhoods (IMK, 2015). One third of the persons who left

---

[5] Even if there is not much left of *Occupy in* 2019, one thing this social movement has achieved is that it has tried to establish a new positive narrative directed against the threat of capitalist globalization, in which there could be a time after capitalism. The approvals that Bernie Sanders received for his demands for social justice in the primaries for the 2016 US presidential election, especially among younger voters, can certainly be interpreted as an echo of this new narrative (also Žižek, 2018, p. 20).

[6] In 2015, *Peter R. Neumann* (2015, p. 90) believes that one must even assume up to 200,000 fighters in the ranks of the so-called Islamic State and take into account, in addition to approximately 30,000 to 40,000 people in the core organization of the IS, also helpers on the ground, but who have not taken an oath, and other tribal militias as well as smaller groups with which the IS cooperates.

the country were criminals before the start of their Islamist or Jihadist careers and had already been convicted of violent offences, property offences and offences against the Narcotics Act (Biene et al., 2016).

It has often been doubted that the refugees who have increasingly come to Germany since 2015 could also be potential terrorists (Mascolo, 2015). In the summer of 2016, however, there were increasing signs that the so-called Islamic State was calling on its followers to carry out acts of violence in Germany as well. On 18 July 2016, a man who had come to Germany as a refugee in 2015 injured five people with a hatchet; on 24 July 2016, a Syrian refugee detonated a backpack bomb in Ansbach, injuring 15 people; on 10 October 2016, a Syrian man was arrested by three compatriots after police mishaps in the manhunt. According to police, the arrested man had contact with IS and was preparing a terrorist attack in Germany. Although, according to German Interior Minister *Thomas de Maizière* after this arrest, the terror threat to Germany had not increased, the "threat posed by international terrorism" remained high.

On 19 December 2016, the threat became a deadly reality. At around 8 p.m., an Islamist bomber steered a truck into a crowd of people at the Christmas market at Berlin's Gedächtniskirche. Eleven visitors to the Christmas market were killed and 55 people were injured, some seriously. The truck had previously been attacked by the assassin and the Polish truck driver murdered by him. The assassin was able to flee and was shot dead days later in Milan by the police there.

The "dark threat" of international and transnational terrorism has left effects. Key events, such as the financial crisis in 2008, Islamist-inspired terrorist attacks or the refugee movements in 2015, as well as the penetration of capitalist principles of utility and exploitation into social relations have left large parts of the population with feelings of threat, disturbance, feelings of disadvantage. These key events were and are certainly not *fixed points* for finding security and support in difficult times.

The time-diagnostic descriptions of the present focus on the unpredictable realities that confront individual actors as well as groups, organizations, states, globally operating associations, or cultural communities. The unpredictable realities have to do not only with terrorist threats and migration, but also with mass unemployment, social degradation, environmental destruction, food risks, the dissolution of traditional social relations, fundamentalism, economic and digital networking, climate change, and so on. Whereas, incidentally, few seem to know what all will change with the increasing digitalization of the world. Air taxis alone will probably not be it.

There is no doubt that digitalization will change the world of work. The loss of traditional jobs, but also the creation of new jobs, is to be expected (Dengler & Matthes, 2015). Automation and robotics will replace some manual tasks. Simple work, those activities that do not require relevant vocational training and can be performed after short qualification or familiarization processes (e.g. in agriculture, healthcare, crafts or public administration), could all but disappear (Hirsch-Kreinsen, 2016). Everyday life will also not remain unaffected; not because Alexa knows our wishes before we ourselves wish for something. But because we will be confronted with new education and training requirements, new consumer offers or new conditions in health care.

In a survey conducted by *infratest dimap,* one in four German citizens said that increasing digitalization is mainly associated with opportunities, 17% see it mainly as a risk, and a majority of 53% thought that opportunities and risks are more or less balanced (infratest dimap, 2019).

At the end of the 1990s and in the transition to the twenty-first century, the "dark threats" in the West apparently reached a diversity and multiformity that it is not absurd to speak of a new age: an *age of diversified threats.* The apparent factual or post-factual threats posed by "Islam", "the" Muslims or "the" influx of refugees are only the surface of a new era.

On November 8, 2016, the elections for the US president took place and *Donald Trump* achieved the necessary majority of the electoral college. An election campaign came to an end that was unparalleled from the point of view of the feuilleton; and into the White House in Washington moved a man who is considered dangerous, unpredictable, sexist, racist, and hostile to Islam and Muslims. The right-wing populists in Germany and Europe welcomed the election results in the USA and see themselves strengthened in their fight against the political elites, the "lying press" and the "flood of migrants" (Fig. 6.3).

On November 3, 2020, Joe Biden was elected as the new US President. Will this change anything?

Bernd Ulrich is not so wrong in his assessment when he writes:

We live in an epochal upheaval, where you can choose what and who you want – the world as we knew it, it is no longer up for choice. The tides of time are sweeping us along like a waterfall. But how does one deal with it? (Ulrich, 2016).

Where are the fixed points?

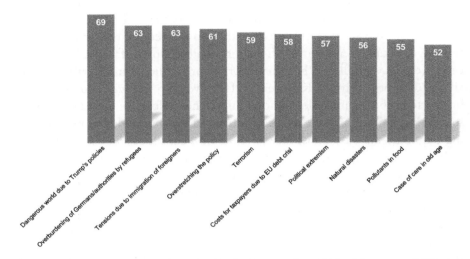

Fig. 6.3 Germans' top ten fears in 2018. (Source: R + V Versicherung., 2018; own representation)

References

Bade, K. J., & Jochen, O. (2005). *Flucht und Asyl seit 1990.* Bundeszentrale für politische Aufklärung. http://www.bpb.de/gesellschaft/migration/dossier-migration-ALT/56443/flucht-und-asyl-seit-1990. Accessed: 21. Okt. 2016.

Baecker, D. (2011). Die Sehnsucht, wieder einmal neu anzufangen. *The European.* https://www.theeuropean.de/dirk-baecker/8593-die-occupy-bewegung. Accessed: 28. März. 2019.

Baudrillard, J. (2003). *Der Geist des Terrorismus.* Wien: Passagen. English Version: The Spirit of Terrorism (2002), London, New York: Verso.

Biene, J., Daase, C., Junk, Julian, & Müller, H. (Hrsg.). (2016). Salafismus und Dschihadismus in Deutschland. Frankfurt a. M.: Campus.

Bock, A. (2009). *Terrorismus.* Paderborn: Fink.

Bonanno, G. A., & Jost, J. T. (2006). Conservative shift among high exposure survivors of the September 11th terrorist attacks. *Basic and Applied Social Psychology, 28,* 311–323.

Borradori, G. (2006). Vorwort. In J. Habermas & J. Derrida (Hrsg.), Philosophie in Zeiten des Terrors. Zwei Gespräche, geführt, eingeleitet und kommentiert von Giovanna Borradori (S. 9–17). Hamburg: Europäische Verlagsanstalt.

Bundesregierung. (2015). Besprechung der Bundeskanzlerin mit den Regierungschefinnen und Regierungschefs der Länder zur Asyl- und

Flüchtlingspolitik am 24. *September 2015.* https://www.bundesregierung.de/resource/blob/976072/432086/a0892e3d6adfceffbefc537c19c25d99/2015-09-24-bund-laender-fluechtlinge-beschluss-data.pdf?download=1. Accessed: 8. Dec. 2016.

Busse, T. (2000). *Weltuntergang als Erlebnis. Apokalyptische Erzählungen in den Massenmedien.* Wiesbaden: Deutscher Universitäts-Verlag.

Cheung-Blunden, V., & Blunden, B. (2008). The emotional construal of war: Anger, fear, and other negative emotions. *Peace and Conflict: Journal of Peace Psychology, 14*(2), 123–149.

Dengler, K., & Matthes, B. (2015). Folgen der Digitalisierung für die Arbeitswelt: Substituierbarkeitspotenziale von Berufen in Deutschland., (No. 11/2015). IAB-Forschungsbericht Nürnberg: IAB.

Derrida, J. (2000). *Apokalypse.* Wien: Passagen.

Destatis. (2015). Bevölkerung und Erwerbstätigkeit. Ausländische Bevölkerung. Ergebnisse des Ausländerzentralregisters. https://www.destatis.de/DE/Themen/Gesellschaft-Umwelt/Bevoelkerung/Migration-Integration/_inhalt.html?__blob=publicationFileaufgerufen. Accessed: 13. Dec. 2016.

Frindte, W., & Dietrich, N. (Eds.). (2017). *Muslime, Flüchtlinge und Pegida. Sozialpsychologische und kommunikationswissenschaftliche Studien in Zeiten globaler Bedrohungen.* Wiesbaden: Springer VS.

Frindte, W., & Haußecker, N. (2010). *Inszenierter Terrorismus.* Wiesbaden: VS Verlag.

Gaisbauer, G. (2000). *Weltendämmerungen: Endzeitvisionen und Apokalypsevorstellungen in der Literatur.* Passau: Erster Deutscher Fantasy Club.

Glaab, S. (Hrsg.). (2007). Medien und Terrorismus – Auf den Spuren einer symbiotischen Beziehung. Berlin: Berliner Wissenschaftsverlag.

Global Terrorism Database. (2017). https://www.start.umd.edu/gtd/. Accessed: 16. Dec. 2018.

Goethe, J. W. (1973). *Faust. Der Tragödie erster Teil* (Bd. 8)., Berliner Ausgabe Berlin: Aufbau Verlag.

Götz, R. (2006). *Russlands Wirtschaftsentwicklung. Abhängig vom Ölpreis oder der staatlichen Politik? SWP-Diskussionspapiere.* Berlin: Stiftung Wissenschaft und Politik. https://www.swp-berlin.org/fileadmin/contents/products/arbeitspapiere/gtz_russldwirtsch_ks.pdf. Accessed: 24. Okt. 2016.

Hirsch-Kreinsen, H. (2016). *Digitalisierung und Einfacharbeit.* Bonn: Friedrich-Ebert-Stiftung. https://library.fes.de/pdf-files/wiso/12645.pdf. Accessed: 1. März. 2019.

Hirschmann, K. (2006). *Internationaler Terrorismus.*, Informationen zur politischen Bildung, Nr. 291 Bonn: Bundeszentrale für politische Bildung.

Hoffmann, H., & Schoeller, W. F. (2001). *Wendepunkt 11. September. Terror, Islam und Demokratie.* Köln: DuMont.

Honegger, C., & Rychner, M. (1998). *Das Ende der Gemütlichkeit.* Zürich: Limmat.

IMK (Ständige Konferenz der Innenminister und -senatoren der Länder). (2015). *Analyse der Radikalisierungshintergründe und -verläufe der Personen, die aus islamistischer Motivation aus Deutschland in Richtung Syrien oder Irak ausgereist sind.* Fortschreibung 2015. http://www.innenministerkonferenz.de/IMK/DE/termine/to-beschluesse/2015-12-03_04/anlage_analyse.pdf?__blob=publicationFile&v=2. Accessed: 12. März. 2019.

Infratest dimap. (2019). ARD-DeutschlandTrend. https://www.infratest-dimap.de/umfragen-analysen/bundesweit/ard-deutschlandtrend/2019/januar/. Accessed: 10. Feb. 2019.

Kam, C. D., & Kinder, D. R. (2007). Terror and ethnocentrism: Foundations of American support for the war on terrorism. *The Journal of Politics, 69*(2), 320–338.

Letter to Baghdadi. (2014). Open letter to Dr. Ibrahim Awwad Al-Badri, alias 'Abu Bakr Al-Baghdadi', and to the fighters and followers of the self-declared 'Islamic State'. Internet Archive. http://web.archive.org/web/20160724162358/http://www.lettertobaghdadi.com. Accessed: 8. Dec. 2016.

Lyotard, J.-F. (1986). *Das postmoderne Wissen.* Graz: Böhlau. English version: The postmodern condition: A report on knowledge (1984), Minnesota: University of Minnesota Press. French original: La condition postmoderne: Rapport Sur le savoir, 1979.

Mascolo, G. (2015). Die Mär vom eingeschlichenen Terroristen. *Süddeutsche Zeitung.* https://www.sueddeutsche.de/politik/fluechtlinge-in-deutschland-die-maer-vom-eingeschlichenen-terroristen-1.2691972. Accessed: 7. Dec. 2016.

Merkur.de. (2015). Extremer Zulauf für Terrorgruppe Islamischer Staat. https://www.merkur.de/politik/extremer-zulauf-terrorgruppe-islamischer-staat-zr-3806698.html. Accessed: 18. Sept. 2015.

Neumann, P. R. (2015). *Die neuen Dschihadisten. IS, Europa und die nächste Welle des Terrorismus.* Berlin: Econ.

R+V Versicherung. (2016). Die Ängste der Deutschen 2016. Infocenter der R+V Versicherung. https://www.ruv.de/static-files/ruvde/downloads/presse/aengste-der-deutschen-2016/ruv-aengste-2016-grafiken-bundesweit.pdf. Accessed: 7. Dec. 2016.

R+V Versicherung. (2018). Die Ängste der Deutschen. https://www.ruv.de/presse/aengste-der-deutschen. Accessed: 1. Feb. 2019.

Schneckener, U. (2006). *Transnationaler Terrorismus.* Frankfurt a. M.: Suhrkamp.

Schulz, E. H., & Sempert, F. P. (2013). *Die Jahr-2000-Krise: Herausforderungen und Chancen für Gesellschaft und Unternehmen.* Wiesbaden: Gabler.

Sennett, R. (1998). *The corrosion of character: The personal consequences of work in the new capitalism.* London: W. W. Norton.

Der Spiegel. (1992). Ansturm vom Balkan. Wer nimmt die Flüchtlinge?. *Der Spiegel, 31.* http://www.spiegel.de/spiegel/print/index-1992-31.html. Accessed: 24. Okt. 2016.

Der Spiegel. (1998). Zu viele Ausländer?. Der Spiegel, 48. http://www.spiegel.de/spiegel/print/index-1998-48.html. Accessed: 6. Dec. 2016.

Der Spiegel. (2008). Showdown in Pristina. https://www.spiegel.de/politik/ausland/russischer-einmarsch-1999-showdown-in-pristina-a-535801.html. Accessed: 19. Apr. 2019.

Ulrich, B. (2016). Mutentbrannt. Zeit Online. https://www.zeit.de/2016/31/globale-krisen-brexit-europa-tuerkei-chaos-terrorismus-putsch. Accessed: 7. März. 2019.

Žižek, S. (2018). *Der Mut der Hoffnungslosigkeit*. Frankfurt a. M.: Fischer. English version: „the courage of hopelessness" (2017), London: Allen lane.

Part II

Threats 2.0: Post-factual and Factual Stories

7

Fake News and Three Stories

> **The First Story Goes Like This**
>
> "A man from Gothenburg had a strange feeling in the morning when he was shaving in the bathroom, as if someone was watching him. But when he turned around, there was no one there. One morning he gets that feeling again and turns around quickly. Just then he sees a boa pull its head in and disappear into the toilet bowl. Turns out the snake belonged to a neighbor from the apartment next door. He had gone away for a week and had locked the animal in his bathroom. There it had wormed its way into the toilet bowl and was thus able to get into other apartments via the drainage network" (Klintberg, 1990, p. 56).

So Much for the Narrative, and Now the Commentary

"In December 1973 I gave a guest lecture at the Ethnological Institute in Gothenburg on folk tales of our time. Among other things, I told about the alligators in the New York sewers. Afterwards, two students, Ylva Bengtsson and Inger Erikson, each wrote down the same story – the one about the boa in the toilet. As they said, it was often heard in Gothenburg [...]. On 6.7.1974 Aftonbladet reported what AP (Associated Press; WF/IF) had known to report from Sidney: *A python snake a good 2.5 m long disappeared into Sidney's sewage system and reappeared in the toilet of an apartment four blocks away* [...]. On 31.10. 1978 Aftonbladet again ran an article on the subject. This time the news was big, because it had happened in Gothenburg. The headline read: *A boa on the toilet!* [...]. On 30.6.1980 Dagens Nyheter had the following news: *Python escaped. To be joined in the bathroom by a python snake is something that can happen at any time. At least in Gothenburg and at least theoretically. There, a python escaped from its owner through the drain. It is three and a half meters*

© The Author(s), under exclusive license to Springer Fachmedien Wiesbaden GmbH, part
of Springer Nature 2022
W. Frindte, I. Frindte, *Support in Times of No Support*,
https://doi.org/10.1007/978-3-658-38637-5_7

long and weighs 13 K [...]. No, the story of large snakes in the drainage network are creations of human imagination" (Klintberg 1990, p. 57 f.; emphasis in the original).

By the way: On August 2, 1995, the "Ostthüringer Zeitung" passes on the following dpa report: "A python snake one and a half meters long has terrified a Spanish family in Madrid. The 16-year-old Natalia found the reptile in the bathtub. Police transported the animal away, which will now be housed in a zoo. How the python got into the bathtub is still unclear."

So be careful the next time you take a seat on the toilet bowl!

The Second Story Is a Quote from *Donald Trump*

In mid-June 2019, the then-U.S. president opened the campaign for his 2020 re-election, telling 20,000 supporters in Florida, "Our radical Democratic opponents are driven by hatred, prejudice and anger ... They want to destroy you, and they want to destroy our country as we know it" (Time Online, 2019).

On the Third Story

In March 2017, the AfD district association Stormarn (in Schleswig-Holstein) published a travel warning for Sweden on Facebook:

> "Trump was right: Foreign Office issues travel warning for Sweden! Since the beginning of March, Sweden has been on a heightened terror alert" (Merkur.de, 2017). A few days earlier, said Donald Trump had spoken of alleged problems with refugees in Sweden during a speech in Florida: "Look at what's happening in Germany, look at what happened in Sweden last night. Sweden, would you believe it? Sweden. They took in huge numbers, and now they have problems they never thought possible" (Welt.de, 2017). Former Swedish Prime Minister *Carl Bildt* asked on Twitter, "Sweden? Terror attack? What was he smoking?"

What Connects the Stories?

They are "newspaper ducks", lies or fake news. The first story is told by *Bengt af Klintberg* in his beautiful book "The Rat in the Pizza and Other Modern Tales and Urban Myths" (1990). The stories of large snakes in the drainage network are creations of the human imagination. As such, they are both titillating and terrifying. If we are to read a symbolic meaning into this story, it has to do with an existential insecurity of our time. The second story is – as I said – a statement by Donald Trump. Whether the AfD (the German political party "Alternative für Deutschland") made up the third story or "just" diligently spread it around cannot be determined. What is certain, however, is that it is a lie, which the German Federal Foreign Office immediately corrected. There was no travel warning for Sweden: "The Foreign Office pointed out a year ago that the Swedish government had lowered the terror alert level. Sorry if that sounds less interesting" (Merkur.de, 2017).

> *Fake news* usually refers to launched and published false reports that spread predominantly on the Internet, especially on social networks and other social media, sometimes virally.

But fake news is not always fake news. In communication studies, a distinction is made between fake news as a *label* and as a *genre* (Zimmermann & Kohring, 2018). Fake news is a label when it is used for political instrumentalization. For example, when the former US president, in his inimitable logic that would make the old Greek *Aristotle* turn in his grave, claims: "…the news is fake, because so much of the news is fake" (Trump at a press conference on 16 February 2017; Independent, 2017). One has to think about this sentence for its logic: News is fake because so much of the news is fake. Even when scolding the "lying press", a label is used for political instrumentalization and defamation.

As a *genre,* fake news belongs to disinformation, i.e. fake news or false reports spread by the media.

Fake news is now seen as symptoms of a post-factual era.

In February 2017, Bitkom (2017), Germany's digital association, published the results of an online survey (involving 1009 people), according to which 74% of respondents agreed with the statement that fake news could play an important role in the upcoming federal election campaign (i.e. in autumn 2017). And in summer 2017, *Christian Reuter* and colleagues asked a representative sample of 1023 adult Germans aged 18–64 about their attitudes towards fake news (Reuter et al. 2019). Figure 7.1 provides an excerpt from the findings. According to this, more than 80% of respondents believe that fake news poses a threat and 78% fear that fake news could threaten democracy.

Early in 2019, *Dimitra Liotsiou, Bence Kollanyi,* and *Philip N. Howard* (2019) present a "Junk News Aggregator," an interactive web tool that aims to make it possible to check, in real time, anything posted publicly on Facebook in English to see if it is factual.

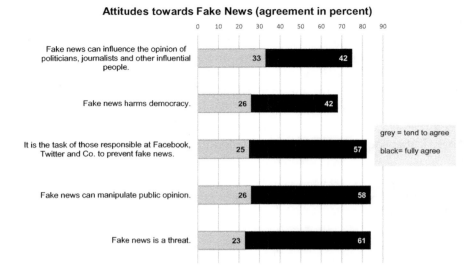

Fig. 7.1 Attitude towards Fake News. (After Reuter et al., 2019; own presentation)

The question of the value of such an app is obvious. Do we need technical support to protect us from Fake News or do we depend on Fake News to protect our beliefs?

References

Bitkom. (2017). Bitkom mahnt zu Besonnenheit im Umgang mit Fake News. https://www.bitkom.org/Presse/Presseinformation/Bitkom-mahnt-zu-Besonnenheit-im-Umgang-mit-Fake-News.html. Accessed: 30. Juni 2017.

Independent. (2017). Donald Trump: 'The leaks are absolutely real. The news is fake'. https://www.independent.co.uk/news/world/americas/us-politics/donald-trump-russia-leaks-fake-news-claims-quote-a7584516.html. Accessed: 24. März 2019.

Klintberg, B. (1990). *Die Ratte in der Pizza – Und andere moderne Sagen und Großstadtmythen.* Kiel: Butt Verlag. Swedish Original: Råttan i pizzan. Stockholm: Norstedts.

Liotsiou, D., Kollanyi, B., & Howard, P. N. (2019). The junk news aggregator: Examining junk news posted on Facebook, starting with the 2018 US midterm elections. arXiv:1901.07920. Accessed: 12. Apr. 2019.

Merkur.de. (2017). Fake News: Auswärtiges Amt dementiert Reisewarnung für Schweden. https://www.merkur.de/reise/fake-news-auswaertiges-amt-dementiert-reisewarnung-fuer-schweden-zr-7509217.html. Accessed: 18. März 2019.

Reuter, C., Hartwig, K., Kirchner, J., & Schlegel, N. (2019). Fake news perception in Germany: A representative study of people's attitudes and approaches to counteract disinformation. In *Proceedings of the 14th International Conference on Wirtschaftsinformatik, February 24–27, 2019.*

Welt.de. (2017). "Schaut euch an, was gestern Abend in Schweden passiert ist". https://www.welt.de/politik/ausland/article162200796/Schaut-euch-an-was-gestern-Abend-in-Schweden-passiert-ist.html. Accessed: 18. März 2019.

Zeit Online. (2019). Donald Trump ruft im Wahlkampf gegen „zerstörerische Demokraten" auf. https://www.zeit.de/politik/ausland/2019-06/usa-donald-trump-wahlkampf-2020-auftakt-orlando. Accessed: 6. Juli 2019.

Zimmermann, F., & Kohring, M. (2018). "Fake News" als aktuelle Desinformation. Systematische Bestimmung eines heterogenen Begriffs. *M&K Medien & Kommunikationswissenschaft, 66*(4), 526–541.

8

In the Post-factual Age?

As is well known, it is difficult to determine what an age or era is, when it will end and a new age or era will begin. Let us take modernity, for example. Are we dealing with an epoch in which economy, politics, science, culture and all important areas of life are ordered and criticized according to rational criteria, i.e. the main task of modernity is the establishment of order, as the sociologist *Zygmunt Bauman* thinks (1992, p. 16)? Or are we dealing with various concepts of modernity, with which *Wolfgang Welsch* already struggled years ago (Welsch, 1991, p. 46 ff.)? After the various modernities, the modernity of the Enlightenment and of rationalism, the modernity of industrialization as well as the modernity of the emancipation of mankind, does postmodernity now follow or is it rather a Second Modernity? The term *Second Modernity* was introduced into academic debates primarily by the sociologist *Ulrich Beck*. After Beck pointed out the risks knowingly produced by humans (environmental pollution, forest dieback, nuclear power, etc.) and their consequences in his book "Risk Society" (1986) at the end of the 1980s, *Beck* later extended his analysis to the comprehensive globalized risks and opportunities of world society (Beck, 1997, 2007).

The concept of *postmodernism*, however, is a matter of some sort. The term has a long history, which – if one follows *Wolfgang Welsch* (1991, p. 9 ff.) again – already appears before 1918, found increasing currency in the North American literary debates in the 1960s, and was vehemently introduced into everyday life by the architect *Charles Jencks* (1978) at the latest in the mid-1970s.

W. Frindte, I. Frindte, *Support in Times of No Support*, https://doi.org/10.1007/978-3-658-38637-5_8

"Postmodernism," according to Welsch, "occurs where a fundamental pluralism of languages, models, modes of procedure is practiced, and not merely in different works side by side, but in one and the same work" (Welsch, 1991, p. 16 f.).

Postmodern conceptions, from whatever scientific or non-scientific corner, appeared in the 1980s and 1990s from this point of view as colorful patchworks, as set pieces from which anyone who liked it (and who detested order) could select what he liked at will.

However, we join *Wolfgang Welsch in* opposing an equation of eclecticism and postmodernism. In the postmodern concepts that Welsch obviously likes and that are also very clear to us, it was and is not just about *crazy quilts,* about colorful patchwork carpets. Not the conceptless accumulation of ideas, but the equal existence of different ideas, the practiced pluralism is still a basic value of postmodern conceptions that are to be taken seriously.

Influential German thinkers have often seen things quite differently. The Tübingen philosopher *Manfred Frank,* for example, sees close parallels between the postmodern views of the French Jean-François Lyotard or Jacques Derrida and Social Darwinism, and even thinks that with the conceptions of French postmodernism "the dark (and denied) underside of our own (the German, W.F. & I.F.) philosophical culture is coming back to us" (Frank, 1993, p. 123). This is strong stuff. The rather undifferentiated equation of postmodernism and neoconservatism by *Jürgen Habermas* is almost benevolent (Habermas, 1981). *Samuel Salzborn* is even of the opinion that postmodernism pays homage to cultural relativism and has completely rejected the dialectic of enlightenment (Salzborn, 2018, p. 100).

This could be countered: The influential conceptions of postmodern thinkers (e.g. *Jacques Derrida, Gilles Deleuze, Umberto Eco, Michel Foucault, Paul Feyerabend, Jean-Francois Lyotard,* and many others) are not about throwing the dialectic of the Enlightenment completely overboard, but about the equal existence of different ideas and about a practiced pluralism, which is also part of the ambivalences of modernity.

Whether postmodernism as a social phenomenon can claim the status of an epoch or an age, or whether it was only an ideological patchwork that has long since faded, remains a matter of debate (e.g. Eagleton, 1997; Krause, 2007). *Umberto Eco*, who, not to be forgotten, also paid homage to postmodernism with his works, meanwhile believes "that "postmodern" is not a current that can be limited in time, but a state of mind or, more precisely, an approach, a *will to art.* One could almost say that every epoch has its own postmodernism" (Eco, 1986, p. 77; emphasis in original).

And what comes next, post-postmodernism, the third modernity or the post-factual age?

Perhaps there is even a much more concise, scientifically sound and for mankind more important division of the ages. In June 2019, geologists met in Berlin to search for facts that could point to the fact that we, i.e. mankind, have entered a new epoch (Häntzschel, 2019). According to said geologists, we are at the end of an Earth age they call the *Holocene*. This is the last 12,000 years, which may have been the most fertile for humanity. Now, they say, we are entering the *Anthropocene*, an age in which humans are exploiting and destroying their habitat to a degree that has previously only occurred through meteorite impacts and volcanic eruptions. Humans have become a force of nature from which they may perish.

Since 2015 at the latest, one has been reading in the German feuilletons that we have left the age of factual reasoning behind us and are now in the *post-factual age*. Even the German Chancellor – who was still in office at the time of writing – spoke of post-factual times, in which people are no longer interested in facts but seem to follow their feelings (Der Spiegel, 2016).

The Gesellschaft für deutsche Sprache (Society for the German Language) chose *post-factual as* its word of the year for 2016, stating: "The artificial word *post-factual* […] refers to the fact that political and social discussions today are increasingly about emotions instead of facts. Ever larger segments of the population, in their distaste for "those up there", are prepared to ignore facts and even willingly accept obvious lies. It is not the claim to truth, but the utterance of the "felt truth" that leads to success in the "post-factual age"" (Gesellschaft für deutsche Sprache, 2016, emphasis in original).

In 2016, Oxford University Press also elevated the word *post-truth* (comparable to the German word *postfaktisch*) to word of the year.

Talk of the post-factual age has also arrived in academic discourse, even if the term is usually placed in quotation marks. Political scientists, for example, write about the new requirements for political education in the "post-factual age" (Deichmann & May, 2019), social scientists are concerned about authoritarian attitudes in this very age (Milbradt, 2018), or media scientists, such as *Bernhard Pörksen* (2018), see in the talk of the post-factual age a word of resignation that immediately turns an experienced crisis of truth into an incontrovertible outcome of human history.

First, let's look again at some catchy and impactful examples:

One of the oldest disinformation, which spread rapidly and left effects, might be the story of the *Queen Esther*, her cousin and adoptive father *Mordecai* and the Jew-hater Haman: The story is reported in the Book of Esther, the historical reliability of which is, admittedly, well debatable. *Ahasuerus,* actually Artaxerxes (possibly 464 to 424 B.C.), who was King from the Indus to the Nile, had taken the beautiful Jewess Esther, who had been raised as an orphan by her cousin Mordecai, as his wife, without knowing of her Jewish origin. Mordecai, having uncovered a plot to murder Ahasuerus, refused to bend the knee before Haman, the chief priest, that is, to pay him homage. Haman, who in turn had learned of Mordecai's Jewishness, became full of fury and spoke to the King that there was a people in the Kingdom who were different from all peoples and did not respect the King's laws. With this false claim, Haman succeeded in persuading the king to issue a decree for the destruction of the Jews.

> And letters were sent by the runners into all the King's countries, to destroy, to kill, and to put to death all the Jews, young and old, children and women, in one day, even in the 13th day of the twelfth month, which is the month Adar, and to spoil their goods and chattels. (Esther, 3: 13-14)

The exact time of the massacre was to be determined by lot – hence the name Purim (lots). Mordecai also learned of the decree and did everything in his power to inform his foster daughter Ester of the planned murder of the Jews. She finally succeeded in convincing the Persian King to revoke his decree. Haman was executed on the gallows and the King had the decree reversed; the Jews were now allowed to take revenge on their enemies throughout the empire; they killed "75000 of their enemies; but to the goods they laid not their hands" (Esther, 9: 17). Mordecai and Esther then declared the Festival of Purim a holiday of Jewish salvation.

Purim has thus become a commemoration of the salvation of the Jewish people from imminent danger in the Persian diaspora. In the synagogue, on this occasion, the festival scroll of the Book of Esther is read aloud and whenever the name of *Haman is* mentioned, as much noise as possible may be made with hoots and rattles. Haman's name became a symbol of hostility to the Jews, and Haman's planned murder is one of the first, historically unattested, examples of the orchestrated extermination of the Jews. Out of anger about the refused homage by the *one* Jew Mordechai, false images about the Jews, fake news, are constructed and spread to justify the extermination.

For the National Socialists, the festival of Purim was again and again an occasion to accuse the Jews of murdering their enemies and to regale the German people with old legends about alleged "Purim murders" committed

by the Jews against non-Jews. Thus in 1934 the Germans could read in the
11th issue of the "Stürmer" under the headline "Die Mordnacht – Das
Geheimnis des jüdischen Purimfestes ist enthüllt" (The Night of Murder –
The Secret of the Jewish Purim Festival is Revealed) among other things the
following:

> Many a mysterious murder, which could not be uncovered, is nothing else than
> a sacrificial murder for the *Purim festival*. In March of the year 1929 (at the time
> of the Purim festival), in Gladbeck, the Primaner Helmut Daube, a splendid
> blond boy, was killed by butcher cuts. His body was found in front of his par-
> ents' house. And in March of the year 1932 (also at the time of the Purim festi-
> val) the maid Kaspar in Paderborn was also butchered by the Jews Meyer (father
> and son) and cut into small pound-sized pieces of meat. Both murders were
> Purimfest sacrificial murders. And thousands and thousands of murders could
> be added to these. And we know the one great Purim murder that all world
> Jewry craves is the murder of the Fuhrer and his comrades in arms… The Jews
> will be wrong. The great turn of the world has come. The turning point in which
> the Jew will no longer be victorious, but the *Aryan*. But this victory, we know
> and Alljuda suspects: *this victory means the downfall of the Jewish world enemy.*
> ("Der Stürmer" 1934, No. 11; all emphasis in the original)

It is surely not necessary to add that none of these legends about alleged
Purim murders were based on facts; or is it necessary to emphasize it; is it
necessary to say it again and again that with the accusation of Purim and ritual
murders the murdering only started, the mass murder of the Jews?

The "Protocols of the Wise Men of Zion" are a more recent example of
anti-Semitism orchestrated by means of fake news. In this anti-Semitic collection of alleged transcripts of Jewish secret meetings, published in the press of
Tsarist Russia in 1903, it was claimed that the Jews were striving for "world
domination".

So says a passage that tells of a midnight meeting of representatives of the
12 Jewish tribes:

> On the day when we shall have made ourselves the sole possessors of all the gold
> in the world, the real power will be in our hands, and then the promises made
> to Abraham will be fulfilled. (From the *Rabbi's speech*; quoted in Cohn,
> 1998, p. 293)[1]

---

[1] *Norman Cohn* proves that this passage appears in a modified form as early as 1868 in a novel by Hermann
Goedsche, who wrote under the pseudonym Sir John Retclif, and was then reproduced in a Russian
pamphlet in 1876 and later found its way into the "Protocols".

This collection is a forgery that may have been created in France between 1894 and 1899, the period in which a new wave of anti-Semitism arose in France with the Dreyfus Affair. After the First World War, the text was disseminated internationally. In Germany, a translation was published in 1920 by Baron Müller von Hausen, who was a captain on Ludendorff's staff during World War 1 and served as publisher of an anti-Semitic journal. This German edition reached a circulation of 120,000. Another edition, also from 1920, reached a circulation of about 100,000 (Hein, 1996). Although the "Protocols" had already been exposed as a forgery in the London "Times" in 1921, a total of 33 editions of the text appeared in Germany until 1933. The "Protocols" were also distributed in large numbers in France, Britain, and the United States in the 1920s, becoming the most widely read anti-Semitic writing of the twentieth century. Henry Ford, founder of the Ford Motor Company, had millions of copies of the "Protocols" printed in 1920. Adolf Hitler quotes from the "Protocols" in "Mein Kampf." And even today many anti-Semites and conspiracy theorists refer to these "Protocols". In the Islamic world, they are still among the bestsellers.

Anti-Semitism is not only based on false projections, it projects false images. With the "Protocols", the anti-Semites present a fake drama to the astonished audience, in which the Jews are constructed as the people who are per se hostile to their own people or nation.

By the way: Umberto Eco's novel "The Cemetery in Prague" (Eco, 2013) is worth reading, even if it is a bit exhausting in parts. With the usual mixture of history, criminal, sabotage, spiritual and fictional, Eco tells how a single man at the end of the nineteenth century spun up the "Protocols of the Wise Men of Zion" in France, wrote them and sold them to the Russian secret service.

> Let's come to a tentative conclusion: the post-factual age does not begin with *Donald Trump*, nor with the current doubts about scientific truths, nor with social media. Propaganda and disinformation are nothing new. Perhaps humans have always lived in a post-factual age (Harari, 2018), or to paraphrase *Umberto Eco* (1986, p. 77): Perhaps every era has its post-factual time.

There are other historical examples for this thesis. One thinks for instance of the *Donation of Constantine*. According to a document – so it is reported – Emperor Constantine in the years 315/317 AD, out of gratitude that he was cured of leprosy through baptism, transferred the western half of the Roman Empire to Pope Silvester I and all his successors by means of a donation.

Constantine thus held court in Constantinople in the future and ruled over the Eastern Roman Empire, while Silvester assumed power in the Western Roman Empire. Only two scholars of the fifteenth century, first in 1433 the German theologian and philosopher *Nicholas of Cusa* and then around 1440 the Italian humanist *Lorenzo Valla,* proved that the donation was a forgery (Miethke, 2008).

The lie with which Adolf Hitler justified the Wehrmacht's attack on Poland in front of the Reichstag in Berlin on September 1, 1939, also belongs to the historical fake news with terrible sustainability. Allegedly, Polish soldiers had attacked the radio station in Gliwice. "Since 5:45 a.m. they have now been firing back," Hitler told. In fact, the SS staged this raid.

On June 15, 1961, the GDR's head of state and party leader, *Walter Ulbricht*, speaks to several hundred journalists from around the world. When asked by the Berlin correspondent of the Frankfurter Rundschau, Annamarie Doherr, whether the GDR wanted to build a state border at the Brandenburg Gate, Ulbricht answered after a short pause with the famous sentence: "Nobody has the intention to build a wall" (Zeit Online, 2011). It would have been nice, but we are dealing with disinformation in the style of fake news, as it turned out two months later[2].

Indeed, according to *Yuval Noah Harari* (2018, p. 310), humans have always lived in an era of the post-factual. Therefore, not only from a historical perspective, it hardly seems appropriate to call the current age the era of the post-factual. From a psychological perspective, the narrative about a current post-factual age is also unlikely to be tenable. People do not simply map the world in which they live. Everything people feel, think, and do is the result of individual and social constructions that are negotiated against the backdrop of self-referential mental processes in social understanding. The individually and socially created constructions of the world can certainly be described as post-factual images of reality. The problem of the post-factual, however, is by no means settled with this.

References

Bauman, Z. (1992). *Moderne und Ambivalenz.* Hamburg: Junius. English Version: Modernity and ambivalence. Ithaca, N.Y: Cornell University Press.

---

[2] However, one can argue whether *Walter Ulbricht* uttered this sentence consciously or whether it was a Freudian slip (Welt.de 2011). This does not change anything.

Beck, U. (1986). *Risikogesellschaft – Auf dem Weg in eine andere Moderne*. Frankfurt a. M.: Suhrkamp. English Version: Risk society – Towards a new modernity. London: Sage.

Beck, U. (1997). *Was ist Globalisierung?* Frankfurt a. M.: Suhrkamp. English Version: What is globalization? Cambridge, Oxford: Polity.

Beck, U. (2007). *Weltrisikogesellschaft: Auf der Suche nach der verlorenen Sicherheit*. Frankfurt a. M.: Suhrkamp. English Version: World risk society. Cambridge, Oxford: Polity.

Cohn, N. (1998). *"Die Protokolle der Weisen von Zion". Der Mythos der jüdischen Weltverschwörung*. Baden-Baden: Elster Verlag.

Deichmann, C., & May, M. (Hrsg.). (2019). *Orientierungen politischer Bildung im "postfaktischen Zeitalter"*. Wiesbaden: Springer VS.

Der Spiegel. (2016). *"Postfaktisch" ist das internationale Wort des Jahres*. http://www.spiegel.de/kultur/gesellschaft/postfaktisch-internationales-wort-des-jahres-a-1121598.html. Accessed 22 Dec 2016.

Der Stürmer. (1934). *Nr. 11*. http://www.humanist.de/kriminalmuseum/st-t3411.htm. Accessed 25 März 2019.

Eagleton, T. (1997). *Die Illusionen der Postmoderne*. Stuttgart: J. B. Metzler. English Version: The illusions of postmodernism. Hoboken, N.J.: Wiley-Blackwell.

Eco, U. (1986). *Nachschrift zum "Namen der Rose"*. München: Deutscher Taschenbuch Verlag.

Eco, U. (2013). *Der Friedhof in Prag*. München: Deutscher Taschenbuch Verlag.

Frank, M. (1993). *Conditio moderna*. Leipzig: Reclam.

Gesellschaft für deutsche Sprache. (2016). *GfdS wählt "postfaktisch" zum Wort des Jahres 2016*. http://gfds.de/wort-des-jahres-2016. Accessed 9 Dec 2016.

Habermas, J. (1981). *Die Moderne – ein unvollendetes. Kleine politische Schriften I-IV* (S. 444–464). Frankfurt a. M.: Suhrkamp.

Häntzschel, J. (2019). Menschengewalt. *Süddeutsche Zeitung* vom 1./2. Juni 2019.

Harari, Y. N. (2018). *21 Lektionen für das 21. Jahrhundert*. München: C. H. Beck. English Version: 21 lessons for the 21st century. London: Random House.

Hein, A. (1996). *"Es ist viel 'Hitler' in Wagner": Rassismus und antisemitische Deutschtumsideologie in den "Bayreuther Blättern"*. Tübingen: Niemeyer.

Jencks, C. (1978). *Die Sprache der postmodernen Architektur*. Stuttgart: DVA. English Version: the language of postmodern architecture. New York: Rizzoli.

Krause, D. (2007). *Postmoderne – Über die Untauglichkeit eines Begriffs der Philosophie, Architekturtheorie und Literaturtheorie*. Frankfurt a. M.: Peter Lang.

Miethke, J. (2008). Die "Konstantinische Schenkung" in der mittelalterlichen Diskussion Ausgewählte Kapitel einer verschlungenen Rezeptionsgeschichte. In A. Goltz & H. Schlange-Schöningen (Hrsg.), *Konstantin der Große, Das Bild des Kaisers im Wandel der Zeiten* (S. 35–109). Köln: Böhlau.

Milbradt, B. (2018). *Über autoritäre Haltungen in, postfaktischen Zeiten*. Opladen: Verlag Barbara Budrich.

Pörksen, B. (2018). Die Deregulierung des Wahrheitsmarktes Von der Macht der Desinformation im digitalen Zeitalter. In G. Blamberger, A. Freimuth, & P. Strohschneider (Hrsg.), *Vom Umgang mit Fakten: Antworten aus Natur-, Sozial- und Geisteswissenschaften*. Paderborn: Fink Verlag.

Salzborn, S. (2018). *Globaler Antisemitismus. Eine Spurensuche in den Abgründen der Moderne*. Weinheim: Beltz Juventa.

Welsch, W. (1991). *Unsere postmoderne Moderne* (3. Aufl. Aufl.). Weinheim: VCH, Acta Humaniora.

Welt.de. (2011). *Niemand hat die Absicht, eine Mauer zu errichten*. https://www.welt.de/kultur/history/article13428422/Niemand-hat-die-Absicht-eine-Mauer-zu-errichten.html. Accessed 23 März 2019.

Zeit Online. (2011). *Niemand hat die Absicht, eine Mauer zu errichten*. https://www.zeit.de/wissen/geschichte/2011-06/mauerbau-ddr-geschichte. Accessed 05 Feb 2019.

9

Factual and Fake News on Climate Change

Since the end of December 2018, a social movement of pupils and students has been forming under the label "Fridays for Future". With their movement, the young people want to draw attention to climate policy grievances and demand that fundamental measures for climate protection be adopted immediately and that the Paris Agreement on climate protection from 2015 finally be translated into practically effective action. To this end, they take to the streets weekly, always on Fridays and during school hours. The demonstrations are creative and peaceful. The public and political reactions more than diverse. Large parts of the German and international public, including numerous scientists, support the actions, for example through the action "Scientists-for-Future", which has been joined by about 23,000 scientists from Germany, Austria and Switzerland until March 2019. Another part accuses the young people of ignorance and disregard for compulsory education. The initiator of the movement, the Swedish schoolgirl *Greta Thunberg*, is described either as the idol of a new extra-parliamentary opposition or as the victim of a profit-oriented PR initiative.

Factually, the problems of climate change are among the greatest challenges and risks. Global climate change and global warming are largely man-made and threaten humanity in all parts of the world (UN Intergovernmental Panel on Climate Change, 2018). Heavy rainfall events and floods in Europe, the increase of drought not only in Africa, rising sea levels in the Pacific region, increasing glacier melt in Antarctica or the Alps, destructive hurricanes in North America – all these are clear indications of the dangers. The UN Intergovernmental Panel on Climate Change (IPCC) – an independent

W. Frindte, I. Frindte, *Support in Times of No Support*,
https://doi.org/10.1007/978-3-658-38637-5_9

scientific body in which hundreds of scientists from all over the world partici-pate – states in a recent report that global warming will probably increase by 1.5 °C between 2030 and 2052. This is associated with further increases in climate-related risks to health, livelihood security, food and water security, human security and economic growth. If global warming were to increase by more than 2 °C, these risks and dangers would become even greater. What would be needed, among other things, would be a reduction in global CO_2 emissions well before 2030 (UN Intergovernmental Panel on Climate Change, 2018). If global warming were to increase by 4°, sea levels could rise up to 11 m in a few decades, threatening the homes of up to 800 million people (Climate Central, 2019).

Although climate data shows that it is "5 to 12" and humanity has little time left to aggressively pursue climate action radically, now and not 20 years from now, there are people and institutions that doubt man-made climate threats and call it Fake News. In June 2017 the former US President *Donald Trump* announced he was pulling out of the Paris climate agreement. In November 2018, he had dismissed US officials' warning about the economic consequences and damages caused by global warming, saying he did not believe what scientists from the *National Climate Assessment* had published. When it comes to the man-made dangers of climate change, Trump speaks of hoaxes and fake news.

Alexander Gauland said in early 2019 at the state party conference of the AfD in Brandenburg that he did not believe the "fairy tale of man-made climate change" (Hannoversche Allgemeine, 2019). In the hot summer of 2018, Beatrix von Storch, deputy parliamentary group leader of the AfD in the German Bundestag, tweeted, "Yes. It is warm. Very much so. But this hysterical climate crisis screeching of the climate Nazis is really unbearable. Even if we all walk instead of building cars, all gendergagists will just eat broccoli: the sun doesn't care" (Huffingtonpost, 2018; comma errors and abbreviations in original). Ms. von Storch gets 1312 "likes" for her tweet. Now that is admittedly not the masses. The AfD's influence as a climate change denier, however, is not small.

In Europe, it is mainly the supporters of the right-wing populist parties, the German AfD, the Austrian FPÖ, the British Ukip or the Dutch PVV, who dispute the scientific findings on climate change. *Stella Schaller* and *Alexander Carius of* the Berlin-based think tank *adelphi* have studied the voting behavior of right-wing and right-wing populist parties in the European Parliament on climate change issues. The authors conclude that two out of three right-wing populist MEPs regularly vote against climate and energy policy measures. Half of all votes against resolutions on climate and energy come from the right-wing populist party spectrum. In this context, the AfD appears particularly as a representative of local initiatives that seek to prevent wind farms (Schaller & Carius, 2019).

According to a survey by the US polling institute *Pew Research Center,* 71% of Germans see climate change as the greatest threat to their security and prosperity, while 59% in the USA and 67% worldwide are very concerned about climate change (Pew Reserarch, 2018). Supporters and adherents of right-wing populist parties are more climate change skeptical – compared to the majority population. For example, perceived threats in the face of climate change are 28% points lower among supporters of the AfD than among the average population. Supporters of the Front National in France or the British anti-European UKIP are also more climate change skeptical than the respective national average.

Pew Research Center data provide interesting insights into the relationship between conservative or liberal ideological beliefs (of US Americans) and attitudes towards climate change (Benegal, 2018). While liberal and very liberal individuals are convinced of man-made climate change, conservative or very conservative individuals deny human influence on climate change and instead believe it is a natural process. *Aaron McCright and Riley Dunlap* (2011), after analyzing Gallup polls from 2001 to 2010 – i.e. before the "Trump era" – conclude that those who would deny climate change in the USA are primarily conservative white males. To speak of a "conservative white male effect" is therefore not so far-fetched (McCright & Dunlap, 2013).

In addition to climate change, people around the world felt threatened by the US under President Trump's leadership – at least until early 2021. In Germany in particular, the number of people who perceived the USA under Trump as a global threat increased dramatically. The results of R + V Versicherung's annual survey of German fears indicate – as we mentioned earlier (see Chap. 6) – that Germans have a pronounced fear of the USA under *Donald Trump.* As a reminder: In 2018, 69% of Germans said their greatest fear was fed by the "dangerous world caused by Trump's policies".

In most other European countries, too, people felt more threatened by the USA and *Donald Trump* than by Russia and Vladimir Putin (cf. Tagesschau. de, 2019).[1]

Christian Crandall, Jason Miller and Mark White (2018) even speak of a *Trump effect,* which was initiated by the election of the US president and is reflected above all in the change in the social climate and can be measured by the increase in prejudice against ethnic minorities and attacks on migrants and refugees.

---

[1] That may have changed since February 24, 2022, after Russia attacked Ukraine.

However, the perceived threats from the US and *Donald Trump* are only signs that stand for something else – for the dark sides of globalization, for the attacks on basic democratic and humanistic values, for authoritarian capitalism, for authoritarian national radicalism (Heitmeyer, 2018).

References

Benegal, S. D. (2018). The impact of unemployment and economic risk perceptions on attitudes towards anthropogenic climate change. *Journal of Environmental Studies and Sciences, 8*(3), 300–311.

Climate Central. (2019). *Surging seas.* http://sealevel.climatecentral.org/. Accessed 25 März 2019.

Crandall, C. S., Miller, J. M., & White, M. H. (2018). Changing norms following the 2016 US presidential election: The Trump effect on prejudice. *Social Psychological and Personality Science, 9*(2), 186–192.

Hannoversche Allgemeine. (2019). *AfD gehört in Europa zu den härtesten Klimawandel-Leugnern.* http://www.haz.de/Nachrichten/Politik/Deutschland-Welt/AfD-gehoert-in-Europa-zu-den-haertesten-Klimawandel-Leugnern. Accessed 25 März 2019.

Heitmeyer, W. (2018). *Autoritäre Versuchungen: Signaturen der Bedrohung I.* Berlin: Suhrkamp Verlag.

Huffingtonpost. (2018). *Von Storch steigt Hitze zu Kopf: AfD-Frau wütet gegen "Klimanazis".* https://www.huffingtonpost.de/entry/von-storch-steigt-hitze-zu-kopf-afd-frau-wutet-gegen-klimanazis_de_5b602636e4b0fd5c73d2eac5. Accessed 20 Sept 2018.

McCright, A. M., & Dunlap, R. E. (2011). Cool dudes: The denial of climate change among conservative white males in the United States. *Global Environmental Change, 21*(4), 1163–1172.

McCright, A. M., & Dunlap, R. E. (2013). Bringing ideology in: The conservative white male effect on worry about environmental problems in the USA. *Journal of Risk Research, 16*(2), 211–226.

Pew Reserarch. (2018). *Climate change still seen as the top global threat, but cyberattacks a rising concern.* https://www.pewglobal.org/2019/02/10/climate-change-still-seen-as-the-top-global-threat-but-cyberattacks-a-rising-concern/. Accessed 26 März 2019.

Schaller, S., & Carius, A. (2019). *Convenient Truths. Mapping climate agendas of right-wing populist parties in Europe.* Berlin: Adelphi consult GmbH.

Tagesschau.de. (2019). *Die Welt hat Angst vor dem Klimawandel.* https://www.tagesschau.de/ausland/umfrage-klimawandel-pew-101.html. Accessed 26 März 2019.

UN-Weltklimarat. (2018). *IPCC-Sonderbericht über 1,5°C globale Erwärmung.* https://www.de-ipcc.de/media/content/Hauptaussagen_IPCC_SR15.pdf. Accessed 25 März 2019.

10

"Play It Again, Sam": From the Clash of Civilizations

Who Is Responsible for the Financial Crisis in 2008, Who Is to Blame for the Risky Handling of the Social Market Economy?

In the search for answers to these questions, one encounters definitional bat-tles between rival interest groups everywhere. For some, bankers, their bonuses and risky credit transactions caused the financial crisis in 2008. For others, fiscal policy and the high debt levels of Europe's southern countries are respon-sible. And as is so often the case, once again it has been the Jews and the American "East Coast". Shortly after the global economic crisis in 2008, the Anti-Defamation League (2009) conducted a representative survey of 3500 adults in seven European countries. It showed that about 31% of the respon-dents blamed the Jews for the crisis.

Why this example? Along with the ecological crisis, international terrorism and religiously motivated or justified conflicts, the financial crisis is certainly one of the most serious global risks at present. A risk, and here we follow *Ulrich Beck* (2007, p. 29), is, as we know, *"not synonymous* with catastrophe. Risk means the *anticipation of* catastrophe". Global risks, such as the threats posed by international terrorism, are not catastrophes that have already occurred, but the anticipation of future calamities.

More:

© The Author(s), under exclusive license to Springer Fachmedien Wiesbaden GmbH, part of Springer Nature 2022
W. Frindte, I. Frindte, *Support in Times of No Support*,
https://doi.org/10.1007/978-3-658-38637-5_10

Risks are social constructions and definitions on the background of corresponding definitional relations. They (i.e. risks, WF/IF) exist in the form of (scientific and alternative-scientific) knowledge. Consequently, their 'reality' can be dramatized or minimized, transformed or simply denied according to the norms according to which knowledge and non-knowledge are decided. (Beck, 2007, p. 66)

However, the definitional struggles and conflicts are not only about different anticipations of possible catastrophes, as Ulrich Beck believes. There are also disputes and struggles about attributions, i.e. about the reasons for and responsibilities of risks and future catastrophes.

Responsible for the crises and global risks are – from a socio-psychological perspective – always the others. These are – again from a socio-psychological perspective – so-called attribution distortions, i.e. distorted explanations of causes and responsibilities. Such distortions ultimately serve to enhance one's own identity and one's own community. We will come back to this in Chap. 19.

Of course, the dissemination media play a special role in these struggles for the interpretation of the world. They create the conditions for local events to achieve global effects and to be perceived and judged as events by a global audience. On the basis of news factors,[1] the importance of which is defined by media-creating communities (of journalists, media scientists, politicians), a selection is made from the range of global events and a decision is made as to what becomes news as an event and what does not.

On September 15, 2004, *Elisabeth Noelle* reported in the Frankfurter Allgemeine Zeitung on the results of a new Allensbach study (Noelle, 2004). In the period from 26 August to 6 September 2004, the Allensbach Institute for Demoscopy (IfD) had conducted an opinion poll among Germans. The surveys took place before and after a hostage-taking in the North Ossetian city of Beslan. During this hostage-taking of 1100 children and adults by Chechen terrorists and the subsequent liberation by Russian forces, more than 330 hostages lost their lives. The IfD now asked the German respondents in personal interviews, among other things, the following question: "One sometimes hears the term 'clash of civilizations'. This refers to a serious

---

[1] News factors are the selection criteria according to which journalists decide what becomes news and what does not. E.g. spatial proximity, negativity, surprise, reference to elite persons or elite nations, etc. (can be found, among others, in Ruhrmann & Woelke, 2003).

conflict between Christianity and Islam. What do you think: Do we currently have such a clash of civilizations, or would you say not?". In summary, *Elisabeth Noelle* writes, among other things:

"Those interviewed before the events in Beslan were 44% with 35% opposed that we were having such a clash of civilizations. Those interviewed after September 3 were 62% with 25% opposed that we were experiencing a clash of civilizations" (Noelle, 2004, p. 5).

In other words, between 40 and 60% of Germans believe there is a "clash of civilizations".

Two years later, *Elisabeth Noelle* and *Thomas Petersen* again report in the Frankfurter Allgemeine Zeitung on another survey by the Allensbach Institute for Public Opinion Research (Noelle & Petersen, 2006). Now 56% still affirm the question "Do we currently have a clash of civilizations between Christianity and Islam?". The authors interpret:

If one looks at the results [...] in May 2006 [...], one cannot help feeling that the very process of alienation between the occidental and Islamic world as well as that between the traditional population and the Muslims living in the country itself is taking place in Germany, which, if one looks at it pessimistically, can be seen as the beginning of a spiral of conflict. (Noelle & Petersen, 2006, p. 5).

On 21 November 2012, the Frankfurter Allgemeine Zeitung published the findings of a new representative survey by the Allensbach Institute for Public Opinion Research. Again, the question was asked about the "clash of civilizations" and 43% of the respondents thought that there was such a clash.

That's the lowest percentage in eight years, but still a relative majority. Only 34% explicitly disagree with the thesis. Consistently, only 36% of Germans think that Christianity and Islam can peacefully coexist. 53%, on the other hand, believe that there will always be serious conflicts between these two religions. (Petersen 2012, p. 10).

It almost seems as if *Samuel Huntington* (1996) has redefined the semantics of systemic contradictions and chosen the "West" and "Islam" as the new protagonists in the "clash of civilizations". Samuel Huntington first published his ideas about the new course of the world after the collapse of communism in

1993 in *Foreign Affairs* magazine in an article entitled "The Clash of Civilizations?" (Huntington, 1993). In 1996, the book was published with the same title but without a question mark. In the same year it was published in German under the misleading title "Battle of Civilizations" and the subtitle "The Reshaping of World Politics in the 21st Century".[2] According to Huntington (2002, p. 35), the illusions of incipient harmony between countries, nations, and political interest groups were disappointed by the numerous ethnic conflicts, by the resurgence of neo-communist and neo-fascist movements, by the intensification of religious fundamentalisms, and by the inability of the United Nations to prevent bloody conflicts. Above all, he argues, the conflict between Islam and the West came to a head at the end of the twentieth century, leading to a clash of civilizations. Huntington's theses have been widely cited and criticized (e.g. Gray, 1998; Henderson, 2005 and many others). And yet it is precisely this narrative (of the "clash of civilizations") that could have become suitable for everyday use at the end of the twentieth century, because it seems to reflect a cultural pessimism that is shared not only by academics.

Readers, even those who have only heard of the inaccurate German book title, readily resort to this semantics, either approvingly or critically. With this semantics and the myth of the "West", "Islam" and the "clash of civilizations", new possibilities are offered with which the seemingly uncertain realities can be interpreted (cf. Husain & O'Brien, 2000, p. 2).

One could say that what goes around comes around. Psychologists like to speak of *self-fulfilling prophecies* in such contexts. All you have to do is talk and report about the "clash of civilizations" as often as possible, and it will happen of its own accord. And with reference to Huntington's book "Clash of Civilization" one could claim – following *Kurt Lewin* (1969, p. 41, original: 1936): real is what works.[3]

The controversy over the Mohammed cartoons has shown that media coverage plays a not unimportant role in the construction of the "clash of civilizations".

---

[2] In the following, we refer to the seventh German edition from 2002.

[3] Kurt Lewin (1890–1947) is one of the great German Gestalt psychologists who had a major influence on modern psychology. From 1927 to 1933 he was an associate professor at the Berlin Institute of Psychology. In 1933 he fled Nazi Germany in time to lay the foundations for modern social psychology in the USA.

A reminder: On 30 September 2005, the Danish daily *Jyllands-Posten* published 12 drawings of the Prophet Mohammed. With this publication Denmark plunged into the most serious foreign policy crisis since the end of the Second World War. What was intended by the newspaper as a provocation to protect freedom of expression in Denmark ultimately led to an economic boycott of Danish goods in the Middle East, burning embassies, death and bomb threats against journalists, mass demonstrations and violent riots in which numerous people lost their lives. This crisis, now known as the *Muhammad cartoon controversy*, provoked a heated public debate about the tension between liberal democratic values on the West's side and the protection of religious symbols on the other. In protest against the Muhammad cartoons and the provocative behavior of *Jyllands-Posten*, some 3000–5000 people demonstrated peacefully in Copenhagen on 14 October 2005 against the "abuse of press freedom". In the same period, however, the first death threats are received against the cartoonists, whereupon they are placed under police protection. On 19 October ambassadors of 11 Islamic countries asked for a meeting with the Danish Prime Minister Rasmussen to discuss with him the publication of the caricatures and the Islamophobic mood in Denmark (see Gamillscheg, 2006). The latter, however, refused to meet with him, saying that the country's freedom of the press was inviolable. On 28 October 2005 Danish Muslims filed criminal charges against the *Jyllands-Posten*; but the proceedings were later dropped by the public prosecutor's office. A joint protest letter from 27 organizations to the Minister of Culture Mikkelsen remains unanswered. Since the outrage over the insult to the Prophet seems to fall on deaf ears in Denmark, a delegation of Danish Imams travels to Egypt from December 3 to 11 to solicit support. The Egyptian government contacts the Arab League and the World Islamic Congress on the matter. Demonstrations on the cartoon controversy take place in Pakistan on 7 December. A second delegation of Danish Imams is touring Lebanon, Turkey, Sudan, Morocco, Algeria and Qatar from December 17–31 to draw attention to the cartoons. Both delegations have a 42-page dossier in their luggage during their travels, which in addition to the Mohammed cartoons of the *Jyllands-Posten* contains three other, previously unpublished pictures. At the end of January, first Saudi Arabia and shortly afterwards Libya withdraw their ambassadors from Denmark. Egypt, Syria, Iran, Indonesia, Pakistan and Bosnia-Herzegovina file formal complaints with the Danish government. Libya threatens an economic boycott; other Muslim countries also call for boycotts of Danish goods. On January 30, 2006, the first violent action takes place in Gaza. Armed fighters of the Al-Aqsa Brigades attack the EU office and demand an apology from the Danish government concerning the cartoon affair. There are also first attacks on individuals in Mecca. *Jyllands-Posten* then apologizes on its homepage for hurting feelings, but not for printing the cartoons themselves. Shortly afterwards, *Jyllands-Posten* in Aarhaus receives a bomb threat. In total, 143 newspapers in 56 countries print at least one of the cartoons by the end of February (see Ata, 2011, p. 95). The scale of demonstrations and violent riots related to the affair rises massively in February. In the Middle East, Asia and North Africa there are more demonstrations, some with tens of thousands of participants. In Syria the Danish and Norwegian embassies are attacked, in Lebanon the Danish embassy is set on fire and a Christian quarter of Beirut is vandalized. The Danish and Austrian embassies in Tehran are also threatened. In Afghanistan and Somalia, several people are killed by security forces during demonstrations. A few days later, several demonstrators are also killed in Pakistan and Libya. On 18 February 2006, 16 people died in Nigeria in attacks on Christian churches and shops. The ensuing wave of mutual violence kills around 200 more people. In February 2008, the cartoon controversy became the focus of media coverage for a second time when three people were arrested for planning an assassination attempt against one of the drafters of the *Jyllands-Posten* cartoons.

Clash of Cultures or Clash of Prejudices?

Interesting findings can be found in the "Global Attitudes Project", which has been carried out by the Pew Research Center since 2002. In the global survey conducted in 2008, adults in Great Britain, France, Germany, Poland and Spain (about 750 in each country) were asked about their attitudes towards Muslims (Pew Research, 2008). In the evaluation of the answers, the authors of the study come to the conclusion, among other things, that in Spain 52%, in Germany 50%, in Poland 38% and in Great Britain 23% of the respondents have a negative attitude towards Muslims and that these attitudes have worsened since 2004.

In another 2011 survey (Pew Research, 2011), which polled about 1000 adults in each of 23 countries, 62% of the French, 61% of the Germans, 58% of the Spanish, and 52% of the British said relations between the "West" and "Muslims" were generally bad. Respondents from Muslim-majority countries expressed similar views: in Jordan, 58% of respondents said relations between the "West" and "Muslims" were generally bad; in Turkey, 62% felt this way; in Lebanon, also 62%; and in the Palestinian territories, 72%. Moreover, 73% of Germans, 70% of Britons, 68% of French and 61% of Spaniards said they were worried about Islamist extremists in their own country. However, the majority of respondents in the Palestinian Territories (78%), Lebanon (73%) or Turkey (52%) were also concerned about Islamist extremists in their own country.

In the 2011 survey, the *Pew Research Center* researchers also asked about attributions of responsibility for the "generally poor" relations between the "West" and "Muslims". And – as expected – the respondents each blame the "others" for the miserable relations. An extract from these findings can be found in *Table* (Table 10.1).

That "those in the West" (i.e., from France, Germany, Spain, and Britain) are somewhat more reticent in their attributions than Muslims (from the Palestinian Territories, Lebanon, Jordan, and Turkey) regarding responsibility for the relationship mess is not particularly reassuring, but may also be a survey artifact. More problematic, if one engages with this data, are likely to be the findings that point to the fact that at least some Muslims in the countries identified above also blame "the Jews" for the poor relations between "the West" and "the Muslims." Westerners, on the other hand, apparently do not attribute any responsibility to "the Jews" for the poor relations between "the West" and "the Muslims."

In the survey, the researchers also presented respondents from predominantly Muslim and non-Muslim countries with a list of characteristics and asked them to assess the extent to which these characteristics apply to the respective "others". The following *table* shows the results (Table 10.2).

Table 10.1 Agreement that relations between "the West" and "the Muslims" are bad and attribution of responsibility

| Countries | Those who say relations are bad (%) | Who is most responsible for the bad relations between the "West" and the "Muslims"? (%) | | | |
		Muslims	Westerners	Both	Jews
France	62	56	26	15	
Germany	61	48	15	24	
Spain	58	49	15	29	
United Kingdom	52	34	26	24	
Palestinian territories	72	17	61	4	17
Lebanon	62	18	38	5	35
Jordan	58	2	65	3	29
Turkey	62	5	75	9	5

Prepared according to *Pew Research Center* (2011, p. 13)

Table 10.2 Mutual attributions of characteristics by Muslims and non-Muslims

Features	Extent to which Muslims in Muslim-majority countries attribute characteristics to people from "the West" (%)	Extent to which non-Muslims in the U.S., Russia, and Western Europe attribute characteristics to Muslims (%)
Selfish	68	35
Violent	66	50
Greedy	64	20
Immoral	61	23
Arrogant	57	39
Fanatical	53	58
Respectful towards women	44	22
Honestly	33	51
Tolerant	31	30
Generous	29	41

Prepared according to *Pew Research Center* (2011, p. 19)

It is clearly evident that well over 50% of Muslims from Muslim-majority countries regard people from "the West" as selfish, violent, greedy, immoral and fanatical. The non-Muslims from the USA, Russia and Western Europe, on the other hand, offer a somewhat more positive view of Muslims in Muslim countries. It is striking, however, that both sides describe the other to a high degree as *violent* and *fanatical*.

From a socio-psychological perspective, as far as relations between Muslims and non-Muslims are concerned, we are not dealing with a *"clash of civilizations"*, but simply with a "clash of prejudices" (of two social communities).

In order to understand the functions and effects of prejudice between *the West* and *Islam,* we look around academic social psychology and first encounter the *Theory of Social Identity* (Tajfel & Turner, 1986; see also Frindte & Geschke, 2019, p. 313 ff.). This theory, which is quite well known and appreciated in and outside social psychology, assumes that people categorize their social world (persons, objects, and events) in order to reduce the complexity of reality. For example, we distinguish between people with red hair and those with bald heads, between diesel drivers and cyclists, between Germans and French, or between "the Muslims" and "the Christians".

Through social categorization, people assign their fellow human beings and themselves to certain social groups. Social categorization is usually automatic, enables quick orientation in reality, and has an important function for the individual. He or she perceives himself or herself as a member of social categories, identifies with these categories, defines his or her social place within the categories and, under certain circumstances, distinguishes himself or herself from people assigned to other categories. Self- and other-definitions based on social categories are helpful in enabling individuals and social communities to locate themselves in the social environment. The more pronounced such self- and other-categorizations on the basis of social categories are, the more likely it is that the respective others, i.e. the strangers, will be perceived and evaluated in a stereotypical manner as being very similar to one another. One also speaks of a perceived homogeneity of foreign groups (Islam, Muslims, the West and those in the West).

Simplified, one could also say that people use social categories (such as *the West* or *Islam*) in their definitions of themselves and others if they see a sense in them in order to secure themselves and their social identity. This also means that people apparently resort to corresponding stereotypical definitions of themselves and others (*We Muslims* or *We in Islam* or *We in the West*) when they feel insecure in the context of their social community. Such insecurities can be the consequences of perceived threats: for example, *the West* feels threatened by Islamist terrorism and *Islam* feels threatened by the *war on terror* waged by the *West*.

If, because of such or otherwise perceived threats, people rely on stereotyped social categories to identify with (*the West* or *Islam*) and to reject, discriminate against, and possibly fight against the supposed members of those social communities that identify with other, opposing social categories In order to reject, discriminate against, and possibly fight the perceived members of those social communities who identify with other, opposing social categories, one simple question that arises is this: what do people rely on in order to determine and claim that the norms, values, and ideologies of their own social community are more legitimate, *true*, and *valid* than the norms and ideologies of the other community?

A rather catchy answer to this question is provided by the *Ingroup Projection Model* (Waldzus & Wenzel, 2008). This model is based on the *aforementioned Social Identity Theory* and can be described as follows: Members of one group or community (e.g., non-Muslims) compare themselves to members of another group (e.g., Muslims) by referring to a (supposedly) common super-ordinate group (e.g., human civilization or religion). Non-Muslims might thus ask in such a case, are Muslims good or bad representatives of human civilization; Muslims might ask the mirror-image question to find out whether they are better than non-Muslims. The crux of such a question now lies in the fact that in such a comparison the members of the individual groups or communities *project* their *own* respective characteristics, norms, values or ideologies onto the imagined common superordinate community or category and only then make the comparison with the other community.

But what does this mean now for the categories of *the West, Muslims* or *Islam*? The following scenario is conceivable: When people who identify with *the West* compare themselves with the *Muslims* or *Islam*, drawing on the supposedly superordinate social category of *human civilization,* they (i.e., *the Westerners*) project their own notions of human civilization (e.g., the notion of *universal human rights*) onto this superordinate category. These projections are then used to make comparisons with *Muslims* or *Islam.* The results of such a comparison are obvious. Since Sharia law, among other things, is not compatible with UN standards of equality and religious freedom, the *Islamic understanding of human rights* cannot be compatible with the UN understanding of human rights either. In other words, with regard to the understanding of human rights, *the West is* likely to appear as the superior victor compared to *Islam.*

But this scenario is also conceivable: When people who identify themselves as Muslims with Islam compare themselves with the *West* and thereby resort to the supposedly superordinate social category of *religion,* they (i.e. *Muslims*) project their own ideas of religion onto this superordinate category. The results of this comparison are now likely to be clearly in favor of Islam.

No matter how you look at it, whenever people, whether they feel threatened or not, identify themselves with *the West* or *Islam in order* to compare themselves with the respective other social community, they do not find a "green branch" and a common denominator. The result is always a fatal comparison: "we" are better than the "others" and they represent a threat to "us".

To return once again to Samuel Huntington: The talk of a "clash of civilizations" is hardly likely to be suitable for adequately describing and explaining the global fault lines and conflicts between the "West" and "Islam". It is not a clash of civilizations that is taking place. It is rather a struggle for influence, power and interpretative sovereignty (cf. also Riesebrodt, 2000).

The causes of this struggle are, of course, also open to considerable debate. But we will deny ourselves that at this point and ask: whether and to what extent the clash of prejudices also has to do with media coverage? In the search for an answer, we will also have to look at the role of the media as possible *fixed points*.

References

Anti-Defamation League. (2009). *Attitudes toward Jews in seven European countries*. http://www.adl.org/assets/pdf/israel-international/Public-ADL-Anti-Semitism-Presentation-February-2009-_3_.pdf. Accessed 14 Okt 2014.

Ata, M. (2011). *Der Mohammed-Karikaturenstreit in den deutschen und türkischen Medien*. Wiesbaden: VS Verlag.

Beck, U. (2007). *Weltrisikogesellschaft: Auf der Suche nach der verlorenen Sicherheit*. Frankfurt a. M.: Suhrkamp. English Version: World risk society. Cambridge, Oxford: Polity.

Frindte, W., & Geschke, D. (2019). *Lehrbuch Kommunikationspsychologie*. Weinheim: Beltz.

Gamillscheg, H. (2006). Chronik eines erhofften Streits. Vom Kinderbuch zum Flächenbrand: Wie die erbitterte Auseinandersetzung um Mohammed-Karikaturen entstand. Frankfurter Rundschau vom 25. Februar 2006, S. 3.

Henderson, E. A. (2005). Not letting evidence get in the way of assumptions: Testing the clash of civilizations thesis with more recent data. *International Politics, 42*, 458–469.

Huntington, S. P. (1993). The clash of civilizations? *Foreign Affairs, 72*(3), 22–49.

Huntington, S. P. (1996). *The clash of civilizations*. New York: Simon & Schuster.

Huntington, S. P. (2002). *Kampf der Kulturen. Die Neugestaltung der Weltpolitik im 21. Jahrhundert*. München: Goldmann.

Husain, F., & O'Brien, M. (2000). Muslim communities in europe: Reconstruction and transformation. *Current Sociology, 48*(1), 1–13.

Gray, J. (1998). Global utopias and clashing civilizations: Misunderstanding the present. *International Affairs, 74*(1), 149–163.

Lewin, K. (1969). *Grundzüge der topologischen Psychologie*. Bern: Huber (Original: 1936).

Noelle, E. (2004). *Der Kampf der Kulturen*. Frankfurter Allgemeine Zeitung vom 15.9.2004, S. 5.

Noelle, E., & Petersen, T. (2006). Eine fremde, bedrohliche Welt. *Frankfurter Allgemeine Zeitung* vom 17.5.2006, S. 5.

Petersen, T. (2012). Die Furcht vor dem Morgenland im Abendland. *Frankfurter Allgemeine Zeitung* vom 21.11.2012, S. 10.

Pew Research. (2008). *Unfavorable views of Jews and Muslims on the increase in Europe.* Pew Research Center. http://www.pewglobal.org/files/2008/09/Pew-2008-Pew-Global-Attitudes-Report-3-September-17-2pm.pdf. Accessed 26 Nov 2012.

Pew Research. (2011). *Muslim-Western tensions persist.* Pew Research Center. http://www.pewglobal.org/files/2011/07/Pew-Global-Attitudes-Muslim-Western-Relations-FINAL-FOR-PRINT-July-21-2011.pdf. Accessed: 26 Nov 2012.

Riesebrodt, M. (2000). *Die Rückkehr der Religionen: Fundamentalismus und der "Kampf der Kulturen".* München: Beck.

Ruhrmann, G., & Woelke, J. (2003). Der Wert von Nachrichten. Ein Modell zur Validierung von Nachrichtenfaktoren. In G. Ruhrmann, J. Woelke, M. Maier, & N. Diehlmann (Hrsg.), *Der Wert von Nachrichten im deutschen Fernsehen* (S. 13–26). Opladen: Leske + Budrich.

Tajfel, H., & Turner, J. (1986). The social identity theory of intergroup behavior. In S. Worchel & W. G. Austin (Hrsg.), *Psychology of intergroup relations* (2. Aufl., S. 7–24). Chicago: Nelson-Hall.

Waldzus, S., & Wenzel, M. (2008). Das Modell der Eigengruppenprojektion. In L.-E. Petersen & B. Six (Hrsg.), *Stereotype, Vorurteile und soziale Diskriminierung.* Weinheim: Beltz.

11

Media and Prejudices

Hey, I can't find nothing on the radio. (R.E.M. 1991).

German society is a media society. No question about it. On a weekday, Germans aged 14 and over spend an average of around nine and a half hours (566 min) with classic and digital media. In most cases, several media are used simultaneously. "The time budget of nine and a half hours or 566 min is distributed among the four daily media television, radio, daily newspaper and Internet, which together account for 511 min and thus 90% of media consumption, as well as books, magazines and storage media for audio (sound carriers) and video" (Breunig & van Eimeren, 2015, p. 506).

Obviously, there are both time-of-day and age differences in media use. Figure 11.1 first illustrates the differences in time of day.

While the radio is mostly played in the background during the morning hours, the television is – as expected – mainly switched on in the evening hours. Meanwhile, Germans are quite active online throughout the day. However, this applies primarily to the younger age group of 14–29 year olds. However, with a daily usage time of 221 min in 2017 (Verband Privater Medien, 2018), *television* is still the medium most frequently used by the German population. Traditional television use has therefore not lost any of its appeal recently.

In view of the intensive use of media, what is the situation regarding users' attitudes and their trust in the media in general?

The question is not so far-fetched because of the loud criticism of the "same-socialized lying press", especially by the supporters of the self-proclaimed "Patriotic Europeans against the Islamization of the Occident" (PEGIDA).

© The Author(s), under exclusive license to Springer Fachmedien Wiesbaden GmbH, part of Springer Nature 2022
W. Frindte, I. Frindte, *Support in Times of No Support*,
https://doi.org/10.1007/978-3-658-38637-5_11

In January 2015, the word *Lügenpresse* was chosen by the "Sprachkritische Aktion das Unwort des Jahres" as the *Unwort des Jahres 2014*. Thus, a word was chosen that has a long and unfortunate history. In 1835, the word probably first appeared in the press, in the *Wiener Zeitung*. The newspaper reported on the discussion in the French Chamber of Deputies on a press law. According to the Wiener Zeitung, a French deputy had spoken of the dictatorship of journalists during this discussion and was then quoted as saying: "Only by suppressing the lying press can the true press be helped up" (Wiener Zeitung, 2 September 1835).

During the March Revolution in 1848, conservative Catholic politicians insult the liberal democratic press as the *Jewish lying press* (Journalistikon, 2018). Before and during World War I, the word *lying press* was used in Germany and Austria-Hungary to denigrate the press of enemy states, namely the press of France. Under National Socialism, *Lügenpresse* was the catchword used to defame the *infiltration of* the press by *world Jewry*. In the GDR, the media in the *West were* regarded as organs of the *capitalist lying press*.

In the course of this history, *Lügenpresse* became the label for a conspiracy theory in which a secret, conspiratorial collaboration of (state) media,

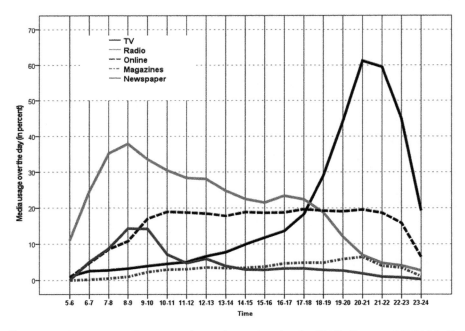

Fig. 11.1 Average media usage throughout the day in 2017. (Source: VPRT Media Usage Analysis, 2017)

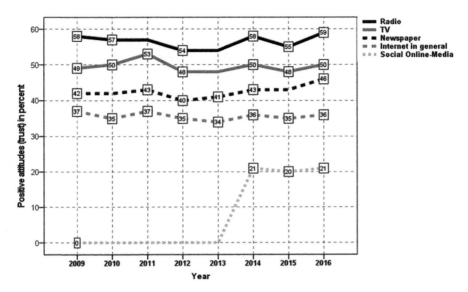

Fig. 11.2 Trust in media. (Source: Eurobarometer Standard, 2016; trust in online social media was only asked about from 2013 onwards)

political elites, state institutions, or secret groups, carried out with illegitimate intentions and directed against the *people,* is assumed (Seidler, 2016).

Since autumn 2014, activists of the PEGIDA movement and the AfD in particular have used the conspiracy theory of the *lying press to* accuse the *system media* or the *system press*[1] and official politics in Germany of conspiring to deal with migrants and the refugee problem. The media (especially public television) and politics (namely the German federal government) are accused, among other things, of having secretly agreed not to take problems of migration and immigration of Muslims seriously and thus of supporting an increasing *Islamization of the Occident.* However, it is not that simple.

Figure 11.2 illustrates that trust in traditional and digital media in Europe is not too bad. This is a representative study in all 28 EU countries and five other EU candidate countries. Approximately 1000 adults were surveyed in each country in November 2016.

Radio is the most trusted medium among European citizens. Television follows in second place. After slightly declining figures in 2015, trust in all the media surveyed rose again in 2016.

---

[1] "System media" or "system press" are also terms used by right-wing populists and right-wing extremists in analogy to the "lying press", which ultimately go back to the language of the National Socialists (Schmitz-Berning, 1998).

Similar findings can also be demonstrated in Germany. In a study published at the beginning of 2018 by the Institute for Journalism at the Johannes Gutenberg University in Mainz, 1200 adult Germans were asked, among other things, the following question "What is it like when it comes to really important things – such as environmental problems, health hazards, political scandals. How much can you trust the media there?" 41% of respondents answered with "partly-partly" and 42% with "One can trust rather/fully" (Schemer et al., 2018).

However, the problem of trust or mistrust in the media is not a problem of society as a whole, but rather one that is particularly pronounced in certain political milieus and groups of people and less so in other groupings. This is indicated by the findings of the representative *Leipzig Center Studies, which* are conducted every 2 years in Germany on behalf of the Heinrich Böll Foundation and the Otto Brenner Foundation. In 2016, the authors were able to show that distrust of the classic media (newspapers, radio and television) is particularly prevalent among supporters of the right-wing populist AfD (see Fig. 11.3).

Dissemination media, such as television, radio or the newspaper and social media, inform and speculate about reality; they criticize, construct and stage reality; they can also radicalize, polarize and socialize.

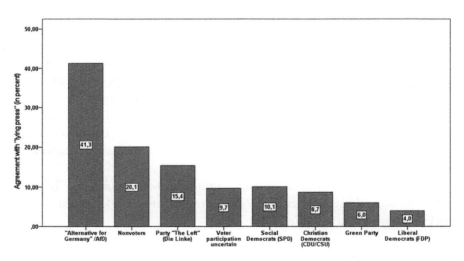

Fig. 11.3 Agreement with the statement "When you think of newspapers, radio and television" in Germany, would you personally speak of a lying press or not?" and party preference (in %). (Adapted from Decker et al., 2016, p. 89)

At the latest with the terrorist attacks of September 11, 2001, the connection between the experience of threat in the face of terrorist risks and media coverage became the focus of scientific research.

Propper et al. (2007), for example, show that it is mainly people in the USA who report stress and stress symptoms who did not actually experience the terrorist attacks of 11 September 2001 themselves, but who followed the media reports intensively and attentively. *Jennifer Ahern* and colleagues (2002), who interviewed more than 1000 New Yorkers by telephone in October and November 2001, found more post-traumatic stress phenomena and more depressive tendencies in people who remembered the dramatic and emotionalized images of the terrorist attacks in New York ("people falling or jumping from the towers of the World Trade Center") than in those who remembered fewer or hardly any such images. Other authors (e.g. Das et al., 2009) report findings that indicate that and how media coverage of terrorism can reinforce prejudices and fears about foreign groups.

Since 9/11, the image of Islam in international reporting has also come under greater scrutiny in the social sciences. *Antje Glück* (2007), for example, proves in a content-analytical evaluation of German and Arabic newspaper reports on the attacks in London and Sharm El-Sheikh (in 2005) that stereotypes towards Arabs and Muslims refer exclusively to the threat potential of Islam. *Georg Ruhrmann* et al. (2006) confirm that international terrorism also influences news coverage of domestic issues due to its high relevance and emotional power. More than one third of the migrant topics show a connection to the terrorism debate in the reporting. Differentiations between religion, Islamism, extremism, fundamentalism and terrorism are also rarely made in terrorism reporting, as the study by *Sascha Werthes* et al. (2002) suggests. After 9/11, *Georg Seeßlen* and *Markus Metz* (2002) even speak of "visual declarations of war" on Islam.

Numerous studies show, however, that people tend to ignore and suppress information that contradicts their attitudes and sensitivities. In psychology, this tendency is known as *confirmation bias* (Peter & Brosius, 2013, p. 467). In this context, it is assumed that media coverage in tolerant societies does not have a major influence on prejudices against, for example, Muslims or refugees, but that the media influence on attitudes towards migrants is primarily dependent on the socio-demographic characteristics of media users (employment status, education, political orientation, etc.) (e.g. Boomgaarden & Vliegenthart, 2009).

In recent years, we have also investigated the mutual prejudices of Muslims and non-Muslims in Germany and the influence of media use (e.g. Frindte & Haußecker, 2010; Frindte & Dietrich, 2017). In panel studies (surveys with the same individuals at multiple survey points), German non-Muslims and Muslims were interviewed and asked about their media preferences. Persons with a Turkish migration background favor German-language television; however, Turkish programs also play a weighty role. Between 45 and 50% of persons with a Turkish migration background state that they prefer the Turkish channel *Kanal D* above all. Among the German television channels, the private stations ProSieben and RTL rank ahead of the public television channels (ARD with 18% and ZDF with 16%). In addition to television, the Internet with its various applications and various print media also play a not insignificant role (cf. also Feierabend et al., 2016; Simon & Kloppenburg, 2010).

What influence does this diverse and intensive media use have on the mutual attitudes of non-Muslims and Muslims?

Our panel studies, which are *not* representative of the entire German population, allow some assumptions to be made. As is well known, panel studies allow causal analyses, i.e. the question of cause-effect relationships.[2]

The following four figure illustrate the summary findings of our panel studies.

Let us start with the first figure (Fig. 11.4). This is a summary of the results of panel surveys with people aged 14–75. One of the main questions we sought to answer with these studies was: What psychological processes underlie the negative attitudes towards Muslims and ultimately lead to the demand that the immigration of Muslims must be stopped?

In our studies prior to 2015, around 10% of the German non-Muslims surveyed were in favor of an immigration stop; in 2016/17, around 15% were in favor of such a stop. Measured against the results of representative surveys, we are dealing with relatively low values. In 2017, the British think tank *Chatham House* asked around 10,000 Europeans in ten countries, among other questions, *"Should all further immigration from predominantly Muslim countries be stopped?"* In Germany, 53% answered in the affirmative, in France 61%, in Belgium 64%, in Hungary also 64%, in Austria 65% and in Poland

---

[2] In panel studies or longitudinal studies, in contrast to cross-sectional studies, people are surveyed or interviewed at several points in time or waves and the results of the individual survey waves are compared. If the same people are repeatedly asked the same questions over time, as is usually the case in panel studies, it is possible to analyze not only correlations, but also changes and possibly even causal processes. An important prerequisite for causal relationships is that the causal condition (i.e. the independent variable, which is surveyed in a first wave, for example) must precede the effect (the dependent variable in a second wave) in time. This is exactly what we have guaranteed in panel studies. And some more information for experts: The data collected were evaluated using complex statistical testing procedures, including cross-lagged panel analyses, structural equation models, and mediator analyses. A mediator analysis examines whether the influence of variable X on variable Y can be partially explained by another variable – a mediator.

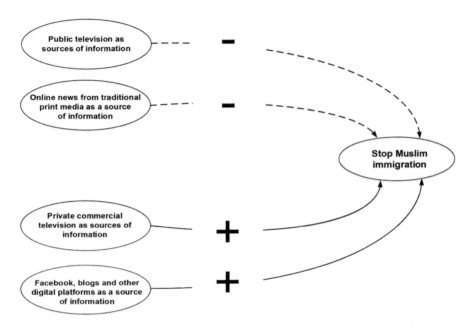

Fig. 11.4 Influence of classical and digital media on attitudes towards Muslims; the plus signs indicate a promoting and the minus signs an inhibiting influence on the approval of an immigration stop (cf. also Frindte, 2013)

71%%. Only in Spain (41%) and the UK (47%) was the figure less than 50% in each case (Chatham House, 2017).

What influence do media preferences have on the approval or rejection of an immigration stop? Figure 11.4 shows the media preferences that proved to be *effective in* the analyses.

Initially, two effects become apparent: People who at time A mainly inform themselves via private television (e.g. RTL-Aktuell or SAT.1 Nachrichten) and/or via digital platforms (Facebook, Instagram, blogs, etc.) agree significantly more often at a later time B with statements such as that the influx of Muslims must be stopped absolutely and completely. The solid lines with the plus signs are intended to illustrate this connection. The dashed lines between public television (ARD-Tagesschau or ZDF-Heute) and the online news of traditional print media (e.g. Zeit-Online, Spiegel-Online, online portals of the Frankfurter Allgemeine Zeitung or the Süddeutsche Zeitung) on the one hand and the statement about stopping immigration on the other point to a second effect. This effect means that people who are more likely to reject an immigration freeze prefer public television and/or the said online news as sources of information. Somewhat flippantly, one could claim that the "do-gooders" get their information primarily from public television or from the

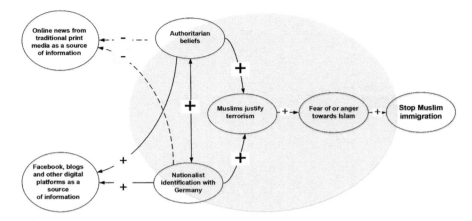

Fig. 11.5 Influence of classical and digital media on attitudes towards Muslims – mediated via authoritarian and nationalist beliefs

digital offerings of established newspapers and magazines. But those who would prefer Muslims not to be in the country tend to get their information about God and the world from private television or social media. And depending on what is offered there and then as information, the more or less informed people are then either for or against the immigration of Muslims. As I said, one could argue that.

However, such an assertion stands on shaky ground. Reality is – as so often – somewhat more complicated. A section of this complexity is illustrated in Fig. 11.5, which – admittedly – requires some explanation.

An arrow with a plus sign is drawn between the statements "Fear of or anger towards Islam" and "Stop immigration of Muslims" (on the right of the image). This means that our panel studies suggest that above all those who are either afraid of Islam or angry at Islam want to stop the immigration of Muslims to Germany. Fear of Islam was expressed by between 15% and 20% in our studies; anger, on the other hand, by just under 5%.

Fear or anger seems to be fed by one source, namely the assumption of the respondents that Muslims per se justify terrorism. Such assumptions are held above all by the adults surveyed who agree with authoritarian and nationalist statements and opinions. These are people who would, for example, approve of Germany once again having a "strong leader" and who think that Germans can only be those who have "German ancestry". If people regard being German as an important, perhaps even central, part of their identity, and at the same time are convinced that power and subordination are important foundations for a social polity, then the likelihood is not small that they regard Muslims per se as potential terrorists.

Overview

National-authoritarian convictions refer to a theoretical concept that has a long history and has been revived in recent years. It is a concept that *Heinrich Mann* already talks about in the novel "Der Untertan" (Mann, 1918). "If you want to kick, you have to let yourself be kicked," says *Diederich Heßling,* the main hero in the novel. *Kurt Tucholsky* reviewed the novel in the "Weltbühne" in 1919, calling the book the "herbarium of the German man." "For," said *Tucholsky,* "these two character traits are in *Heßling,* are developed in the German in the most subtle way: a slavish sense of subordination and a slavish desire for domination. He needs powers, powers to which he bows like a natural man before a thunderstorm, powers which he himself seeks to gain in order to duck others" (*Tucholsky,* 1919, here quoted in Tucholsky, 1972, p. 409).

Heinrich Mann describes the socialization and dangerousness of a social character that was scientifically explained a few years later by *Erich Fromm, Max Horkheimer, Wilhelm Reich* and then fundamentally in "Escape from Freedom" (Fromm, 1941) and "The Authoritarian Personality" (Adorno et al., 1950) and was to become a terrible regime-bearing reality during National Socialism: the social character of the authoritarian. It is still around – the authoritarian specter. It haunts the scientific and pseudo-scientific landscapes, changes its appearance now and then, and serves as a foil to develop explanations about prejudice structures and their dynamics. An innovative step in the study of authoritarianism occurred in the 1980s. The publication of *Robert Altemeyer's* book "Right-wing Authoritarianism" (1981) is regarded as a turning point and the beginning of modern authoritarianism research.

According to *Altemeyer,* right-wing authoritarianism is an individual difference variable according to which people submit to authority to a greater or lesser extent, act against outsiders, and consistently conform to conventional norms. With this approach to authoritarianism, Altemeyer has brought back into play the image of the *cyclist* as a metaphor for the typical authoritarian: highly authoritarian individuals are like the legendary, tradition-conscious German "cyclists" who hump up, kick down, and move in well-worn tracks.

In modern social psychological literature, authoritarian beliefs are described as generalized attitudes or ideological beliefs that are very stable and generalized over time.

Since 2017 and 2018 there has been a push in authoritarianism research. *Volker Weiß* describes the new right-wing movements in his book "Die autoritäre Revolte" (Weiß, 2017). Contemporaneous with the volume "Flucht ins Autoritäre - Right-wing Extremist Dynamics in the Middle of Society" by *Oliver Decker* and *Elmar Brähler* (2018), *Wilhelm Heitmeyer* publishes a book entitled "Authoritarian Temptations. Signatures of Threat I" (Heitmeyer, 2018). *Christian Fuchs* (2018), a communications scholar at the University of Westminster, titles his book "Digital Demagogy. Authoritarian Capitalism in Times of Trump and Twitter". Books with titles such as "The Terror of Neoliberalism. Authoritarianism and the Eclipse of Democracy" (Giroux, 2018) or "Saving the Sacred Sea: The Power of Civil Society in an Age of Authoritarianism and Globalization" (Brown, 2018) are being published in the USA.

Certainly, social science publications on the topic of "authoritarianism" have been booming for years, both nationally and internationally. So the question is obvious: why the continuing interest in an old concept? Key events, such as the financial crisis in 2008, Islamist-inspired terrorist attacks or the refugee movements in 2015, as well as the penetration of capitalist principles of utility and exploitation into social relations have left large parts of the population with feelings of threat, disturbance, feelings of disadvantage. Such disturbances can lead to a flight into the supposed security "…promised by authoritarian political actors with their dichotomous images of the world and society" (Heitmeyer, 2018, p. 112).

Turning again to Fig. 11.5, the attitudinal facets in the figure illustrate a process by which, step by step, the likelihood grows that people will agree with the view that the immigration of Muslims to Germany should be stopped. In order to hold such a view, *being German* (as an important part of one's own identity) must be accompanied by *national-authoritarian convictions,* entrenched *attitudes that* Muslims justify terrorism, and either *fear of Islam* or *anger towards Islam.*

Certainly, other conditions and influences play a role in whether people react to Islam and Muslims with rejection. However, the conditions and relationships listed in the figure have been shown to be very robust explanators in numerous national and international studies (as an overview: Beck & Plant, 2018; Logvinov, 2017).

But what remains of the influence of the media and media use? Interestingly, preferences for public or private television channels as sources of political information no longer appear in Fig. 11.5. The influence of these preferences is – statistically – completely eclipsed by authoritarian beliefs, nationalist orientations and Muslim-related attitudes. What remains – in a statistically significant sense – are relationships between online news from traditional print media and digital platforms as possible sources of political information on the one hand, and authoritarian-nationalist beliefs on the other. In contrast to Fig. 11.4, these relationships now run in *reverse* – from authoritarian and nationalist beliefs and attitudes to preferences for online news and digital platforms, respectively. How can these inverse relationships, which are moreover marked with plus and minus signs, be explained?

Let us first take a look at the arrows with the plus signs. Our panel studies suggest that people who are characterized by *low* authoritarian convictions and a weaker nationalist orientation at the first time of the survey primarily seek political information in the online news of traditional print media at the second time of the survey. Highly authoritarian and strongly nationalistically oriented persons, on the other hand, tend to turn to digital platforms such as Facebook, blogs, etc. when looking for political information.

In general, it can be concluded that the *connection* between *authoritarian convictions, nationalistic identification with Germany, prejudiced attitudes and negative emotions towards Muslims* (Muslims justify terrorism; fear or anger) forms the *individual pattern of interpretation for* rejecting the immigration of Muslims to Germany. It is a relatively stable and largely self-contained cognitive-emotional pattern with which Muslims and Islam are interpreted and reinterpreted. Media offerings, such as those on digital platforms, are only sought out if they are suitable as echoes to confirm one's own individual, authoritarian-nationalist pattern of interpretation.

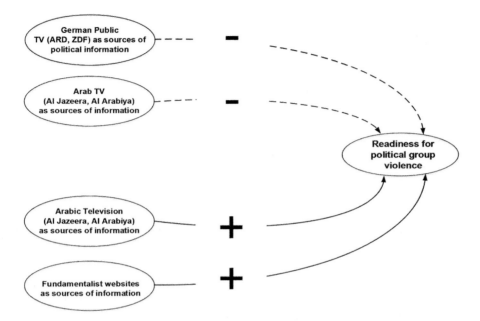

Fig. 11.6 Influence of classical and digital media on the willingness of young Muslims to use political violence

The findings from our panel studies with young Muslims from Germany aged 14–32 initially reveal a similar picture (Fig. 11.6). Young Muslims who obtain information primarily from Turkish television or fundamentalist websites (wave 1 in the panel) are also more likely to accept ideological group violence, such as terrorism (wave 2).

By contrast, young Muslims who state that they obtain information primarily from German public television or the Arabic news channels Al Jazeera or Al Arabiya tend to reject political violence.

The – for German television – flattering picture changes again when further convictions and attitudes of the young Muslims are taken into account.

Let us take a look at the following Fig. 11.7. The willingness to participate in political group violence is again driven by a complex cognitive-emotional pattern of interpretation. This interpretive pattern includes (a) hatred and anger towards the West, (b) the idea or belief that the dominance of the West is the cause of terrorism, (c) an omnipresent identification with Islam, and (d) pronounced authoritarian convictions.

Social identification with Islam is omnipresent when it takes place almost exclusively through identification with a social category (here with Muslims and the Muslim community, the ummah) and identification with other social

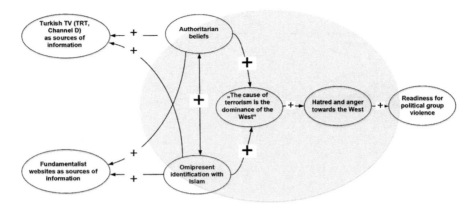

Fig. 11.7 Factors influencing the willingness of young Muslims to use political violence

categories (e.g. with a nation or a professional group) is not considered important at all. That is, everything is subordinated to belonging to and identifying with the Muslim community. Everything else does not count.

Possible influences of preferences for German or Arabic television news disappear again – statistically speaking – behind the strong influence of the interpretive pattern of hatred and anger towards the West, the belief that the dominance of the West is the cause of terrorism, the omnipresent identification with Islam and authoritarian convictions. In contrast, relationships are found between preferences for Turkish television and for fundamentalist websites on the one hand, and authoritarian beliefs and omnipresent identification with Islam on the other. However – similar to Fig. 11.5 – in the *opposite* direction and to a statistically significant but small extent.

Exaggerated interpretation: Muslims with authoritarian convictions and dominant identification with the Muslim community, as well as strong anti-Western emotions, are more likely to accept ideological group violence (such as terrorist actions) and look for those media echoes to confirm their world views (cf. extensively Frindte et al., 2016). This is not a new message; however, it is not harmless.

The parallels between young Muslims with authoritarian convictions and authoritarian non-Muslims cannot be overlooked. In both cases we are dealing with individual patterns of interpretation that can possibly provide *support in difficult times*, but in a fatal way only function as filter bubbles to ignore and suppress everything that contradicts one's own attitudes and sensitivities.

Unfortunately, public opinion depends more than one believes on the journals. (Heine, 1975, p. 385; original: Letter to Karl August Varnhagen v. Ense, 28 February 1830).

However, the influence of the media cannot be completely dismissed. As is well known, the media, with their reporting, provide forms or frames with which reality can be interpreted. *Media frames* are, so to speak, the forms in which media productions take place and appear. In reporting on spectacular events, the complexity of what happened is often reduced to simple structures ("good" versus "bad"; victims versus perpetrators, Muslims versus the West), visualized, emotionalized and dramatized accordingly, so that potential recipients are more likely to identify with the "good" and have more understanding for the fight against the "bad".

Frames and framing are old but still wearable and helpful hats in communication studies. The framing concept has become popular in the last 20–30 years in political science, sociology, communication studies or psychology. An indication of this is the vast number of publications (e.g. Dahinden, 2006; Matthes, 2014; Scheufele, 2003 and many others).

A few years ago, we carried out, among other things, an analysis of terrorism frames in a very elaborate manner over a longer period of time and, for this purpose, recorded and evaluated the content of 4160 main news programs from eight television channels (ARD Tagesschau, ZDF heute, RTL aktuell, Sat.1 Nachrichten, the Turkish TRT Türk and Kanal D as well as the Arabic-language channels Al Jazeera, Al Arabiya) (Frindte & Haußecker, 2010). In addition, coverage of specific events was analyzed. These events were the murder of the pregnant Egyptian Marwa al-Sherbini in a Dresden courtroom (July 1, 2009), the air strike on two hijacked tankers near Kunduz/ Afghanistan (September 4, 2009), the referendum on a ban on minarets in Switzerland (November 29, 2009), and Israel's attack on six ships carrying aid supplies for the Gaza Strip (May 31, 2010). A dramatization index was created for these reports. This index indicates the extent to which the news reports are characterized by dramatic speech (e.g., explosive vocabulary), emotionalizing effects (e.g., sound effects or specific noises), or strong visuals (e.g., close-ups of victims). In addition, it was recorded whether "Islam" is portrayed as a threat in the reports and to what extent the "West" is reported as a threat.[3]

---

[3] In order to be able to compare the data obtained, they were z-transformed. The z-transformation is a statistical tool to make values from different data sources (or samples) comparable.

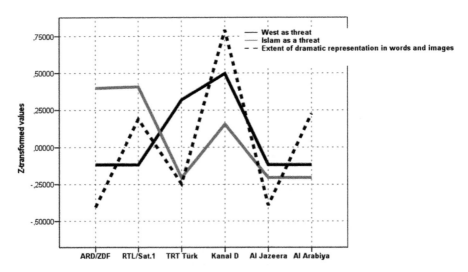

Fig. 11.8 "Islam" and "the West" as a threat and dramatization in the various news channels (Frindte, 2015)

Figure 11.8 illustrates that the reports of the Turkish channel *Kanal D* show the highest dramatization values. Moreover, in the reports of the Turkish stations, the "West" is primarily portrayed as a threat. On the other hand, and in a mirror image, "Islam" appears as a threat in the event reports of the German public and private broadcasters – and hardly at all in the reports of the other broadcasters. And – this is also recognizable – the German private broadcasters report more dramatically than the public broadcasters on the respective events; the differences are statistically significant.

And so the circle almost closes: "The West" and "Islam" presumably form the categorical basis for judging one's own community and that of the "others" in a stereotypical manner, especially in supposed crisis situations. Media constructions about "the West" and "Islam" often provide the framework (the frames) for interpreting one's own and other people's realities in this way. Above all – it could now be said – spectacular events in which conflicts between Muslims and non-Muslims are thematized and focused on can be experienced as threatening to one's own community.

Through the media staging of such events, the myths about "Islam" and "the West" can become significant as self-attributions and attributions to others and come into play as reference systems for mutual prejudices. Of course, the dissemination media play a special role in these competitive battles. They create the conditions for local events to achieve global effects and to be perceived and judged as events by a global audience.

On the other hand, we know so much about the mass media that we cannot trust these sources. We defend ourselves with a suspicion of manipulation, which, however, does not lead to any significant consequences, since the knowledge taken from the mass media coalesces as if by itself into a self-reinforcing structure. (Luhmann, 1996, p. 9).

In the end, there can be no talk of a clash of civilizations, but there can be talk of the aforementioned clash of prejudices. And this clash is currently preventing the protagonists from engaging in a conflict over the appropriate and suitable cultural systems. Instead, a large part of Muslims and non-Muslims seem to accept the self-presentation and external presentation of "the West" and "Islam". It is a staging precisely because it is also a staging of a conflictual relationship whose positive potential is simultaneously concealed and veiled. The Muslims and the non-Muslims have an image of the other group that has hardly anything to do with the Muslims or the non-Muslims. They are "false" images and constructions that only work because they are based on prejudices and myths whose mechanism of origin and effect is difficult to understand.

Stagings of the "West" and of "Islam" work because they are suitable as propaganda to impress a hitherto uninvolved audience (e.g. the non-religious Muslims or the hitherto not "Islamophobic" non-Muslims). In order to be useful as identification aids, such stagings have to correspond to the frame conceptions of the audience. Then the media productions are also suitable as *firm, secure points* in difficult times.

A tried and tested means of using anti-Islamic or anti-Western productions to meet the framework ideas and expectations of an audience and to provide aids to identification is the staged and dramatized use of generally known, traditional symbols, metaphors and myths. A scandalous Mohammed caricature or an invective video about the Prophet provide the "image", the metaphor of "Western" wickedness that no longer needs to be justified. The staged argumentation of "Islamist terrorism" is apparently enough to activate the myths of Muslims all wanting jihad.

References

Adorno, T. W., Frenkel-Brunswick, E., Levinson, J. D., & Sanford, R. N. (1950). *The authoritarian personality*. New York: Harper & Row.

Altemeyer, R. (1981). *Right-wing authoritarianism*. Winnipeg: University of Manitoba Press.

Beck, C. L., & Plant, A. E. (2018). The implications of right-wing authoritarianism for non-Muslims' aggression toward Muslims in the United States. *Analyses of Social Issues and Public Policy, 18*(1), 353–377.

Boomgaarden, H. G., & Vliegenthart, R. (2009). How news content influences anti-immigration attitudes: Germany, 1993–2005. *European Journal of Political Research, 48*(4), 516–542.

Breunig, C., & van Eimeren, B. (2015). 50 Jahre "Massenkommunikation": Trends in der Nutzung und Bewertung der Medien. *Media Perspektiven, 11*(2015), 505–525.

Brown, K. P. (2018). *Saving the sacred sea: The power of civil society in an age of authoritarianism and globalization.* New York: Oxford University Press.

Chatham House. (2017). *What do Europeans think about muslim immigration?* Quelle: https://www.chathamhouse.org/expert/comment/what-do-europeans-think-about-muslim-immigration. Accessed 29 März 2019.

Dahinden, U. (2006). *Framing. Eine integrative Theorie der Massenkommunikation.* Konstanz: UVK.

Das, E., Bushman, B. J., Bezemer, M. D., Kerkhof, P., & Vermeulen, I. E. (2009). How terrorism news reports increase prejudice against outgroups: A terror management account. *Journal of Experimental Social Psychology, 45*(3), 453–459.

Decker, O., & Brähler, E. (Eds.). (2018). *Flucht ins Autoritäre. Rechtsextreme Dynamiken in der Mitte der Gesellschaft. Die Leipziger Autoritarismus-Studie.* Gießen: Psychosozial-Verlag.

Decker, O., Kiess, J., & Brähler, E. (2016). *Die enthemmte Mitte. Autoritäre und rechtsextreme Einstellung in Deutschland. Die Leipziger Mitte-Studie 2016.* Gießen: Psychosozial-Verlag.

Eurobarometer Standard. (2016). *Media use in the European Union.* Quelle: https://ec.europa.eu/commfrontoffice/publicopinion/…/79405. Accessed 21 Juni 2017.

Feierabend, S., Plankenhorn, T., & Rathgeb, T. (2016). Social media im Alltag von Kindern und Jugendlichen. *Studies in Communication Sciences, 16*(2), 150–162.

Frindte, W. (2013). *Der Islam und der Westen. Sozialpsychologische Aspekte einer Inszenierung.* Wiesbaden: Springer VS.

Frindte, W. (2015). "Das Risiko sind immer die anderen": Mediale Inszenierungen interkultureller Risiken. In P. Zoche, S. Kaufmann, & H. Arnold (Hrsg.), *Sichere Zeiten? Gesellschaftliche Dimensionen der Sicherheitsforschung.* Berlin: LIT.

Frindte, W., & Dietrich, N. (Eds.). (2017). *Muslime, Flüchtlinge und Pegida. Sozialpsychologische und kommunikationswissenschaftliche Studien in Zeiten globaler Bedrohungen.* Wiesbaden: Springer VS.

Frindte, W., & Haußecker, N. (2010). *Inszenierter Terrorismus.* Wiesbaden: VS Verlag.

Frindte, W., Ben Slama, B., Dietrich, N., Pisiou, D., Uhlmann, M., & Kausch, M. (2016). Motivationen und Karrieren salafistischer Dschihadistinnen und Dschihadisten. In J. Biene, C. Daase, J. Junk, & H. Müller (Hrsg.), *Salafismus und Dschihadismus in Deutschland.* Frankfurt a. M.: Campus.

Fromm, E. (1941). *Escape from Freedom* (Deutsche Übersetzung: In R. Funk (Hrsg.), (1999). *Erich Fromm Gesamtausgabe in 12 Bänden* (Bd. 1). Stuttgart: Deutsche Verlags-Anstalt). New York: Farrar & Rinehart.

Fuchs, C. (2018). *Digitale Demagogie. Autoritärer Kapitalismus in Zeiten von Trump und Twitter.* Hamburg: Verlag Hamburg.

Giroux, H. A. (2018). *Terror of neoliberalism: Authoritarianism and the eclipse of democracy*. New York: Routledge.

Glück, A. (2007). *Terror im Kopf. Terrorismusberichterstattung in der deutschen und arabischen Elitepresse*. Berlin: Frank & Timme.

Heine, H. (1975). *Säkularausgabe. Werke, Briefwechsel, Lebenszeugnisse* (Bd. 20). Berlin: Akademie-Verlag.

Heitmeyer, W. (2018). *Autoritäre Versuchungen: Signaturen der Bedrohung I*. Berlin: Suhrkamp.

Journalistikon. (2018). *Das Wörterbuch der Journalistik*. Quelle: http://journalistikon. de/luegenpresse. Accessed 25 Mai 2018.

Logvinov, M. (2017). *Muslim- und Islamfeindlichkeit in Deutschland: Begriffe und Befunde im europäischen Vergleich*. Wiesbaden: Springer VS.

Luhmann, N. (1996). *Die Realität der Massenmedien* (2. Aufl.). Opladen: Westdeutscher Verlag.

Mann, H. (1918). *Der Untertan*. Leipzig: Kurt Wolff Verlag.

Matthes, J. (2014). *Framing*. Baden-Baden: Nomos.

Peter, C., & Brosius, H. (2013). Wahrnehmungsphänomene. In W. Schweiger & A. Fahr (Hrsg.), *Handbuch Medienwirkungsforschung* (S. 463–480). Wiesbaden: Springer VS.

Propper, R., Stickgold, R., Keeley, R., & Christman, S. (2007). Is television traumatic?: Dreams, stress, and media exposure in the aftermath of September 11, 2001. *Psychological Science, 18*(4), 334–340.

R.E.M. (1991). "Hey, I can't find nothing on the radio". Songtext aus dem Album "Out of Time", Songwriter: Bill Berry, Peter Buck, Michael Mills & Michael Stipe. Radio Song © Universal Music Publishing Group.

Ruhrmann, G., Sommer, D., & Uhlemann, H. (2006). TV-Nachrichtenberichterstattung über Migranten – Von der Politik zum Terror. In R. Geißler (Hrsg.), *Integration durch Massenmedien. Medien und Migration im internationalen Vergleich* (S. 45–75). Bielefeld: Transcript.

Schemer, C., Jackob, N., Quiring, O., Schultz, T., Ziegele, M., & Granow, V. (2018). *Medienvertrauen in Deutschland 2017*. Quelle: http://www.uni-mainz.de/downloads_presse/02_publizistik_medienvertrauen_grafiken.pdf. Accessed 10 März 2019.

Scheufele, B. (2003). *Frames – Framing – Framing-Effekte. Theoretische und methodische Grundlegung sowie empirische Befunde zur Nachrichtenproduktion*. Wiesbaden: Westdeutscher Verlag.

Schmitz-Berning, C. (1998). *Vokabular des Nationalsozialismus*. Berlin: de Gruyter.

Seeßlen, G., & Metz, M. (2002). *Krieg der Bilder, Bilder des Krieges: Abhandlung über die Katastrophe und die mediale Wirklichkeit*. Berlin: Tiamat.

Seidler, J. D. (2016). *Die Verschwörung der Massenmedien: Eine Kulturgeschichte vom Buchhändler-Komplott bis zur Lügenpresse*. Bielefeld: Transcript.

Simon, E., & Kloppenburg, G. (2010). Kanal D, Pro Sieben oder Das Erste? Determinanten der Fernsehprogrammnutzung junger Zuschauer mit türkischem Zuwanderungshintergrund. *Medien & Kommunikationswissenschaft, 58*(3), 388–405.

Tucholsky, K. (1972). *"Der Untertan". Kurt Tucholsky Ausgewählte Werke* (Bd. 1). Berlin: Verlag Volk und Welt (Original: 1919).

Verband Privater Medien. (2018). *Fernsehnutzung in Europa bleibt konstant auf hohem Niveau.* Quelle: https://www.vau.net/tv-nutzung/content/fernsehnutzung-europa-bleibt-konstant-hohem-niveau. Accessed 27 März 2019.

VPRT-Mediennutzungsanalyse. (2017). *Mediennutzung in Deutschland.* Quelle: https://www.vau.net/system/files/documents/vprt_mediennutzung-in-deutschland-2017.pdf. Accessed 1 Juni 2018.

Weiß, V. (2017). *Die autoritäre Revolte. Die neue Rechte und der Untergang des Abendlandes.* Stuttgart: Klett-Cotta.

Werthes, S., Kim, R., & Conrad, C. (2002). Die Terrorkrise als Medienereignis? In C. Schicha & C. Brosda (Hrsg.), *Medien und Terrorismus. Reaktionen auf den 11. September 2001* (S. 80–93). Münster: LIT.

12

The Impact of Social Media

It is true that the net allows even those who say unreasonable things to express their opinions, but the excess of stupidity clogs the channels. (Eco, 2016, p. 218)

The US-American computer scientist, musician, author, inventor and winner of the Peace Prize of the German Book Trade *Jaron Lanier* demanded some time ago that we should all delete our social media accounts as soon as possible (Lanier, 2018). Do you know what it means should you heed Lanier's call? Your access to the world of bits and bytes would be gone. You would no longer be able to make brunch dates with your girlfriends via WhatsApp; your latest cat pictures would no longer find a place on Facebook; tweeting with your political enemies would no longer be possible; you wouldn't have to post selfies on Instagram either. You'd be thrown back into the *brave old world*. You would have to do without the support of the virtual communities of social media.

Jaron Lanier provides perfectly understandable (and long-known) arguments for his claim. For example, he points out that social media promote inequality, that our data would only increase the profits of Google and Facebook, that we would be subtly manipulated by social media.

But it all started out so well and visionary. When the *World Wide Web was* just trying to emerge from its infancy, many saw in the coming global networking great opportunities for a pluralization of our information and communication possibilities (keywords: teleworking, telebanking, teleshopping, telemedicine, teleteaching, open channels, direct democracy, etc.). Computer-mediated communications could enable users to multiply their social relations and to enter into media-mediated contact and exchange information

W. Frindte, I. Frindte, *Support in Times of No Support*,
https://doi.org/10.1007/978-3-658-38637-5_12

with thousands of people at the same time. The content and forms of social exchange would rapidly expand and multiply. We were of this opinion at the time (Frindte & Köhler, 1999).

Net optimists such as *Nicholas Negroponte, Alvin Toffler, Marvin Minsky* and *Seymour Papert* saw a "post-information age" dawning that would bring not only dark sides (e.g. digital vandalism, software piracy, data thievery, loss of many jobs) but also, and above all, bright times (e.g. Negroponte, 1995). With global networking, organizational hierarchies could be dismantled, societies globalized, controls decentralized, and people harmonized. Above all, however, the individual could determine for himself what and how he communicates, what he informs himself about and allows himself to be informed about.

"Der Spiegel" reported on the positive aspects of these computer-mediated communications using the example of international computer networks for schools:

"Children from all continents exchange measurements in biology lessons, values about the oxygen content of lakes and rivers or about the acidity of rain. And instead of learning about the customs of foreign cultures from boring geography or language textbooks, they prefer to get information from their peers on the ground. Thus, German children are not only in contact with the Bronx via data networks, but also with classes in Hong Kong, New Delhi or Tokyo. In a matter of seconds, they chase their electronic letters to the other end of the world, where young people are just as eager to read the news from screens and answer them immediately" (Der Spiegel, issue 9, 1994, p. 101).

Critics of the new virtual networks were quick to respond, such as *Joseph Weizenbaum, Neil Postman, Luciana* Castellina, and *Howard Rheingold.* In 1993, *Howard Rheingold* writes*:*

> Every time we travel or shop or communicate, citizens of the credit-card society contribute to streams of information that travel between point of purchase, remote credit bureaus, municipal and federal information systems, crime information databases, central transaction databases. And all these other forms of cyberspace interaction take place via the same packet-switched, high-bandwidth network technology – those packets can contain transactions as well as video clips and text files. When these streams of information begin to connect together, the unscrupulous or would-be tyrants can use the Net to catch citizens in a more ominous kind of net. (Rheingold, 2000, p. 300; Original: 1993).

And then, at the beginning of the twenty-first century, *Web 2.0* came along. The virtual world became more interactive and collaborative. Users could now, without much software knowledge, not only consume the content of the virtual networks, but actively shape it themselves and network with virtual communities.

Very soon, the term Web 2.0 was replaced by the term *social media*. Social media are all those internet-based interactive web applications through which users can network with each other and share (self-designed) content with each other. Social media can be divided into social networking sites (such as Facebook or Google), multimedia platforms (Pinterest, Snapchat, Instagram, YouTube), webblogs/microblogs (Tumblr, WordPress, Twitter) and instant messengers (Telegram or WhatsApp) (Frindte & Geschke, 2019, p. 410).

In January 2004, the first version of *Facebook* went online and now has more than two million users per month. Just like Facebook, Twitter, YouTube, Instagram, etc. are also part of the social media that are shaping our current epoch. In this new epoch, the lines between what used to be called the real reality and the virtual reality are blurring. Our everyday communications are both real and virtual. What does this do to us and what do we do with these communicative border crossings?

Self-revelation and self-portrayal play an important role in social media. In addition to blog posts, news, status messages, selfies, photos that users take of themselves and then publish on social media, are among the most popular forms of self-expression.

Why do Facebook users post cat pictures so often? Why do you read on the websites of business consultants that you have to stage yourself in order to make a career? Or why does a colleague only share references to his or her current publications on Facebook? And why does a US president tweet that he is not only clever, but brilliant and a very consistent genius at that (@realDonaldTrump, 06.01.2018)?

Incidentally, pronounced tendencies to use social networking sites more frequently are found in people with low self-esteem, high narcissism values and strongly pronounced feelings of loneliness (Liu & Baumeister, 2016). Narcissism is known to manifest itself in self-overestimation, self-centeredness, hypersensitivity to criticism and a lack of empathy (Schütz, 2014).

Yongjun Sung and colleagues (Sung et al., 2016, p. 260) highlight four motivational patterns in addition to narcissism that explain the posting of selfies on social media: (a) seeking attention, (b) to communicate with friends, family members, or others, (c) to capture and archive specific moments, everyday events, or stages of life, and (d) to entertain and relieve boredom.

Facebook earns money by showing users the most suitable advertising possible, for which companies or other organizations pay. In this respect, Facebook is interested in learning as much as possible about the preferences and interests of its users. On the basis of digital algorithms, Facebook recommends content to users that they – i.e. the users – have already viewed or received in this or a similar way at previous times, or that is preferred by similar people. In this way, users on Facebook are provided with information that is precisely tailored to them.

> In the long run, they end up in their own personalized filter bubble (Filter Bubble; Pariser, 2011) – leaving aside the fact that there are of course other sources of information: A perfectly tailored information universe. (Holtz et al., 2019, p. 427)

In the feature pages, but also in academic discourse, questions are being discussed such as: Are social media a curse or a blessing? Does the world really only consist of selfies and other embarrassment posters? Do shitstorms and hatred on the net lead to the brutalization of our social manners? Can insiders use social media to manipulate elections and overthrow democratic societies? Does the internet make people sick, lazy and violent? Is digitalization leading to a new wave of unemployment? Is social media enabling a new, creative form of learning or are we unlearning learning? Are we doing away with ourselves with artificial intelligence? Etc. etc.

Sure, these are central questions. Not all of them can be answered unequivocally. Some of the questions reflect the uncertainties and indeed the sense of threat that many people express when confronted with the new digital challenges. But some questions have been answered unambiguously by serious researchers, for example:

- The Internet does not make us sad or lonely (Appel & Schreiner, 2014).
- The use of digital technologies and social networks is not harmful per se (Przybylski & Weinstein, 2017). However, the German Federal Center for Health Education (BZgA) points out, on the basis of its own surveys from 2015, that 5.8% of all 12- to 17-year-old adolescents can be assumed to be addicted to computer games or the Internet. Girls aged 12–17 are statistically significantly more affected (7.1%) than male adolescents in this age group (4.5%) (cf. Mortler, 2018, p. 276).
- Internet addiction is a problem that not only stems from excessive use of Internet-based applications, but is associated with symptom burdens in numerous areas, e.g. increased depressiveness and anxiety, motivational and drive deficits (e.g. Lemmens et al., 2011).
- The digitalization of learning cannot solve all the problems of the education system, nor can it teach the skills that pupils and students need on

their path through life (empathy, interest, confidence, morality). However, digital learning can contribute to giving everyone the opportunities to acquire and expand knowledge and to develop their own talents (Dräger & Müller-Eiselt, 2018).

- Internet users tend to be more socially engaged than non-users (Skoric et al., 2016).
- In turn, people with high narcissism scores are not only able to become U.S. president, but they are much more likely to post selfies on Facebook or Instagram, and they tweet more often than people with low narcissism scores (Halpern et al., 2016).
- Cyberbullying or cybermobbing is a problem that is only made possible by social media. It is a deliberate and damaging behavior in that people can be defamed, exposed or have their social relationships damaged via the internet (Obermaier et al., 2015). Individuals who seek to harm others in this way have a generally lower capacity for empathy (Pfetsch et al., 2014).
- The largest German representative online survey to date, with 7349 participants aged between 18 and 95, showed in 2019 that one in 12 people surveyed had already personally experienced hate speech online, i.e. had been verbally attacked or threatened with violence by other people. In particular, younger people aged 18–24 (17%) and people from immigrant families (14%) are significantly more likely to report having experienced aggressive and derogatory comments on social media compared to other groups (Geschke et al., 2019).
- Right-wing extremist and right-wing populist statements about refugees and migrants on Facebook can promote hate crimes against refugees (Müller & Schwarz, 2017).

Information from social networks (e.g. Facebook, Twitter) that deliberately spreads misinformation, fake news, is problematic. The frequent consumption of such false information encourages users to believe in conspiracy theories (Mocanu et al., 2015). More on this in Chap. 15.

Brian L. Ott concludes that the increasing use of such networks can lead to an oversimplification of communication and a brutalization of manners. In doing so, he has the former US president *Donald Trump* and the consequences of his Twittering in mind. After an analysis of 2550 messages sent by Donald Trump via Twitter between October 2015 and May 2016, i.e. before the beginning of his presidency, Ott (2017, p. 64 f.) states: Trump's messages are simplistic, offensive, bossy, uncivilized, predominantly negatively connoted, sexist, racist and xenophobic.

However, everyday life on the Internet and social media is no better, but also no worse than the everyday life of traditional face-to-face encounters in real life. It's just that touching doesn't really work on the Internet yet.

If we are to lament the demise of freedom, humanity, and normativity in social media, we should first and foremost change real reality. If we emphasize the advantages of computer-mediated communication, then these advantages must first benefit people in real reality. These digital forms of social interaction are real because they work. Whether they are threatening or beneficial, whether they are helpful and can provide support and security, is in the eye of the beholder.

References

Appel, M., & Schreiner, C. (2014). Digitale Demenz? Mythen und wissenschaftliche Befundlage zur Auswirkung von Internetnutzung. *Psychologische Rundschau, 65,* 1–10.

Der Spiegel. (1994). *Revolution des Lernens, 9,* S. 9–113.

Dräger, J., & Müller-Eiselt, R. (2018). *Die digitale Bildungsrevolution.* München: Deutsche-Verlags-Anstalt.

Eco, U. (2016). *Pape Satàn.* München: Hanser.

Frindte, W., & Geschke, D. (2019). *Lehrbuch Kommunikationspsychologie.* Weinheim: Beltz.

Frindte, W., & Köhler, T. (Hrsg.). (1999). *Kommunikation im Internet.* Frankfurt a. M.: Lang.

Geschke, D., Klaßen, A., Quent, M., & Richter, C. (2019).*#Hass im Netz: Der schleichende Angriff auf unsere Demokratie – eine bundesweite repräsentative Untersuchung.* Institut für Demokratie und Zivilgesellschaft. Quelle: https://www.idz-jena.de/fileadmin/user_upload/_Hass_im_Netz_-_Der_schleichende_Angriff.pdf. Accessed 8 Sept 2019.

Halpern, D., Valenzuela, S., & Katz, J. E. (2016). "Selfie-ists" or "Narci-selfiers"?: A cross-lagged panel analysis of selfie taking and narcissism. *Personality and Individual Differences, 97,* 98–101.

Holtz, P., von Hoyer, J., & Frindte, W. (2019). Soziale Medien als Bühne des 21. Jahrhunderts. In W. Frindte & D. Geschke (Hrsg.), *Lehrbuch Kommunikationspsychologie.* Weinheim: Beltz.

Lanier, J. (2018). *Zehn Gründe, warum du deine Social Media Accounts sofort löschen musst.* Hamburg: Hoffmann und Campe.

Lemmens, J. S., Valkenburg, P. M., & Peter, J. (2011). Psychosocial causes and consequences of pathological gaming. *Computers in Human Behavior, 27*(1), 144–152.

Liu, D., & Baumeister, R. F. (2016). Social networking online and personality of self-worth: A meta-analysis. *Journal of Research in Personality, 64,* 79–89.

Mocanu, D., Rossi, L., Zhang, Q., Karsai, M., & Quattrociocchi, W. (2015). Collective attention in the age of (mis) information. *Computers in Human Behavior, 51*, 1198–1204.

Mortler, M. (2018). Digitale Medien – Fortschritt ohne Schattenseiten? In C. Bär, G. Thomas, & R. Mayr (Hrsg.), *Digitalisierung im Spannungsfeld von Politik, Wirtschaft, Wissenschaft und Recht* (S. 275–284). Berlin: Springer Gabler.

Müller, K., & Schwarz, C. (2017). *Fanning the flames of hate: Social media and hate crime.* Quelle: https://pdfs.semanticscholar.org/b19c/8a6eb0a519749a724a3 4b677aa7d3cf24e74.pdf. Accessed 15 März 2019.

Negroponte, N. (1995). *Being digital.* New York: Knopf.

Obermaier, M., Fawzi, N., & Koch, T. (2015). Bystanderintervention bei Cybermobbing. Warum spezifische Merkmale computervermittelter Kommunikation prosoziales Eingreifen von Bystandern einerseits hemmen und andererseits fördern. *Studies in Commuication and Media, 4*, 28–52.

Ott, B. L. (2017). The age of twitter: Donald J. Trump and the politics of debasement. *Critical Studies in Media Communication, 34*(1), 59–68.

Pariser, E. (2011). *The filter bubble: What the internet is hiding from you.* London: Penguin.

Pfetsch, J., Müller, C. R., & Ittel, A. (2014). Cyberbullying und Empathie: Affektive, kognitive und medienbasierte Empathie im Kontext von cyberbullying im Kindes- und Jugendalter. *Diskurs Kindheits-und Jugendforschung, 9*(1), 23–37.

Przybylski, A. K., & Weinstein, N. (2017). A large-scale test of the goldilocks hypothesis: Quantifying the relations between digital-screen use and the mental well-being of adolescents. *Psychological Science, 28*(2), 204–215.

Rheingold, H. (2000; Original: 1993). *The virtual community.* Cambridge, London: The MIT Press. German Version: *Virtuelle Gemeinschaft.* Bonn: Addisson Wesley (Deutschland).

Schütz, A. (2014). Narzissmus. In M. A. Wirtz (Hrsg.), *Dorsch – Lexikon der Psychologie* (18. Aufl.). Bern: Hogrefe.

Skoric, M. M., Zhu, Q., Goh, D., & Pang, N. (2016). Social media and citizen engagement: A meta-analytic review. *New Media & Society, 18*(9), 1817–1839.

Sung, Y., Lee, J., Kim, E., & Choi, S. M. (2016). Why we post selfies: Understanding motivations for posting pictures of oneself. *Personality and Individual Differences, 97*, 260–265.

Part III

The Great Narratives Still Exist

13

Reminder of the Meta-Narratives

Great is the confusion under heaven. Strange things happen in these times.
(Eco, 2012, p. 213).

What is the value of talking about "the West", "Islam" or the "Clash of Civilizations"? The thesis we like to put forward is: that this talk is part of a meta-narrative with which speakers and listeners try to explain and find a *foothold* in realities and their own place in these realities.

In order to substantiate this thesis, we first have to expect the reader to take an excursion into postmodern language games. The following chapter therefore requires a little philosophical leisure.

In 1979, the French philosopher *Jean-François Lyotard* (1924–1998) published the book "The Postmodern Condition", commissioned by the University Council of the Government of Québec in Canada. A thorough German translation was published in 1986 by the Austrian publisher Passagen Verlag. According to Lyotard (1986), the modern era or modernity has produced at least two major explanations of the world, meta-narratives, through which science and scientific work have been legitimized and justified: a speculative and an emancipatory legitimacy narrative. The *speculative model* is very closely related to Humboldt's ideal of education. According to this model, an unselfish search for knowledge is inherent in the human spirit. Science legitimates

In this chapter, we use passages that we have already published in the book "Muslime, Flüchtlinge und Pegida" (Frindte & Dietrich, 2017) or in "Soziale Konstruktionen" (Frindte, 1998).

itself by representing the form through which the development of the "objective spirit" (Hegel, 1979, original: 1817) ultimately takes place. The *emancipation model,* on the other hand, was primarily a political narrative. According to this model, science has to help people to emancipate themselves and to become free through knowledge. According to Lyotard, both "grand narratives" or meta-narratives have failed: the unfolding of the mind ("spirit") or the unfolding of knowledge is apparently only one of many stories that cannot be substantiated. And the emancipation narrative is also no longer suitable for the justification of science. No prescriptive statements about the making of the world and about the liberation of human beings could be derived from scientific explanations.

However – according to *Lyotard* – while philosophical reflection on the human condition and the sciences in their *claim to totality* have reached their end, scientific-technical development per se has not. Lyotard refers here above all to the rapid developments in the computer sciences and speaks – like many others – of the developing information society, to which he has a rather ambivalent relationship. At the very least, he sees two possibilities for countering the increasing and irreversible informatization of society: Either in the future those privileged minorities who succeed in having the information media at their disposal will control and regulate the social systems with power and terror. Or, through the comprehensive informatization of society, the public will have free access to all memories and databases (Lyotard, 1986, p. 192) in order to be able to enter into a comprehensive dispute about the human possibilities for the future. The vision of the two possibilities had, it must be admitted today, something prophetic about it.

The metaphor of "grand narratives" has become commonplace. In general, one could say that grand narratives or meta-narratives have at least the following characteristics: they analyze the past, formulate diagnoses about the present, and make predictions about the future. *Meta-narratives thus provide constructions to reduce the unpredictability of the world.* They simultaneously predict that the world and being human can have a future under certain conditions. Grand narratives can provide *support* and *security* in more or less untenable times.

Some interpreters of *Jean-François Lyotard* believe that the time of the grand narratives is over. Now only the small narratives are lived, told and believed. "Ego society," "two-thirds society," "society of the unstable," "single society," "loss of public spirit," "release from gender roles," "disintegration of marriage and family," "new poverty," "new privatism," "new freedom," "disenchantment with politics," "social coldness," "risky opportunities," etc. – have emerged over the last three decades as brands to name the small or smaller narratives of our way of life or to describe the individualization processes of the present time, in post-modern industrial societies. In this context, sociologists have drawn attention to serious "individualization thrusts" in the highly developed industrialized countries (Beck, 1986; Heitmeyer et al., 1992). Some years ago, *Elisabeth Beck-Gernsheim* (1994) highlighted the following dimensions of individualization: (a) Liberation from traditional controls, (b) Loss of traditional stabilities, and (c) New bonds, constraints, and controls. The individual is increasingly thrown back on his or her own individual resources. Industrial forms of life (such as social classes and strata), traditional family social structures, but also work and friend groups are increasingly losing and changing their previous identity-forming function in highly industrialized civilizations. Relatively consistent and time-stable social reference groups (and their value structures) are being replaced by a patchwork of social networks in which individuals construct, stage and present their biography and identity on their own responsibility.

Although *Jean-François Lyotard* also speaks of the "disintegration of the social bond" (1986, p. 54), he is primarily interested in the ways in which different ideas and insights can be contested in a highly complex world.

As an analytical tool for finding such possibilities, Lyotard uses *Wittgenstein's* metaphor of language games. According to this metaphor, knowledge can be expressed in many and diverse language games. One thinks, for example, of the linguistic games of telling, explaining, prescribing, promising, commanding, etc. Firstly, all these language games are not compatible with each other: narratives are hardly suitable for the justification of science, from scientific explanations state orders can only be derived to a limited extent, and so on. Secondly, these different language games could hardly be linked and compared with each other by means of any meta-language games (i.e. grand narratives). There is no simple criterion for deciding which of our language games is particularly distinguished from the others.

Again we encounter a pluralism of language and knowledge games to be endured. Or? *Lyotard*, too, wonders whether criteria cannot be found against which we could test our knowledge of the world and our manifold ideas of how to shape our lives. Two criteria seem conceivable to him: The first he calls legitimacy of knowledge (or speaking, WF/IF) through performativity. According to this, today's knowledge would have to be measured more and more by the criterion of efficiency. This makes sense at first and obviously corresponds to our everyday experiences. What is true is what is useful, and what is useful ultimately pays off, or rather: what is useful must pay off. Isn't that one of our main New German rules?

The consequences of applying pure efficiency or performativity criteria, however, are ultimately fatal. According to these criteria, only those knowledge and language games, research and scientific fields as well as political interest groups would have access to the state's money pots that could prove that they and only they could make the state system more effective. Scientific or political efficiency in the service of power – who can't think of enough current examples?

Lyotard, however, offers a second way in which knowledge can be examined and legitimated. He calls this path the legitimation of knowledge through *paralogy*. Paralogy in Greek stands for irrationality and error. All knowledge is accepted as such. Every design has its value. This is the recognition of plural language and knowledge games. Between the different language and knowledge games, scientific as well as non-scientific, there can be no final decision about their ultimate validity and truth. This is what Lyotard means when he says that the emphasis must now be placed on dissensus. "Consensus is a horizon, it is never acquired" (1986, p. 176f.).

Lyotard later summarizes this idea in the concept of *contradiction* (1989). The pluralism of thinking, speaking and living is a constant process of dispute between multiplicities. The friction points of the dispute are found at the borders and conflict zones where the unknown and unfamiliar meet the familiar and conventional. Knowledge is to be measured by the extent to which it is dedicated to the paradoxical, unfamiliar, seemingly erroneous spheres of our conceptions of reality, by the extent to which it is able to produce the unknown instead of the known, i.e. to raise new questions. In this context, minorities in politics and science have an important role to play, since they not only develop new ideas, conceptions and life designs, but can also fuel the dispute and dissent between minorities and majorities (cf. also Lyotard, 1977).

Almost at the same time as Lyotard, the French social psychologist and former director of the Laboratoire Européen de Psychologie Sociale, *Serge Moscovici*, also drew attention to the innovative role of social minorities in social change (Moscovici, 1979). Moscovici was thinking primarily of minorities, who are capable of producing new ideas in politics, philosophy, and art through which societies can become more humane. For Moscovici, the minorities who can achieve possible social change through their alternative viewpoints and consistent behavior are the progressive initiators of social progress. More on this in Chap. 25.

Not always, but more and more often, minorities do not only stand up for social progress. The nationalists in Europe, for example, are not only concerned with restoring the independence of their nations. They also oppose the alleged Islamization of the Christian West; they are, like the former Polish foreign minister *Witold Waszczykowski,* against cyclists, vegetarians, homo-sexuals, and against the "gender craze"; they organize to seal off their countries from refugees; and they dream of taking power in the European Union (e.g. Die Zeit, 2019). Climate change skeptics are equally radical in their rejection of man-made climate change and corresponding radical measures to save the climate. Representatives of these and similar minorities, moreover, have learned. Whether they have read the work of the Frenchman *Moscovici* cannot be verified. What is certain, however, is that their appearance and their suc-cesses in the public arenas correspond to the recipes that scholars, such as *Serge Moscovici,* have derived from their research on successful change through minorities.

More than that, dissent between scientific or political minorities and majorities can be threatening, since their respective representatives usually start from the assumption that their, and only their, view of the world and science is the only true grand narrative. The scientific, political, and journal-istic protagonists who advocate immediate and fundamental new climate policies are as convinced of the greatness of their insights as the climate change deniers are of theirs.

The nationalists in Europe and elsewhere see in the ideology with which they try to glorify their own nation the grand narrative to stigmatize the cos-mopolitans and Brexit opponents as fatherless fellows. The cosmopolitans, for their part, see in their ideas of the equality, freedom and brotherhood of all people the only and great possibility of ensuring the survival of humanity without falling back into barbarism (cf. Beck, 2002).

The anti-Semites are as convinced of the greatness of their tales of the impurity, rapacity and wickedness of the Jews as the Islamists are of the uniqueness of their God and the necessity of a world according to Islamic ideas of order.

The "Clash of Civilization" (Huntington, 2002) also has enough potential to be recognized as a meta-narrative. After all, it is not surprising. If one were to dispense with such meta-narratives, one could indeed claim, with *Francis Fukuyama* (1992), that we have reached the end of history. Meta-narratives are still being produced, at least in political contexts. The new meta-narratives owe their vitality, of course, to the current relevance of the global and the many-voiced talk about globalization.[1]

In addition to nationalism, anti-Semitism and cosmopolitanism, other more or less grand meta-narratives about the future are of course currently

---

[1] *Peter Sloterdijk* says: "The misery of the great narratives of the conventional kind lies not at all in the fact that they were too big, but in the fact that they were not big enough" (2005, p. 14).

being told against the backdrop of the present and the past; for example, the narrative about neoliberalism after the Lehman bankruptcy or about the end of the European Union, the narrative about religious fundamentalism and its temptations, or the narrative about Europe's Christian-Jewish roots, and so on. That the meta-narrative about cosmopolitanism is more sympathetic to us compared to the others does not really need to be justified. At the end of this book, we still do.

References

Beck, U. (1986). *Risikogesellschaft – Auf dem Weg in eine andere Moderne*. Frankfurt a. M.: Suhrkamp. English Version: Risk society – Towards a new modernity. London: Sage.

Beck, U. (2002). *Macht und Gegenmacht im globalen Zeitalter*. Frankfurt a. M.: Suhrkamp. English Version: Power in the global age: A new global political economy. Cambridge, Oxford: Polity.

Beck-Gernsheim, E. (1994). Invidualisierungstheorie: Veränderungen des Lebenslaufs in der Moderne. In H. Keupp (Hrsg.), *Zugänge zum Subjekt – Perspektiven einer reflexiven Sozialpsychologie*. Frankfurt a. M.: Suhrkamp.

Die Zeit. (2019, April 11). *Alles, was rechts ist*, S. 4.

Eco, U. (2012). *Im Krebsgang voran*. München: Deutscher Taschenbuch Verlag.

Frindte, W. (1998). *Soziale Konstruktionen*. Wiesbaden: Westdeutscher Verlag.

Frindte, W., & Dietrich, N. (Hrsg.). (2017). *Muslime, Flüchtlinge und Pegida. Sozialpsychologische und kommunikationswissenschaftliche Studien in Zeiten globaler Bedrohungen*. Wiesbaden: Springer VS.

Fukuyama, F. (1992). *Das Ende der Geschichte*. München: Kindler. English Version (1992): The end of history and the last man. Florence, MA: Free Press.

Hegel, G. W. F. (1979). *Enzyklopädie der philosophischen Wissenschaften im Grundrisse*. Werke, Bd 10. Frankfurt a. M.: Suhrkamp (Original: 1817).

Heitmeyer, W., et al. (1992). *Die Bielefelder Rechtsextremismus-Studie*. Weinheim: Juventa.

Huntington, S. P. (2002). *Kampf der Kulturen. Die Neugestaltung der Weltpolitik im 21. Jahrhundert*. München: Goldmann.

Lyotard, J. (1977). *Das Patchwork der Minderheiten*. Berlin: Merve Verlag.

Lyotard, J. (1986). *Das postmoderne Wissen*. Graz, Wien: Böhlau. English Version: The postmodern condition: A report on knowledge (1984). Minnesota: University of Minnesota Press. French Original: La condition postmoderne: Rapport sur le savoir, 1979.

Lyotard, J. (1989). *Der Widerstreit*. Wilhelm Fink Verlag. French Original: Le différend. Minuit.

Moscovici, S. (1979). *Sozialer Wandel durch Minoritäten*. München: Urban und Schwarzenberg. English Version: Social influence and social change. London: Academic Press.

Sloterdijk, P. (2005). *Im Weltinnenraum des Kapitals*. Frankfurt a. M.: Suhrkamp.

14

Back to the Roots: Fundamentalisms Offer Support and Threaten the Foundations

Certainly (apart from the neo-fascist extremists) something of the fascist heritage has remained in our national character and reappears from time to time – for example, the racism, the homophobia, the strident machismo, the anti-communism and the preference for the right... (Eco, 2016, p. 101f.)

Let's take a closer look at some of the more or less grand narratives with which their protagonists try to reverse the positive developments of globalization.

Nationalism

We begin with *nationalism*, which is once again celebrating joyous reigns not only in Germany with the AfD or the people who take to the streets under the label PEGIDA. Whether in Poland, Hungary, Italy, France, Austria or the Netherlands, in Sweden and Norway, in Spain and, of course, in Great Britain – in most European countries parties and social movements have established themselves that fuel the train of illiberal democracies and try to satisfy a seemingly mass need for national *support* and order. One can also think of the nationalist rumble caused by the former US President Donald Trump's "America first" slogan, or the dream of an Islamic-influenced "Greater Turkish Empire" dreamed by Turkish President *Recep Tayyip Erdoğan*. And of course of the wars that are being waged to put the supposed rights of a nation or people in perspective, in Yemen, Ukraine or the Middle East. This global shift to the right is in contrast to the internationalization and globalization of political, economic, scientific and cultural processes. *Matthias Quent* (2019),

W. Frindte, I. Frindte, *Support in Times of No Support*, https://doi.org/10.1007/978-3-658-38637-5_14

following *Seymour Lipset* (Lipset & Raab, 1971), refers to this shift to the right as *backlash* – the reaction of groups that feel they are losing importance, influence and power due to societal changes and therefore try to reverse or contain these changes. The authoritarians feel that the state refuses to enforce the alleged will of the people; the nationalists see their faith in the nation-state threatened; the anti-Semites try to blame their poverty on the Jews; the Islamists believe that only the "proper" foundations of Islam are suitable to counter the power of the "West".

In order:

Do you, dear readers, still remember the "summer fairy tale 2006". That's right, we mean the football World Cup that took place in Germany that year. Although the German national team only came third, it was celebrated as the "World Champion of Hearts", as was reported in the media. Millions of Germans were captivated by this major event. Foreign countries looked on in part amazement and in part amusement at the German soccer fans, who were enthusiastic about their team but also acted as generous, friendly hosts. It later emerged that the awarding of the World Cup to Germany was not all above board. Leading German football officials were accused of venality and tax evasion. But it was beautiful, the black-red-gold summer fairy tale, so beautiful that it was made into a film. The director *Sönke Wortmann* made a full-length documentary about our German heroes around Jürgen Klinsmann, Joachim Löw, etc., which is well worth seeing.

In the context of the long-term studies on group-focused enmity conducted by *Wilhelm Heitmeyer* and colleagues from 2002 to 2012, *Julia Becker, Ulrich Wagner* and *Oliver Christ* asked themselves whether the World Cup euphoria could also have influenced the Germans' national pride. In order to answer this question, the authors interviewed around 1700 adult Germans in May 2006, i.e. before the World Cup, and repeated the survey with just under 1000 people after the World Cup in August 2006. The *nationalistic* and *patriotic* attitudes of the respondents were measured. In order to measure nationalistic attitudes, respondents were asked to state, among other things, how proud they were of German history and of being German. Patriotic attitudes were measured, among other things, with questions about pride in democracy and social security in Germany.

The results point to a clear effect: "People surveyed after the World Cup were more nationalistic and less patriotic than those surveyed before the World Cup" (Becker et al., 2007, p. 145). Moreover, pronounced nationalist attitudes were found to be closely linked to xenophobia and anti-Semitism. But more on that later.

A somewhat more difficult analysis of the course of nationalist and patriotic attitudes during the 2006 World Cup was attempted by *Klaus Ahlheim* and *Bardo Heger* (2008). They drew on surveys conducted as part of the 2006 General Population Survey (ALLBUS), in which a total of 3421 adult Germans were interviewed. One of the interview questions was "How proud are you to be German?". The following figure illustrates the percentage of those who answered the statement with "very proud" (Fig. 14.1).

In the course of the 2006 World Cup, the pride of being German or Deutscher initially increased until the semi-final against Italy. The German national team lost this match. Thereafter, the proportion of those who are proud of Germany fell significantly and, after the "summer fairy tale", reached the level of the period before the World Cup. *Michael Mutz* rightly points out, however, that the data are cross-sectional surveys and not a longitudinal study with the same people. The number of cases during the individual surveys is also not particularly high (Mutz, 2012, p. 524).

But what can be observed up to the semi-finals has a name in social psychology: *"Basking* in *reflected glory",* basking in the glory of others, in short: BIRG. For example, people "bask" in the success of a particular sports club; they see themselves as part of this success, symbolizing their affiliation, e.g. with club scarves or other signs, in order to openly present their connection

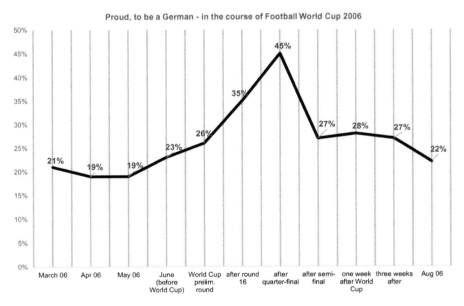

Fig. 14.1 Pride in being German – during the 2006 World Cup. (Source: Ahlheim & Heger, 2008, p. 46; Mutz, 2012, p. 525)

to the successful club. In case of failure, on the other hand, they turn away (*we won – they* lost). In other words, *identification with* the successful can certainly provide support and security. But it is also a fragile matter.

So we have to go further and ask: What are we actually talking about when we talk about nationalism and patriotism? Where is the dividing line between the two? Does it exist at all? Social scientists think they can recognize and identify such a dividing line.

All those ideologies can be classified under nationalism with which the characteristics of one's own ethnic community (language, culture, history) are exaggerated and absolutized in comparison to other communities. *Otto Damm* (1993, p. 20) puts it even more sharply, understanding nationalism as political behavior "… that is not borne by the conviction of the equal value of all people and nations, but rather assesses and treats other peoples and nations as inferior or as enemies".

Nationalist attitudes are linked to convictions of one's own national superiority and to stereotyped devaluations of intra-societal minorities and other nations. In contrast, people with patriotic attitudes strive for diversity within society. Individualization, cultural and religious differences are accepted by them, and minorities within society experience protection, support and solidarity.

In older social psychological studies (e.g., Blank & Schmidt, 1997, 2003; Heyder & Schmidt, 2002), nationalistic attitudes were shown to be a promoting condition for anti-Semitism, xenophobia, and Islamophobia. Patriotic attitudes, on the other hand, tended to be associated with less negative attitudes toward strangers, foreigners, and Jews. In other words, German patriots do not seem to pose a threat to Jews and foreigners. They may continue to be invited to German television talk shows, write books, and speak proudly of the welfare-state benefits and political participation opportunities in Germany.

It's not quite that simple again.

In our own, non-representative study, we asked approximately 350 German adults about their anti-Semitic attitudes. Without wanting to capture the diversity of anti-Semitic attitudes (more on this in the next section), we initially limited ourselves to searching for the extent of modern and politicized anti-Semitic statements (example statement "In Germany, the Jews have too much influence").

We also recorded how strongly the respondents identify with Germany (in the sense of patriotism), how much they agree with German-national ideologies (nationalism in the sense of "völkisch thinking") and how they assess national collective goods (e.g. German history, Germany's political, cultural and economic successes, the German flag, the German anthem, etc.).

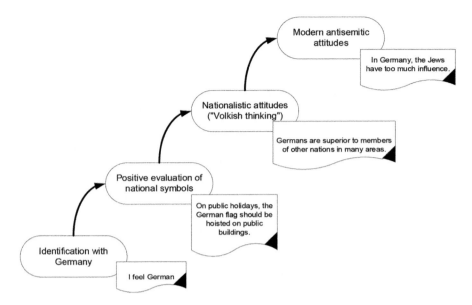

Fig. 14.2 Patriotic, nationalistic and anti-Semitic attitudes. (Illustration of own statistical findings, Frindte & Wammetsberger, 2008)

Without going into the complex test statistical evaluations in detail, we present the results in the summarizing Fig. 14.2[1]: Identification with Germany (e.g., a positive sense of belonging to Germany) and commitment to national goals in the sense of patriotic attitudes do not initially promote German-national attitudes, but do cause a positive evaluation of national symbols (e.g., the German flag or the national anthem). However, the more positively these symbols are valued, the more pronounced are the nationalistic and, as a consequence, the politically tinged anti-Semitic attitudes (see Frindte & Wammetsberger, 2008).

That is, the connection between (patriotic) identification with the German nation and anti-Semitism is mediated through the positive evaluation of German symbols and German-national attitudes.

However, these correlations can only be demonstrated in German contexts. In a European comparison, it seems difficult to find empirical support for this (Schmidt-Denter & Schick, 2007). Not to mention that people from different countries seem to mean something different most of the time when they are asked to answer the question whether they are proud of their country or of democracy in their country (Meitinger, 2018).

---

[1] The basis of this figure are various so-called structural equation models; fit values in the present case as an indication for experts: Chi-Square = 21.72, df = 14, p = 0.085, RMSEA = 0.042.

On the one hand, of course, the findings of a study by the *Open Society Foundation,* the foundation funded by US-American *George Soros,* give cause for optimism. In the *Voices on Values* research project, more than 6000 participants were surveyed in Germany, France, Poland, Hungary, Italy and Greece in 2018. Nearly 90% of Germans surveyed say they are proud of important aspects of their German identity. Respondents from Germany, France, Poland, Hungary, Italy and Greece largely support democratic social values. More than 90% believe that the rule of law, pluralism and the protection of individual rights are essential to a good society. Only 5% support only closed society values. In Germany, support for open society values is highest compared to the other countries. Ninety-six percent of Germans surveyed consider freedom of expression essential; 90% support the rights of minorities to be protected; 96% support the right of the media to criticize the government (Open Society European Policy Institute, 2019).

On the other hand, people in many European countries support authoritarian populist views. This refers to cynical attitudes towards minority rights, rejection of immigration and convictions of one's own national superiority. Almost half of all respondents share such views, according to a 2016 survey by the YouGov polling institute (YouGov, 2016). At the top of the list are Romania (82%), Poland (78%), France (63%) and the Netherlands (55%).

The results point to the voter potential that populist parties have in these countries.

It should be obvious that the populist parties in Germany, France, the Netherlands, Poland or elsewhere are nationalist in the above sense. The most important argumentation pattern, which is repeatedly varied by the representatives of these parties, is the topos of the *people* (Wodak, 2015). The "people" must be protected from "alienation", the blood of the "people" must remain pure, the "people" is invoked to draw attention to a supposed "we", the "people" must be reclaimed. Its rights must be demanded and love for the people and the fatherland is true patriotism, etc. The rhetoric and the argumentation are racial and nationalistic, even if populist speakers try to pretend to be patriotic or found a party called "Aufbruch deutscher Patrioten".

This actually only shows that *patriotism* and *nationalism* are ideologically charged social constructions and can be used as such. Sometimes such a construction promotes social discrimination, but sometimes it prevents such rejections, depending on how and for what purpose they are used by political elites. Any reference to a national affiliation has the potential to be interpreted as nationalistic or patriotic.

Which brings us back to the beginning: A distinction between nationalism and patriotism doesn't seem particularly helpful in giving the *Michel,* who is

proud of his country, a foothold in the right-wing populist, xenophobic and/
or anti-Semitic din. We agree with *Yuval Noah Harari* when he writes:

> It becomes problematic when well-meaning patriotism turns into chauvinistic
> ultranationalism. Instead of believing my nation is unique-which is basically
> true of all nations-I now feel my nation is superior to all others, I owe it all my
> loyalty, and I have no meaningful obligations to anyone else. This is the breed-
> ing ground for violent conflict. (Harari, 2018, p. 158f.)

A productive dispute with the ultra-nationalists is thus ruled out.

Anti-Semitism

Teacher: "Moritz, what race are the Jews?" "Semites." "Good. – And the
Germans?" "Anti-Semites."

On October 27, 2018, a white adult in Pittsburgh, Pennsylvania, shot and
killed 11 people during a naming ceremony at the *Tree of Life* synagogue; at
least six others were injured. This is the most serious attack on Jews in recent
U.S. history. Social and traditional media very soon began a race to explain
the Pittsburgh massacre. For some the only real culprit is US President *Donald
Trump,* whose demagogy has fueled the spiral of violence in the US. Others,
however, see the culprits among those Jews in the US who oppose the US
administration's refugee policy. Among these critics of the US administration
is the Jewish refugee aid organization HIAS (Hebrew Immigrant Aid Society),
which was founded in 1881 with the goal of helping Jews immigrate to the
US. Since 2015, HIAS has also engaged with the concerns and issues of non-
Jewish refugees, establishing itself as part of the opposition movement against
the Trump administration. That the second explanatory pattern reflects the
perpetrator-victim reversal common in modern anti-Semitism, blaming Jews
for anti-Semitic attacks, should not go unmentioned. We, the authors of the
book, found it difficult to seek explanations for the Pittsburgh massacre. More
than that, we refused to take a public stand with punched-up explanations.
We refused because the murder of 11 Jews made no sense, because we were
stunned and saddened. The murder in Pittsburgh was an act motivated by
anti-Semitism, which ultimately only testifies to the spiritual and emotional
poverty of the perpetrator.

Anti-Semitic criminal and violent acts have been increasing rapidly in the
US since 2017. In 2017, there were nearly 2000 physical attacks, threats, and

harassment against Jews, as well as vandalism against Jewish institutions. That was 57% more than in 2016 and the highest overall increase since 1979, the year the *Anti-Defamation League,* a U.S. organization, began recording anti-Semitic incidents. In Germany, the number of anti-Semitic *crimes* increased by 10% in 2018 compared to the previous year. A total of 1646 anti-Semitic crimes were recorded in Germany in 2018, compared to 1504 the year before. Anti-Semitic *acts of violence* actually doubled. In the process, 43 people were injured. In other European countries, the number of anti-Semitic crimes also increased. A total of 541 anti-Semitic crimes were recorded in France in 2018. This is an increase of 74% compared to 2017.

In December 2018, the EU conducted a survey of more than 16,000 Jews in 12 European countries (Eurobarometer Special, 2019). Nine out of ten respondents felt that anti-Semitism had increased in their country, and more than eight out of ten saw anti-Semitism as a serious problem. However, a subsequent EU survey of non-Jews showed how far apart the assessments of Jews and non-Jews are. Across Europe, only 36% of non-Jews thought that anti-Semitism had increased in their country. In Germany and France, countries with a relatively large Jewish population, but also in Sweden, awareness of the problem of anti-Semitism and hostility towards Jews is significantly higher than in other European countries. In Germany, two thirds of the population see anti-Semitism as a problem, in France 72% and in Sweden 81%.

The problems can be observed in everyday life and are well known. In France, for example, Jews such as the philosopher *Alain Finkielkraut* are called anti-Semitic names during the demonstration of the yellow vest movement. In Berlin, it is dangerous to walk as a Jew with a kippa. The president of the Jewish Community in Munich, *Charlotte Knobloch,* receives letters and emails in which the senders, who can be identified by name, express their hatred of the "money-hungry and power-hungry Jews". In Chemnitz, hooded strangers attack a kosher restaurant with rocks and bottles. In Copenhagen, young migrants attack an elderly Jew right next to the synagogue and demand his money. Seventy years after the Shoah, the synagogues, Jewish schools and other Jewish institutions in many European places have to be heavily guarded and protected by the police.

There have been many attempts to define *anti-Semitism.* There have also been warnings against an inflationary use of the term (e.g. Waldenegg, 2000). Nevertheless, the term is now an "established convention" (Almog, 1990, p. 142), which, although it has a false meaning, can hardly be removed from the conceptual inventory of the scientific community and from everyday life. Anti-Semitism – the word coined in 1879 by the German anti-Semite *Wilhelm*

Marr – reflects those false projections with which non-Jews attempt to defame *Jews as Jews* (cf. Horkheimer & Adorno, 1944, here: 1969).

Against the background of increasingly right-wing populist developments in Western Europe, anti-Semitic incidents in Germany and other European countries, and anti-Israeli statements by right-wing political opinion leaders, social scientists, politicians, and journalists have been diagnosing new forms of anti-Semitism and anti-Judaism since the early 1990s (cf. for Germany, e.g. Bergmann & Erb, 2000). Under the guise of public pressure of opinion, new varieties of anti-Semitic attitudes have developed, which are accepted in the private sphere but not in society as a whole. Compared to openly expressed anti-Semitic attitudes, statements of this kind appear more "harmless", but can to the same extent legitimize and encourage extreme attitudes and actions towards foreign minorities. The frequently expressed demand to finally draw a line under the subject of the *Holocaust* and *German guilt* also reflects a relatively new form of anti-Semitism. *Peter Schönbach* already pointed to this form many years ago. When in the winter of 1959/1960 a wave of desecrations of Jewish cemeteries and monuments attracted public attention in the FRG, he, who at that time worked at the Institute for Social Research in Frankfurt a. Main and was concerned with the background and manifestations of these anti-Semitic stagings, coined the term *secondary anti-Semitism*. Schönbach thus diagnosed a reprivatized, non-militant, non-fanatical, and "de-ideologized anti-Semitism" in the Federal Republic of Germany (Schönbach, 1961). When in public statements the Memorial to the Murdered Jews of Europe in Berlin is called a "monument of shame", then secondary anti-Semitism is not far away even today.

At the latest since the "Al-Aqsa Intifada" in 2000, September 11, 2001, and the so-called Muhammad cartoon controversy (see Chap. 10), an increase in anti-Semitic propaganda has been registered in Islamic countries, but also in Europe a *new* or *Islamist anti-Semitism* or *anti-Zionism* has been diagnosed (cf. among others Holz & Kiefer, 2010). In a survey with young Muslims and non-Muslims (aged 14–32) in Germany in 2010, more than 30% of Muslims but only just under 4% of young non-Muslims agreed with the statement: "It would be better if the Jews left the Middle East" (Frindte, 2013).

And after 2015, when just under one million refugees arrived in Germany, the question is again asked how widespread anti-Semitism or anti-Israeli attitudes are among refugees. In the summer of 2016, some 780 refugees in Bavarian asylum shelters answered a standardized questionnaire that also asked about opinions toward Jews and Israel. More than half of the respondents from the predominantly Muslim countries of Afghanistan, Iraq and Syria agreed with the statement "Jews have too much influence in the world", but only slightly more than 5% of the refugees from Eritrea (Hanns Seidel Foundation, 2017).

Following a report by the *European Monitoring Center on Racism and Xenophobia* (*EUMC*, today: European Union Agency for Fundamental Rights), it can be assumed that all definitions of anti-Semitism have one thing in common: Anti-Semitism is about hostile attitudes and/or actions against Jews because they are Jews ("… that the hostility is directed towards Jews 'as Jews'…", EUMC, 2004, p. 12).

In order to describe the differentiations of anti-Semitic attitudes, we have developed a model of anti-Semitic attitudes in our previous research that includes the following facets:

- *Manifest anti-Semitic attitudes* (Example statement: "It would be better for Germany not to have Jews in the country.");
- *Latent anti-Semitism* (Communication latency,[2] example statement: "I'm kind of uncomfortable with the whole topic of Jews.");
- *Secondary anti-Semitism* (Example statement: "Decades after the end of the war, we should stop talking so much about the persecution of the Jews and finally draw a line under the past.");
- *Anti-Zionist attitudes* towards the state of Israel become apparent, among other things, when the state of Israel is denied the right to exist (Example statement: "It would be better if the Jews left the Middle East.");
- *Anti-Israeli attitudes* are expressed, for example, in statements such as the following: "Israel is solely to blame for creating and maintaining the conflicts in the Middle East".

Figure 14.3 illustrates the significant correlations between the facets of anti-Semitic attitudes. These are results of a small, non-representative and somewhat older study of 410 adults aged 18–83 (Petzold, 2003; Frindte et al., 2005). The figures indicate the strength of the correlations between the attitudinal facets. The correlation coefficients can range from −1.00 to +1.00, with the double asterisks after the numbers indicating very significant, i.e. very close, correlations between the facets.

The simple message is that not only latent anti-Semitic and secondary anti-Semitic attitudes are closely linked to manifest anti-Semitic attitudes; anti-Zionist and anti-Israeli attitudes are also often linked to manifest anti-Semitic

---

[2] With the construct of latent anti-Semitism, we have taken up Bergmann and Erb's (1991) approach to the latency of communication in public dealings with anti-Semitic phenomena and use it to describe the attempts to avoid talking publicly about the calculatedly staged discrimination and defamation of Jews as Jews.

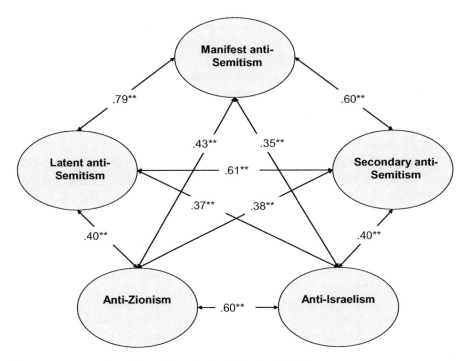

Fig. 14.3 Facets of anti-Semitic attitudes (Frindte, 2006)

attitudes. Anti-Semites use anti-Israeli and anti-Zionist statements to confirm and disguise their prejudices. They resort to anti-Israelism and anti-Zionism in public communication when addressing manifest anti-Jewish attitudes would entail considerable disadvantages.

On the basis of a representative study with approximately 1500 participants from East and West Germany, *Wilhelm Kempf* (2017) concludes, among other things:

> A quarter of Germans are anti-Semitic critics of Israel, for whom anti-Jewish and Islamophobic attitudes go hand in hand, and whose (apparent) partisanship for the Palestinians ultimately serves them only as a means of exposing 'the true face of the Jews'. A good tenth avoid criticizing Israeli policy 'because one is not allowed to say what one really thinks about the Jews', and even that quarter of Germans who are sympathetic to Israel's policy often only do so in order to look good themselves in the eyes of the world. (Kempf, 2017, p. 7).

Anti-Semitism is an anti-Semitism of average citizens who condemn violence against Jews but at the same time would not regret the disappearance of Jews as a special group. They react with manifest, secondary anti-Semitism and with anti-Israelism or anti-Zionism regardless of the real or virtual presence of the Jews.

Modern anti-Semitism uses allusions, metaphors and myths that create references to traditional anti-Semitic resentments and thus reproduce them in a coded and usually weakened form. For example, when "the Jews" are blamed for their expulsion and murder, or when attempts are made to deny or relativize the Holocaust.

The Israeli-Palestinian conflict forms a new field for anti-Semitic substitute actions. Anti-Semitism finds expression here, for example, in the equation of "the Israelis" or "the Jews" with "the Nazis" when describing Israel's policy of repression against the Palestinians.

Incidentally, the *3-D test for anti-Semitism* designed by *Natan Sharansky,* former interior minister and Israeli deputy prime minister, can help distinguish legitimate criticism of Israeli policies from anti-Semitic statements. Sharansky has designed three criteria for this:

- *D for demonization:* The Jews have been demonized for centuries. Comparisons between the Israelis and the Nazis are part of such demonization and are therefore anti-Semitic.
- *D for double standards:* Such double standards refer to anti-Semitism when Israel as a state is judged differently from other states and is criticized for behavior that is not even noted when dealing with other states.
- *D for delegitimization:* Criticism of Israeli policy does not have to be anti-Semitic. But it is whenever the right of the state of Israel to exist is denied. If other peoples have the right to live safely in their homeland, then Jews must also be granted such a right (Sharansky, 2004).

We would also like to say this to the supporters of the BDS campaign. "BDS" stands for Boycott, Divestment and Sanctions. It is a transnational campaign to isolate the State of Israel politically, economically, culturally and scientifically from the rest of the world. As we know, the people of Israel and their state are not identical with the nationalist policies of the current Israeli government. Therefore, what the *BDS* movement is engaged in is ultimately anti-Semitism masquerading only as criticism of Israel. The fact that Roger Waters, co-founder of *Pink Floyd,* is one of the loudest spokesmen for BDS is very regrettable, but it does not change the anti-Semitic nature of BDS.

The Jews do not care whether "Muslim anti-Semitism" is a genuine component of Islam and is based on corresponding suras in the Koran, whether it only hides behind the camouflage of "criticism of Israel", whether it is voiced by right-wing nationalists or by left-wing opponents of globalization. It is always an anti-Semitism that has nothing to do with *Judaism*. It belongs to those social constructions with which the anti-Semites construct themselves in order to somehow find a *foothold* in a world that is untenable for them. No matter where it comes from, the

> Anti-Semitism is exactly what it purports to be: a mortal danger to the Jews and nothing else. (Arendt, 2001, p. 38; original: 1951)[3]

Therefore, we, the authors of this book, exclude a productive dispute with anti-Semites of various stripes. In this case we keep it with *Sigmund Freud*. In a letter to Arnold Zweig dated December 2, 1927, Freud writes:

> On the question of anti-Semitism, I have little desire to seek explanations, feel a strong inclination to abandon myself to my affects, and feel strengthened in the quite unscientific attitude that people are so average and, on the whole, wretched rabble after all. (Freud, 1969, p. 11)

Islamism

Since the beginning of 2019, IS seems to have been defeated in the Middle East. A large number of IS fighters have been killed or captured by Kurdish fighters or Syrian government forces. German IS fighters are also in custody, awaiting sentencing and the opportunity to return to Germany. Potential returnees range from fellow travelers to those with an affinity for violence (Deutscher Bundestag, 2019).

Islamism, however, does not only refer to terrorist groups such as the IS. Islamism includes all those movements of political Islam that refer to the foundations of Islam and hold the view that Allah is the holder of absolute sovereignty (hākimiyya) and, through the Koran and the Prophet with the Sharia, has revealed and bindingly prescribed the indisputable legal framework for the way of life of all people.

That is to say, not only far behind Turkey, to satirize Goethe's Faust (Goethe, 1973, original: 1808), where the peoples clash, an Islamization of public life is demanded. In Germany and other European countries, Islamists are trying to influence social life and the political order – in contrast to the

---

[3] This is the English translation from the German edition. The original American edition states: "Anti-Semitism, far from being a mysterious guarantee for the survival of the Jewish people, has clearly proved to be a threat to their extermination" (Arendt, 2001, p. 8).

constitutional democratic foundations (sovereignty of the people, separation of state and religion, freedom of expression and general equality).

Under the heading "Islamic religious fundamentalism is widespread", *Ruud Koopmans of* the Science Center published in 2013 the results of a study on the fundamentalism of Christians and Muslims in six European countries (Germany, France, the Netherlands, Belgium, Austria and Sweden). A total of 500–600 people were interviewed in each country.

"Nearly 60% of Muslims," Koopmans says, "agree with the statement that Muslims should return to the roots of Islam; 75% believe that there is only one interpretation of the Qur'an that all Muslims should adhere to" (Koopmans, 2013, p. 22).

Detlef Pollack and *Olaf Müller* (2018) report on a survey conducted in 2016 in which 1200 people of Turkish origin and living in Germany aged 16 and over were asked about their attitudes towards Islam. The results show, on the one hand, that an overwhelming majority of 90% profess to feel comfortable in Germany. Feelings of disadvantage do not appear to be more widespread among people of Turkish origin in Germany than in the population as a whole. However, the results also suggest that the proportion of Islamic fundamentalist attitudes is not considerable. Approximately 50% of the respondents support the statement "There is only one true religion". Forty-seven percent consider the observance of the commandments of Islam to be more important than German laws. Thirty-six percent of the first generation (those who came to Germany as adults) and 27% of the second and third generation (those who came to Germany as children or were born here) believe that Muslims should return to a social order like that of Mohammed's time. Forty percent of the first and 33% of the second generation say that only Islam can solve the problems of our time.

Islamist fundamentalism can be understood as a strict form of religiosity,

- in which Islam is not only understood as the basis of one's own life, but also as a fundamental social order, and
- the world is divided into "good" and "evil" in a dualistic way,
- in which commandments and prohibitions are justified by reference to the divine authority of Allah and the Prophet Mohammed, are considered inviolable, and the religious teachings and the underlying texts are to be followed word for word,
- which, however, regards only certain elements of the faith as sacred, while others are ignored or reinterpreted,
- in which the idea of the imminent end of the world or a strong focus on the "hereafter" dominates, and

- with which all other religious (Muslim and non-Muslim) views are rejected and fought against as false and hostile (cf. e.g. Almond et al., 2003; Herriot, 2009).

Fundamentalist movements in Islam, however, vary in the type and extent of politicization and ideologization (Schellhöh et al., 2018). In particular, militant fundamentalism in its various currents (especially Salafism as part of the religion of Sunni Islam or Shiite Islamism in Iran) have gained in importance over the last two decades.

A survey conducted by the *Pew Research Center* a year after 9/11, in 2002, asked about the justification for suicide bombings in predominantly Muslim countries.

Table 14.1 below shows the number of respondents per country and the percentages of those who answered either "yes" or "no" to the question about justifiability.

Apparently, in 2002, a majority in Lebanon and Côte d'Ivoire see suicide bombings to defend Islam as justified. Except for Tanzania, Turkey and Uzbekistan, the remaining countries have between 27 and 47% who affirm such justification. *Christine Fair* and *Bryan Shepherd* (2006) looked for possible deeper explanations based on these 2002 data and found, among other things, the following:

- Women seem more likely to support such terrorist actions.
- The older the respondents are, the less they support such actions.

Table 14.1 Are suicide attacks justified in defense of Islam?

Countries	Number of Respondents	Justified? (%)	
		Yes	No
Lebanon	1000	73	21
Ivory Coast	708	56	44
Nigeria	1000	47	45
Bangladesh	689	44	37
Jordan	1000	43	48
Pakistan	2032	33	43
Mali	697	32	57
Ghana	702	30	57
Uganda	1008	29	63
Senegal	710	28	69
Indonesia	1017	27	70
Tanzania	720	18	70
Turkey	1005	13	71
Uzbekistan	700	7	84

Prepared according to *Pew Research Center* (2002, p. 5)

- Individuals who believe religious leaders should play a greater role in politics also tend to be more supportive of or justify terrorist actions.
- Above all, those Muslims who believe that Islam is under threat support terrorist actions.

Eleven years after the survey by *Pew Research,* the view of suicide attacks in most Muslim-majority countries has changed, in some cases considerably. In 2013, only 3% in Pakistan considered such terrorist attacks justified, in Indonesia 6%, in Nigeria 8%, in Lebanon 33% (Pew Research Center, 2013).

Fenella Fleischmann et al. (2011) surveyed 1543 second-generation Muslims of Turkish and Moroccan origin in Belgium, the Netherlands and Sweden to analyze the potential for support for political/militant Islam and for general political action. One of the findings was that Muslims who perceive themselves as discriminated against are more likely to identify with their religion and that this religious identification also increases sympathies with political/militant Islam.

One could assume the following causal chain: Discrimination against Muslims as a group or religious community by non-Muslims must be perceived by Muslims as group discrimination. The stronger this discrimination is perceived, the more likely Muslims are to identify with their religion. This stronger identification promotes the turn to religious fundamentalist currents in Islam and possibly strengthens sympathies for terrorist groups and their actions.

Such a causal chain would be scientifically appealing, but socially fatal.

Why do Muslims see themselves discriminated against as a group or religious community and why do some identify with Islamic fundamentalism? Because they see the wars in Iraq or Afghanistan as wars against Islam? Or because right-wing populist movements are organizing in Germany and elsewhere against the lives of Muslims? Or because the Swiss have spoken out against the building of minarets? Or because a man writes a book about a country that is abolishing itself because of Muslim migrants? Or because they have taken note of the studies on the Islamophobia of non-Muslims?

All these would be good reasons to feel discriminated against as a group, even if as an individual Muslim or individual Muslim woman one is able to live a perfectly good life in this country.

As is well known, there are neither *the* Jews nor *the* Christians, nor *the* Muslims. In our own non-representative studies with young Muslims in Germany (see Chap. 11), for example, we found three statistically different groupings: A grouping to which about 87% of the interviewed young Muslims aged 14–18 belong, who express hardly any religious-fundamentalist inclinations and virtually no political propensity to violence. Furthermore, a grouping of young Sunnis with strong fundamentalist tendencies and a pronounced potential for violence. 11% of the total sample belong to this group. And finally, a small grouping (approx. 2%) of young Sunnis with likewise pronounced potential for violence, relatively strong prejudices against Germany, but without religious fundamentalist tendencies (Frindte, 2013).

In an extensive study of more than 6500 adult Muslims from 26 countries, *Johannes Beller* and *Christoph Kröger* (2017) are able to demonstrate the close connection between extremist propensity to violence and religious fundamentalist convictions. Muslims who pray frequently, go to mosque often and identify primarily with religious fundamentalist norms and values of Islam express hostile attitudes towards people of other faiths and support extremist violence.

In the very strict system of values and norms of fundamentalist Islam obviously lies its attractiveness *and* its problem. Through the complete commitment to the fundamentalist creeds, a burden is apparently lifted from Muslims who feel they belong to fundamentalist Islam: One knows again for certain who one is and what is expected of one. At the same time, one becomes part of a collective in which strict values and norms create strong feelings of homogeneity, security and *a sense of purpose.* And yet, or precisely because of this, Islamist fundamentalism is a militant ideology that can become the basis for prejudice, negative feelings and a willingness to use violence against all those who do not support and/or reject this ideology.

We want nothing to do with these fundamentalisms.

Interim Summary

Nationalists, anti-Semites and fundamentalist Islamists have at least one thing in common: they want to return to the roots, to what they see as the solid foundations that make human coexistence possible in the first place. The nationalists make use of their own "people", which is exaggerated and stylized in a racist manner in relation to other peoples. Anti-Semites fall back on the apparently historically secured views of *the* Jews as Christ-killers, well-poisoners, child molesters or rapacious capitalists. And the Islamists see in the Koran and the sayings of the Prophet the only true foundations on which life and society are to be built.

In their fundamentalist beliefs, the nationalists, anti-Semites and Islamists effectively combine their radical conservative, racist and chauvinist ideologies with the technological developments of modernity (state-of-the-art weaponry and the social web) for propaganda and war purposes.

Shmuel N. Eisenstadt, for whom fundamentalism is one of the antinomies of modernity, has forcefully pointed out this paradox. The ideology (Eisenstadt speaks of "anti-modern attitude(s)", 1998, p. 84) of the fundamentalist movements is "… not simply a reaction of traditional groups to the seduction by new lifestyles, but a militant ideology that is fundamentally integrated into a highly modern structure". This applies to the "Islamic State", but also to other fundamentalist movements.

The term *fundamentalism* already came into use in the USA in the transition to the twentieth century and since then has meant above all a strict and exclusive interpretation of the (initially Christian) roots of a religion. Between 1910 and 1915 a series of writings appeared under the title "The Fundamentals", in which the return to the fundamentals of the Christian religion was demanded. In 1919 conferences of the World's Christian Fundamentals Association were held on this subject. However, fundamentalism entered the stage of world events only with the end of the "grand narratives" (Lyotard, 1986). At the end of the twentieth century, when the socialist utopia began to falter with the collapse of "real existing socialism" and the ideas about the omnipotence of capitalism, the hour of worldwide fundamentalism rang.

Eisenstadt (1998, p. 121 f.) states: "Fundamentalist movements develop among groups that see their cultures, the basic religious premises of their cultures, as threatened, especially by the influence of reason and, in modern times, by modern civilization. But they gained momentum only in situations and times when there was a certain political and ideological weakening of the influence of Western civilizations or of non-fundamentalist, often reformist regimes in various non-Western societies…".

Fundamentalist are social movements that

- against the democratic and humanistic developments of modernity (universal basic rights, cultural diversity, individual freedom and self-determination),
- divide the world into "good" and "evil",
- declare their own world-, life- and belief-view to be generally valid and inviolable and
- devalue, discriminate against and, if necessary, violently combat those communities and individuals who do not submit to the fundamentalist ideology.

Fundamentalist in this sense are religious movements such as the fundamentalist Christians in the USA (Kirkpatrick, 1993), the ultra-Orthodox Jews in Israel (Bermanis et al., 2004), the fundamentalist Islamists (Meyer, 2011), the nationalists and right-wing extremists who call themselves the "Identitarians" in Germany or Austria (Glösel et al., 2016), and the members of the anti-Semitic "International".

> With their small grand narratives the fundamentalists spread prejudices against minorities, against so-called elites or against people of other faiths. Above all, however, the fundamentalists have a readiness to use violence, which is directed against those who are regarded as enemies of the movement. In this respect, fundamentalists threaten the foundations of democratic communities.

References

Ahlheim, K., & Heger, B. (2008). *Nation und Exklusion: Der Stolz der Deutschen und seine Nebenwirkungen.* Schwalbach: Wochenschau Verlag.

Almog, S. (1990). *Nationalism & anti-Semitism in modern Europe 1815–1945.* Oxford: Pergamon Press.

Almond, G. A., Appleby, S. R., & Sivan, E. (2003). *Strong religion: The rise of fundamentalism around the world.* Chicago: University of Chicago Press.

Arendt, H. (2001). *Elemente und Ursprünge totaler Herrschaft.* München: Piper (Original: The origins of totalitarianism. New York: Harcourt Brace 1951).

Becker, J., Wagner, U., & Christ, O. (2007). Nationalismus und Patriotismus als Ursache für Fremdenfeindlichkeit. In W. Heitmeyer (Hrsg.), *Deutsche Zustände, Folge 5* (S. 131–149). Frankfurt a. M.: Suhrkamp.

Beller, J., & Kröger, C. (2017). Religiosity, religious fundamentalism, and perceived threat as predictors of Muslim support for extremist violence. *Psychology of Religion and Spirituality, 10*(4), 345.

Bergmann, W., & Erb, R. (1991). *Antisemitismus in der Bundesrepublik Deutschland. Ergebnisse der empirischen Forschung 1946–1989.* Opladen: Leske und Budrich.

Bergmann, W., & Erb, R. (2000). Antisemitismus in der Bundesrepublik Deutschland 1996. In R. Alba, P. Schmidt, & M. Wasmer (Hrsg.), *Deutsche und Ausländer: Freunde, Fremde oder Feinde? Empirische Befunde und theoretische Erklärungen* (S. 401–438). Wiesbaden: Westdeutscher Verlag.

Bermanis, S., Canetti-Nisim, D., & Pedahzur, A. (2004). Religious fundamentalism and the extreme right-wing camp in Israel. *Patterns of Prejudice, 38*(2), 159–176.

Blank, T., & Schmidt, P. (1997). Konstruktiver Patriotismus im vereinigten Deutschland? Ergebnisse einer repräsentativen Studie. In A. Mummendey & B. Simon (Hrsg.), *Identität und Verschiedenheit. Zur Sozialpsychologie der Identität in komplexen Gesellschaften* (S. 127–148). Bern: Huber.

Blank, T., & Schmidt, P. (2003). National identity in a united Germany: Nationalism or patriotism? An empirical test with representative data. *Political Psychology, 24,* 289–312.

Damm, O. (1993). *Nation und Nationalismus in Deutschland.* München: C.H. Beck.

Deutscher Bundestag. (2019). *Drucksache 19/8155.* Quelle: http://dip21.bundestag. de/dip21/btd/19/087/1908739.pdf. Accessed 16 Apr 2019.

Eco, U. (2016). *Pape Satàn.* München: Hanser.

Eisenstadt, S. N. (1998). *Die Antinomien der Moderne.* Frankfurt a. M.: Suhrkamp.

EUMC. (2004). *European monitoring centre on racism and xenophobia. Manifestations of Antisemitism in the EU 2002–2003.* Quelle: https://fra.europa.eu/sites/default/ files/fra_uploads/184-AS-Main-report.pdf. Accessed 17 März 2017.

Eurobarometer Special 484. (2019). *Perceptions of antisemitism.* Quelle: http://data. europa.eu/euodp/en/data/dataset/S2220_90_4_484_ENG/resource/42e52d98-ad59-457b-961a-c27980897712. Accessed 16 Apr 2019.

Fair, C. C., & Shepherd, B. (2006). Who supports terrorism? evidence from fourteen muslim countries. *Studies in Conflict & Terrorism, 29,* 51–74.

Fleischmann, F., Phalet, K., & Klein, O. (2011). Religious identification and politicization in the face of discrimination: Support for political Islam and political action among the Turkish and Moroccan second generation in Europe. *British Journal of Social Psychology, 50,* 628–648.

Freud, S. (1969). Brief an Arnold Zweig 1927. In E. L. Freud (Hrsg.), *Sigmund Freud – Arnold Zweig Briefwechsel.* Frankfurt a. M.: Fischer.

Frindte, W. (2006). *Inszenierter Antisemitismus.* Wiesbaden: VS Verlag.

Frindte, W. (2013). *Der Islam und der Westen. Sozialpsychologische Aspekte einer Inszenierung.* Wiesbaden: Springer VS.

Frindte, W., & Wammetsberger, D. (2008). Antisemitismus, Israelkritik, Nationalismus – Empirische Befunde. *Berliner Debatte Initial, 19,* 29–42.

Frindte, W., Wettig, S., & Wammetsberger, D. (2005). Old and new anti-Semitic attitudes in the context of authoritarianism and social dominance orientation – Two studies in Germany. *Peace and: Journal of Peace Psychology, 11*(3), 239–266.

Glösel, K., Strobl, N., & Bruns, J. (2016). *Die Identitären. Handbuch zur Jugendbewegung der Neuen Rechten in Europa.* Münster: Unrast Verlag.

Goethe, J. W. (1973). *Faust. Der Tragödie erster Teil. Berliner Ausgabe* (Bd. 8). Berlin: Aufbau Verlag (Original: 1808).

Hanns Seidel Stiftung. (2017). *Asylsuchende in Bayern.* Quelle: https://www.hss.de/ download/publications/Asylsuchende_in_Bayern.pdf. Accessed 16 Apr 2019.

Harari, Y. N. (2018). *21 Lektionen für das 21 Jahrhundert.* München: C.H. Beck.

Heitmeyer, W. (2002–2012). *Deutsche Zustände. Folge 1 bis 10.* Frankfurt a. M.: Suhrkamp.

Herriot, P. (2009). *Religious fundamentalism: Global, local and personal.* New York: Psychology Press.

Heyder, A., & Schmidt, P. (2002). Deutscher Stolz. Patriotismus wäre besser. In W. Heitmeyer (Hrsg.), *Deutsche Zustände, Folge 1* (S. 71–82). Frankfurt a. M.: Suhrkamp.

Holz, K., & Kiefer, M. (2010). Islamistischer Antisemitismus. In W. Stender, G. Follert, & M. Özdogan (Hrsg.), *Konstellationen des Antisemitismus* (S. 109–137). Wiesbaden: VS Verlag.

Horkheimer, M., & Adorno, T. W. (1969). *Dialektik der Aufklärung*. Frankfurt a. M.: Fischer (Original: 1944).

Kempf, W. (2017). Antisemitismus und Israelkritik. *Diskussionsbeiträge der Projektgruppe Friedensforschung Konstanz, Nr. 79*. Quelle: http://www.regener-online.de/books/diskuss_pdf/79. Accessed 19 Mai 2019.

Kirkpatrick, L. A. (1993). Fundamentalism, Christian orthodoxy, and intrinsic religious orientation as predictors of discriminatory attitudes. *Journal for the Scientific Study of Religion, 32*(3), 256–268.

Koopmans, R. (2013). Fundamentalismus und Fremdenfeindlichkeit Muslime und Christen im europäischen Vergleich. *WZB Mitteilungen, Heft 142*. Quelle: https://www.wzb.eu/en/media/10498. Accessed 12 Juli 2017.

Lipset, S. M., & Raab, E. (1971). *The politics of unreason. Right wing extremism in America, 1790–1970*. London: Heinemann Educational Books.

Lyotard, J. (1986). *Das postmoderne Wissen*. Graz: Böhlau.

Meitinger, K. (2018). What does the general national pride item measure? Insights from web probing. *International Journal of Comparative Sociology, 59*(5–6), 428–450.

Meyer, T. (2011). *Was ist Fundamentalismus?* Wiesbaden: Springer.

Mutz, M. (2012). Patrioten für drei Wochen. Nationale Identifikation und die Fußballeuropameisterschaft 2012. *Berliner Journal für Soziologie, 22*(4), 517–538.

Open Society European Policy Institute. (2019). *Mehr Stolz wagen: Offene Gesellschaft profitiert von "gesundem Nationalstolz"*. Quelle: https://www.presseportal.de/pm/133708/4197492. Accessed 16 Apr 2019.

Petzold, S. (2003). *Antisemitische Einstellungen in Deutschland – Eine Explorationsstudie*. Unveröffentlichte Diplomarbeit, Friedrich-Schiller-Universität Jena.

Pew Research. (2002). *What the world thinks in 2002*. Pew Research Center. Quelle: https://www.pewresearch.org/wp-content/uploads/sites/4/legacy-pdf/165.pdf. Accessed 15 Sept 2017.

Pew Research. (2013). *Muslim publics share concerns about extremist groups*. Pew Research Center. Quelle: https://www.pewglobal.org/2013/09/10/muslim-publics-share-concerns-about-extremist-groups. Accessed 16 Apr 2019.

Pollack, D., & Müller, O. (2018). Religion und Integration aus Sicht der "Mehrheitsgesellschaft" und der Türkeistämmigen in Deutschland. In R. Ceylan & H. Uslucan (Hrsg.), *Transformation religiöser Symbole und religiöser Kommunikation in der Diaspora*. Wiesbaden: Springer VS.

Quent, M. (2019). *Deutschland rechts außen*. München: Piper.

Schellhöh, J., Reichertz, J., Heins, V. M., & Flender, A. (Hrsg.). (2018). *Großerzählungen des Extremen: Neue Rechte, Populismus, Islamismus, War on Terror*. Bielefeld: Tanscript.

Schmidt-Denter, U., & Schick, H. (2007). *Nationalismus und Patriotismus im europäischen Vergleich*. Köln: Forschungsbericht (Quelle: http://www.schmidt-denter.de/forschung/identitaet/pdf-files/FB_25.pdf. Accessed 14 Apr 2019).

Schönbach, P. (1961). *Reaktionen auf die antisemitische Welle im Winter 1959/1960. Frankfurter Beiträge zur Soziologie*. Frankfurt a. M.: Europäische Verlagsanstalt.

Sharansky, N. (2004). *Antisemitismus in 3-D*. Quelle: http://www.hagalil.com/anti-semitismus/europa/sharansky.htm. Accessed 16 Apr 2019.

Waldenegg, G. C. B. (2000). Eine gefährliche Vokabel? Zur Diagnose eines Begriffs. In W. Benz (Hrsg.), *Jahrbuch für Antisemitismusforschung* (Bd. 9). Frankfurt a. M.: Campus.

Wodak, R. E. (2015). "Normalisierung nach rechts": Politischer Diskurs im Spannungsfeld von Neoliberalismus. *Populismus und kritischer Öffentlichkeit. Linguistik Online, 73*(4), 27–44.

YouGov. (2016). *Studie zu Autoritärem Populismus in Europa: Deutsche am wenigsten empfänglich*. Quelle: https://yougov.de/news/2016/11/21/studie-zu-autoritarem-populismus-europa-deutsche-a/. Accessed 16 Apr 2019.

15

"But Otherwise But Otherwise. All Lies!" (Rio Reiser, 1986) – From the Charm of Conspiracy Theories

On the evening of April 15, 2019, the *Notre Dame* church in Paris burned. In addition to the many media reports about the terrible fire, in which the roof truss was destroyed and a wooden tower collapsed, false reports were found very quickly in the social media, with which various explanations were spread about the cause of the fire. There was drivel about an attack by Islamist terrorists. Others blamed members of the Yellow Vest movement, a protest movement in France against the policies of President Macron. Still others wanted to pinpoint the Rothschilds, and thus the French-Jewish establishment, as the culprits (Lobo, 2019).

Such explanations belong to the class of conspiracy theories.

> If one speaks [...] of conspiracy theory, one means the idea of a worldwide plot (in some theories even with cosmic dimensions), according to which all or almost all events in history are directed by a single, mysterious power operating in the dark. (Eco, 2016, p. 82)

The nationalists, anti-Semites and Islamists are also united by the belief in conspiracies that, although different, are all global. The nationalists, for example, see their nation and their people threatened by the European Union, because they regard the EU as an "internationalist aberration". Therefore, for the nationalists, Brexit, Britain's exit from the EU, is "a great thing." *Wilhelm Heitmeyer* (2018, p. 318) points out that a very popular conspiracy theory among national radicals is that of the "Umvolkung" of Germany.

W. Frindte, I. Frindte, *Support in Times of No Support*, https://doi.org/10.1007/978-3-658-38637-5_15

The image of the "Jewish world conspiracy" provides the anti-Semites, but also the Islamists, with the background for their belief in conspiracy. Islamists also like to speak of the "crusade of the West", which threatens Islam and can only be ended by a "holy war" against the infidels. "This battle is not between al Qaeda and the U.S. This is a battle of Muslims against the global crusaders," Bin Laden said in October 2001 (CNN, 2001).

> Conspiracy theories are social constructions with which current or historical events, collective experiences or the development of social structures and processes are interpreted as the result of a conspiracy (a secret, conspiratorial decision by individuals or a small group with mostly illegitimate intentions and for their own benefit) (cf. Anton et al., 2015).

However, hypotheses about actual or possible conspiracies should be distinguished from dubious conspiracy fantasies, in which there is talk of secret powers operating in the dark that control or direct the world or individual events. *Armin Pfahl-Traughber* (2002) differentiates between conspiracy hypotheses, conspiracy ideologies and conspiracy myths. The assumption, for example, that *Vladimir Ilyich Lenin* was able to travel from Switzerland through Germany to Russia on a sealed train at the beginning of April 1917 because the German Reich wanted to use it to fuel the revolution in Russia and to seek a quick peace in the East is a conspiracy hypothesis that is testable and, under certain circumstances, falsifiable. There are also numerous conspiracy hypotheses about the CIA's involvement in the coup against the democratically elected government of Chilean President Salvador Allende in September 1973, which cannot be dismissed out of hand.

In the following we have conspiracy theories in mind in the sense of ideologies and myths. Especially in times of national or global threats, such conspiracy theories are in vogue, because they pretend to be able to give people a *foothold* in untenable times. When the plague devastated Europe in the fourteenth century, the conspiracy theory about the Jews had to be used to accuse them of having caused the plague by poisoning wells. "Normal" German students burned writings by the German-Jewish publicist *Saul Ascher,* among others, at the Wartburg Festival in 1817, shouting, "Woe to the Jews who cling to their Judaism and want to mock and revile our Volksthum and Deutschthum!" (Treß, 2011). The staging of the Holocaust was based on racial-biological conspiracy theories of the Jews as "brutes, usurers, stock market and loan capitalists, and world conspirators" from whom the "Aryan race" had to distance itself as "supermen".

In a not too disguised way, such conspiracy theories (about the "Jewish world conspiracy") can also be found in connection with the terrorist attacks of September 11, 2001 (Jaecker, 2005) or in the context of the global financial crisis of 2008 as well as in current pamphlets, e.g. about the "plundering campaign of the US East Coast". The metaphor of the "US East Coast" is meant to refer to the influence of Jewish finance capital (cf. Rensmann, 2015).

In search of new social narratives, new messages or new fixed points, populists resort to old and new conspiracy theories. It does not seem to be "the hour of the comedians", to recall *Graham Greene's* political thriller, but the hour of the populists (Hartleb, 2017). Populism is becoming the dominant communication strategy through the populists and rabble-rousing is becoming acceptable again. The aim is to exacerbate common prejudices, threat scenarios and enemy images by breaking taboos. Conspiracy theories are particularly well suited to pushing the boundaries of political correctness, for example when the "lying" and "systemic press" is attacked, the swelling "stream" of refugees is written about, or there is talk of a "dictatorship of ideas" at German universities.

Right-wing extremist and neo-right groups and movements, such as the "Identitarian Movement" or PEGIDA, for example, resort to the idea of the "great exchange" or the "Umvolkung" in order to appeal to xenophobic prejudices in the population and to spread racist conspiracy theories. The concept of *the great exchange* was coined by the Frenchman *Renaud Camus* and stylized as a fighting term by the neo-Right in political debates about migration, flight and expulsion. In 2016, Camus' book "Le grand remplacement" was published in German translation with the title "Revolte gegen den Großen Austausch" (Revolt against the Great Exchange) by the small neurechten Antaios Verlag, which is run by Götz Kubitschek, a companion of Björn Höcke.

The new right argues that behind the repopulation is a systematic, secretly planned conspiracy of European elites who have set themselves the goal of settling migrants en masse in Europe in order to break down national cohesion in the respective countries (see also Kopke, 2017).

However, conspiracy theories do not only refer to political events and trials. As is well known, there is also a conspiracy theory about the death of *Wolfgang Amadeus Mozart*, that the court composer Antonio Salieri, who was jealous of the composer, murdered Mozart or had him murdered. Or consider chemtrails, the contrails in the sky created by airplanes. Supporters of the chemtrail theory assume, among other things, that the contrails contain poisonous gases that are deliberately sprayed to reduce people's ability to think and procreate. Somewhat less dramatic, on the other hand, are the assumptions that the chemtrails are intended to reduce the greenhouse effect. As is well known, various conspiracies can be linked to the first moon landing of the Americans: The moon landing did not take place at all, but had been staged in a Hollywood studio.

The examples illustrate the different complexity of conspiracy theories, so that it is obvious to distinguish between event-related conspiracy theories (e.g. concerning the death of Mozart), systematic conspiracy theories (e.g. concerning the "great exchange") and meta-conspiracies (e.g. the Jewish world conspiracy) (cf. also Institute for Democracy and Civil Society, 2019).

Actually, conspiracy theories are not theories, but are more similar to legends and myths. Like these, conspiracy theories are initially nothing more than social constructions with which people seek to describe and interpret their world. However, they seem to be based on pre-existing constructions. Think of the conspiracy theories about the death of *John F. Kennedy,* about the events of 9/11 as well as the "Protocols of the Wise Men of Zion" and the "Jewish world domination" or the "lying press".

All these narratives (or shall we say statements) are based on already existing statements. For example, the conspiracy theory about 9/11 is based on statements such as, "on 9/11/2001 the Twin Towers were destroyed in the USA and about 3000 people were killed", and the conspiracy theory about the lying press feeds on reports and statements about the limitations or one-sidedness of media information.

The underlying or primary statements are widely known, handed down and possibly handed down within social communities. They can be called primary social constructions. Conspiracy theories are based on these primary social constructions. In this respect, conspiracy theories contain statements about statements or social constructions about social constructions.[1]

Since conspiracy theories as social constructions are based on already existing statements (primary social construction), these primary statements or primary social constructions simultaneously function as legitimating instances for the conspiratorial (meta-)constructions. Conspiracy theories, however, are not only based on underlying primary statements or primary social constructions. They also attempt to reinterpret the meanings of these primary social constructions. By means of conspiracy theories, the meanings of primary social constructions are assimilated and subjugated. Social events, collective experiences, or the development of social structures and processes are given the character of decisions made in secret, illegitimate, elite circles through conspiratorial statements. Thus the assassination of John F. Kennedy is

---

[1] At this point, the similarity, if not affinity, between conspiracy theories and myths becomes apparent (Frindte, 1998).

explained either by a plot of the US secret service or by an assassination order from *Fidel Castro*; the terrorist attacks of 9/11 are attributed to the Israeli secret service *Mossad* or to the US government; the financial crisis of 2008 is attributed to the "greed of Jewish finance capital".

Conspiracy theories function not least through their narrative value, and that means:

- The conspiracy theory must be a story that can be told because it emphasizes a striking difference from previous narratives *(conspiratorial story)*.
- Ways and means must be found to be able to spread the conspiracy theory and make it publicly available *(media dissemination)*.
- Narrators and listeners must be found who listen to the conspiratorial narrative, receive it, believe it and retell it *(conspiratorial believers)*.
- The conspiracy theory must fit, reinforce, and justify the prejudices of the narrators and re-narrator *(effective fit)*.

This conspiracy quartet should be present if the conspiracy theory is to have an effect. In this quartet, conspiracy theories acquire those characteristics through which they virtually offer themselves as collective patterns for complexity reduction and as anchors for individual and group-specific world views.

The relationship or the relations between conspiracy theories, media dissemination, recipients (i.e. the adherents of various conspiracy theories) and the individual or group-specific experiences in dealing with the conspiracy theories should therefore not be uninteresting from a (social) psychological perspective.

Various studies suggest that people who believe in one conspiracy theory (e.g. AIDS was developed in US laboratories or the 2008 financial crisis was the result of a conspiracy between bankers and corrupt politicians) are also believers in other conspiracy theories, e.g. the FBI was involved in the assassination of Martin Luther King or man-made climate change is a political hoax (e.g. Van Prooijen, 2017). Belief in conspiracy theories is a rather complex and consistent worldview that seems to be particularly appealing to people with lower education, authoritarian beliefs, and political extremist attitudes (Crocker et al., 1999; Van Prooijen & Van Vugt, 2018). However, as we know, more education does not necessarily protect against conspiracy beliefs. More crucial is likely to be the way in which people engage with conspiracy theories. The more analytically and elaborately they deal with conspiracy theory statements, the less they believe in such statements.

Conspiracy theories are self-esteem and group-serving, i.e. they are intended to protect one's own self-worth and the value of one's community (Federico et al., 2018). People who believe in the validity of conspiracy theories (e.g. that climate change is not happening or is not man-made) are apparently less willing to engage in humanitarian activities (Van der Linden, 2015). The greater the belief in conspiracy theories, the lower the trust in the traditional media, such as newspapers, radio and television (cf. e.g. Jackob et al., 2017; Stempel et al., 2007).

The fact that social media can play a special role in the staging of conspiracy theories is related to the *filter bubbles* or echo chambers created in and through social media. In this sense, social media are important as a means of networking the "believers" and as an instrument for mutually reinforcing the correctness of one's own conspiracy belief (cf. Salzborn, 2017, p. 119 ff.). Social media can produce a homogenization of network content through the media-specific algorithms. Whether such homogenized network content (e.g. on Facebook or Twitter) can exert a homogenizing influence on users depends on their needs and motives. In Chap. 11 we drew attention to the need for confirmation of individual and collectively shared convictions, the *confirmation bias.* Media are also used to confirm individual and collective beliefs (Geschke et al., 2019). Individual and collectively shared beliefs and attitudes form the individual background for the preference and selection of certain media offerings.

In a study published by the Friedrich Ebert Foundation, in which almost 1900 adult Germans were surveyed, almost 46% of those questioned said that there are secret organizations that have a great deal of influence on political decisions. Almost a quarter of the respondents (24.2%) thought that the media and politics were in cahoots. And just over half (50.4%) of respondents said they trust their feelings more than so-called experts. Of those respondents who tended to agree with conspiracy theory statements, 40.3% were inclined towards right-wing populist attitudes (Rees & Lamberty, 2019).

Close correlations between populist attitudes and belief in conspiracy theories are also confirmed in international studies. The opinion research institute YouGov (2019) surveyed more than 1000 adults in each of 19 countries (including Germany, France, China, Saudi Arabia and the USA). People with populist attitudes and opinions (e.g. that the ordinary people face a corrupt elite) are more likely than those with less or non-populist attitudes to be convinced that there is a small group of people who control the world, that the then US government helped the terrorists of 9/11, that man-made climate change is a hoax and that the Holocaust is a lie.

In a nutshell: The charm of conspiracy theories – if one can call them that at all – lies in the fact that they offer explanations with which (a) the complexity of the world can be easily reduced (for example into good and evil), (b) the respective dealings with the good and evil worlds can be morally justified, (c) future developments and future events as well as their causers can already be anticipated today and (d) the pleasant community feeling can be created that others could also see the world in a similar way. Conspiracy theories offer all those who believe in them the "charming" possibility of setting themselves apart from the mainstream, supposed experts or, alternatively, political and cultural elites, and of standing on the side of those who know better. Perhaps that is why the proportion of people who like to indulge in the charm of conspiracy theories is not so small. We too sometimes believe that our neighbor doesn't say hello to us because he's up to something.

> A conspiracy theory in the sense of an ideology, however, then "… becomes material violence as soon as it takes hold of the masses", to satirize Karl Marx (Marx, 1972, p. 385; original: 1844). As small grand narratives, conspiracy theories can, in some circumstances, provide support and security for "unstable" minorities. But they can also promote the radicalization of social groups and be instrumentalized to justify violence against other groups.

References

Anton, A., Schetsche, M., & Walter, M. K. (Hrsg.). (2015). *Konspiration. Soziologie der Verschwörungsdenken*. Wiesbaden: Springer VS.

CNN. (2001). *Quelle.* http://articles.cnn.com/2002-02-05/world/binladen.transcript_1_incitement-fatwas-al-qaeda-organization/2?_s=PM:asiapcf. Accessed 1 Nov 2012.

Crocker, J., Luhtanen, R., Broadnax, S., & Blaine, B. E. (1999). Belief in U.S. government conspiracies against blacks among black and white college students: Powerlessness or system blame? *Personality and Social Psychology Bulletin, 25*(8), 941–953.

Eco, U. (2016). *Pape Satàn*. München: Hanser.

Federico, C. M., Williams, A. L., & Vitriol, J. A. (2018). The role of system identity threat in conspiracy theory endorsement. *European Journal of Social Psychology, 48*(7), 927–938.

Frindte, W. (1998). *Soziale Konstruktionen*. Wiesbaden: Westdeutscher Verlag.

Geschke, D., Lorenz, J., & Holtz, P. (2019). The triple-filter bubble: Using agent-based modelling to test a meta-theoretical framework for the emergence of filter bubbles and echo chambers. *British Journal of Social Psychology, 58*(1), 129–149.

Hartleb, F. (2017). *Die Stunde der Populisten: Wie sich unsere Politik trumpetisiert und was wir dagegen tun können*. Schwalbach: Wochenschau Verlag.

Heitmeyer, W. (2018). *Autoritäre Versuchungen: Signaturen der Bedrohung I*. Berlin: Suhrkamp.

Institut für Demokratie und Zivilgesellschaft. (2019). *Neue Rechte und alte Ideen*. Quelle. https://www.idz-jena.de/index.php?id=131. Accessed 15 Sept 2019.

Jackob, N., Quiring, O., & Schemer, C. (2017). Wölfe im Schafspelz? Warum manche Menschen denken, dass man Journalisten nicht vertrauen darf – und was das mit Verschwörungstheorien zu tun hat. In K. N. Renner, T. Schultz, & J. Wilke (Hrsg.), *Journalismus zwischen Autonomie und Nutzwert* (S. 225–249). Köln: Halem.

Jaecker, T. (2005). *Antisemitische Verschwörungstheorien nach dem 11. September: Neue Varianten eines alten Deutungsmusters*. Münster: LIT.

Kopke, C. (2017). Verschwörungsmythen und Feindbilder in der AfD und in der neuen Protestbewegung von rechts. *NK Neue Kriminalpolitik, 29*(1), 49–61.

Lobo, S. (2019). *Von rechts bis zum Rechtschaffenheitsreflex*. Spiegel Online. Quelle: https://www.spiegel.de/netzwelt/web/notre-dame-in-paris-verschwoerungs theorien-und-rechtschaffenheitsreflexe-a-1263295.html. Accessed 24 Apr 2019.

Marx, K. (1972). *Zur Kritik der Hegelschen Rechtsphilosophie. Marx-Engels Werke* (Bd. 1). Berlin: Dietz (Original: 1844).

Pfahl-Traughber, A. (2002). "Bausteine" zu einer Theorie über "Verschwörungstheorien": Definitionen, Erscheinungsformen, Funktionen und Ursachen. In H. Reinalter (Hrsg.), *Verschwörungstheorien – Theorie, Geschichte, Wirkung*. Innsbruck: Studien Verlag.

Rees, J. H., & Lamberty, P. (2019). Mitreißende Wahrheiten: Verschwörungsmythen als Gefahr für den gesellschaftlichen Zusammenhalt. In A. Zick, B. Küpper, & W. Berghan (Hrsg.), *Verlorene Mitte – feindselige Zustände*. Bonn: Friedrich-Ebert-Stiftung, Verlag Dietz Nachf.

Rensmann, L. (2015). Zion als Chiffre Modernisierter Antisemitismus in aktuellen Diskursen der deutschen politischen Öffentlichkeit. In M. Schwarz-Friesel (Hrsg.), *Gebildeter Antisemitismus Eine Herausforderung für Politik und Zivilgesellschaft* (S. 93–116). Baden-Baden: Nomos.

Salzborn, S. (2017). *Angriff der Antidemokraten*. Weinheim: Beltz.

Stempel, C., Hargrove, T., & Stempel, G. H. (2007). Media use, social structure, and belief in 9/11 conspiracy theories. *Journalism & Mass Communication Quarterly, 84*(2), 353–372.

Treß, W. (2011). Wartburgfest. In W. Benz (Hrsg.), *Handbuch des Antisemitismus, Band 4: Ereignisse, Dekrete, Kontroversen*. Berlin: de Gruyter.

Van der Linden, S. (2015). The conspiracy-effect: Exposure to conspiracy theories (about global warming) decreases pro-social behavior and science acceptance. *Personality and Individual Differences, 87*, 171–173.

Van Prooijen, J. (2017). Why education predicts decreased belief in conspiracy theories. *Applied Cognitive Psychology, 31*(1), 50–58.

Van Prooijen, J., & Van Vugt, M. (2018). Conspiracy theories: Evolved functions and psychological mechanisms. *Perspectives on Psychological Science, 13*(6), 770–788.

YouGov. (2019). *Which conspiracy theories do populists believe?* Quelle: https://yougov. co.uk/topics/politics/articles-reports/2019/05/03/which-conspiracy-theories-do-populists-believe. Accessed 15 Sept 2019.

Part IV

Shelters, Holding Areas and Other Psychological Features

16

Miniskirts, Anti-Semites and Possible Fixed Points

In this and the following chapters we now want to concretize our socio-psychological search for the fixed points, the possibilities of finding a foot-hold. This will not be easy; we are asking a lot of our readers.

And we begin again with a story to help structure our social psychological quest a bit.

In order to bring conspiracy theories to the masses, they must be spread. Rumors are the appropriate means of dissemination for this. Wherever the public wants to understand but does not receive official answers, rumors arise. They are the "black market of information" (Kapferer, 1996, p. 19, emphasis in original). And conspiracy theories are among the "commodities" traded on the black market.

A rumor that has all the ingredients to illustrate the trade of these "goods", the traders, the customers, the social background and the conspiracy-theoretical consequences of the trade, has been described by *Edgar Morin*(Morin et al., 1969), *Paul Watzlawick* (1978) and *Jean-Noël Kapferer* (1996). It is the *rumor of Orléans*. In 1969, one year after the May 1968 pro-tests in Paris, France was experiencing a period of political uncertainty. President *Charles de Gaulle* had announced a referendum on fundamental state reform. The referendum took place on 27 April 1969. By a narrow majority, the French people rejected the reform. As a result, de Gaulle resigned on April 28. The new election of a president then took place in June 1969.

In the period between the referendum and the new elections, a sensational rumor emerged in Orléans that soon gripped the whole city. *Paul Watzlawick* (1978, p. 86 f.) describes it as follows:

© The Author(s), under exclusive license to Springer Fachmedien Wiesbaden GmbH, part of Springer Nature 2022
W. Frindte, I. Frindte, *Support in Times of No Support*,
https://doi.org/10.1007/978-3-658-38637-5_16

Ladies' fashion shops and boutiques in this modern, though provincial, city of 100,000 inhabitants were involved in trafficking in girls. Customers of these shops were overpowered and drugged in the dressing rooms, held captive in cellars until nightfall, then taken through underground passages to the banks of the Loire and from there abducted overseas on a submarine and consigned to a fate 'worse than death.' As early as May 20, additional detailed information was circulating. According to this, 28 young women were already missing; a shoe store used injection devices hidden in shoes to stun the victims, since the hypodermic syringes used in fashion boutiques could understandably not be used in a shoe store, and so much more. The merchants themselves apparently knew nothing of this rumor until May 31, the day before the elections, when hostile groups of people began to gather in the shopping streets. In the preceding days, however, they had received strange calls – in one case, someone inquiring about the address of a brothel in Tangier; in another, the unknown caller ordered 'fresh meat'. As the rumor spread and became more specific, two remarkable details came to light: first, the fashion shops in question sold the new miniskirts and thus represented the provincial mentality in the twilight of a particular eroticism; second, the rumor took on a distinctly anti-Semitic character[1]. The age-old theme of ritual murder surfaced and began to make the rounds. By May 30, the Jewish community's concern about the way things were developing had reached a level that prompted them to ask the authorities to take protective measures. The police were of course already aware of the threatening development, but up to that point they had only dealt with the situation from a purely factual, security-police point of view and had not found any concrete clues. It was clear, for example, that not a single woman, let alone 28, had gone missing in Orléans … The next day, however, the election results brought a first détente, and very soon reason prevailed. The rumor was investigated and found to be unfounded. The local press, private individuals and public associations strongly condemned this sudden outbreak of anti-Semitism, and the rumor died out almost more quickly than it had flared up.

The starting point of the rumor was later located in the girls' classes of local high schools (Morin et al., 1969). A classmate is said to have told her friends that she herself had been overpowered and drugged in the dressing room of a shop in Orléans, but managed to save herself. Based on this tale, the rumor spread rapidly.

In the case of the Rumor of Orleans we are dealing with a social event that can be used to illustrate quite well how real or perceived threats are dealt with and on which levels people in such cases look for an anchor, a fixed point, a foothold, in order to be able to cope with such threats. We call these levels, on

---

[1] All the owners of the accused businesses were Jews.

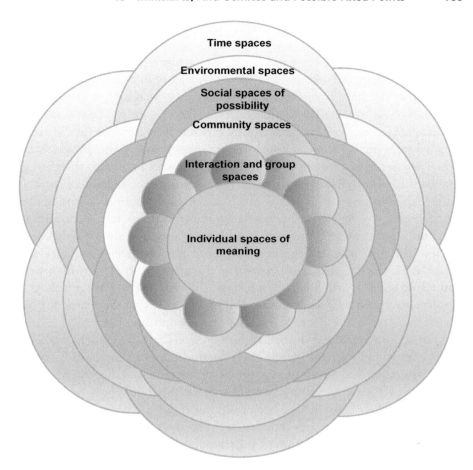

Fig. 16.1   The spaces for "fixed points" (Frindte, 1998)

which support and security are sought and possibly also found, *spaces*. In Fig. 16.1 we have first summarized these spaces in order to explain them in more detail in the following chapters.[2]

First of all, there are the girls in the high schools of Orléans. One or more of them think up a story which, for whatever reason, they tell to their friends. What did the girls see as the point of their tale? Did they want to be envied?

---

[2] In view of this illustration, initiated readers will remember the influential and often cited multi-level concept of *Urie Bronfenbrenner* (1981), and rightly so. In order to systematize the factors influencing human individual development, Bronfenbrenner developed an ecosystematic approach in which different systems are described: the microsystem (e.g., the family), the mesosystem (e.g., the relationships between different groups), the macrosystem (society and culture), the exosystem (in the broadest sense, the environment through which a person is indirectly influenced), and the chronosystem (the temporal dimensions of individual development).

Did they see their narratives as a good opportunity for self-expression (or self-presentation)? Did they want to "reveal" their own problems, experiences, worries, and hardships? How did the girlfriends interpret this story; why did they not dismiss it as hokum? And why such a story in particular?

In the search for answers to these questions we encounter a first problem: everyone obviously sees the world as he/she wants to see it. What one person communicates may be interpreted quite differently by another than what was meant by the first. People do not simply represent the world in which they live. They construct, interpret and interpret the world and also the messages against the background of experiences already made. The individual constructions (depending on the respective motives, reasons for action, attitudes, ideas, etc.) form, as it were, the *individual background* for interpersonal communication and, in our case, for the telling and interpretation of almost unbelievable stories. The girls who tell the invented story proceed from their individual experiences, fears, desires and beliefs, and the others who apparently believed and retold the story do likewise in reverse. This *individual* background is the *first* level we need to look at in order to understand why the search for fixed points takes place as it does. This background is multifaceted.

In order to name these individual backgrounds, we speak about *individual spaces of* meaning (or *sense space*). There we find the first prerequisites *and* the first barriers for the search for support (in more detail in Chap. 17).

If we say, for example, that we are writing this book because, since the death of *Umberto Eco*, we have been thinking about the finiteness of our own lives and about the fixed points in our lives, then we have said something about the meaning of our present experience and actions. With reasons, the meaning of our experiences and actions, we create knots in the web of our feelings and thoughts in order to preserve old ones and to be able to knit new stitches. The reasons secure us (in the truest sense of the word) the hold in the continuation of our life. The psychic web of our feelings, thoughts and intentions is the sense space. A meaning space or *sense space* refers to the extent or expression of the psychological structures and processes (the individual constructions, such as needs, values, beliefs, attitudes, subjective theories, schemas, etc.) with which a person grounds his or her individual view of his or her own past, present, and future life and of the world at large.

But since people do not "live as lonely Robinsons in paradise where we are without sin because we cannot commit any",[3] they with their individual constructions, ideas and narratives about the world and in their search for support inevitably come up against other people who have similar or quite different ideas and expectations of the world and reality.

---

[3] We found this beautiful thought in *Friedrich Engels* (Engels, 1972, p. 143, original: 1894).

We call the forms of *immediate* human *interaction and group spaces*. On this *second* level or in the *second* space, the individual person can share his/her ideas about the world, try them out and test whether and how such stories about the world are understood, believed or rejected by other people (more on this in Chap. 18).

These problems are also illustrated in the story of Orleans. As the girls in the grammar schools talk about the invented stories, which not all of them know are invented, it seems that completely new realities or, in other words, new constructions and narratives about the world are created. The girls who tell the stories may think their friends care about them. The others experience their own importance by continuing to tell these stories about the danger of shoe shops outside their girls' high schools. An important prerequisite for this, however, is that the stories told are believed by the listeners. Only then do they have substance and make sense.

Whether it is useful and meaningful to see the world in this way and not in a different way, to construct it, will only be proven when we seek out the world and try to deal with it interactively. Then it will become clear to what extent our beliefs, attitudes, subjective theories, cognitive schemata fit, our prophecies are self-fulfilling or our stories about the world come to nothing and we perceive our own helplessness.

The girls in the grammar schools of Orléans, not to forget our initial story, were, it can be assumed, not only in loose relationships with each other. They were involved in more or less close friendly relationships, had developed feelings of belonging and thus set themselves apart from other groups.

All of this may have happened in girls' high schools. The stories initially spread as gossip about alleged trafficking in girls may have further reinforced the stability and sense of belonging of the girls' groups. In this or similar ways, social groups in general and the said girls' groups in particular become important reference systems and "fixed points" for individual group members in dealing with perceived threats.

It is well known that people gossip when they meet people and try to communicate face-to-face. "Face-to-face" means: the communication partners mutually identify themselves as really existing. They begin to interpret and communicate about social realities together face-to-face.

Gossip seems at first to be a marginal phenomenon of human communication. When people gossip, they engage in "side conversations" (from their perspective and that of external observers) that seem to have little to do with those topics through which the social relationships of the people involved are constituted.

Gossip is part of life and – according to our thesis – not only enriches the respective current interaction space, but also defines it in a decisive way by charging it with intimacy and intensifying the communicative relations between the communicating persons and ensuring the continuation of their relationships. Gossip literally "claps" the gossiping persons together. Gossip conveys to those who can and are allowed to participate in it, on the one hand, a sense of stability and security through the feeling of belonging to the group of gossipers and, on the other hand, at least an inkling that those who are being gossiped about at a given moment do not belong to it.

At some point, however, gossip in the girls' groups apparently crossed the boundaries of the *interaction and group spaces,* reached the local communities, and became rumor. According to *Ralph Rosnow* (1989), rumors are attempts people make to clarify unresolved situations. For *Rosnow,* individual fears, credulity (i.e. the willingness to believe a rumor to be true), the nature of the rumor (whether it is meaningful or meaningless) and a generally widespread state of uncertainty are decisive and empirically proven factors for the emergence and spread of rumors. Similarly, *Peter R. Hofstätter* formulates in his "Theses on Rumors":

> Rumors occur primarily in situations that are distressing or threatening to larger segments of the population. Their task is to make this situation manageable and understandable in terms of an egocentric causal principle by labeling individual or several responsible persons. (Hofstätter, 1972, p. 165)

As can be seen, with this thesis *Hofstätter* draws attention to another possible characteristic of rumors: the attribution of responsibility for the phenomenon the rumor is about. Social psychologists call this *causal attribution* (Hewstone et al., 2015). People construct rumors to reduce their uncertainty in the face of strange, inexplicable realities. Rumors describe an unfamiliar, strange phenomenon by associating it with a previously unfamiliar, strange interpretation. In rumor, the strange is added to the unfamiliar.

And that seems to have happened in Orléans. The rather private gossip about the alleged trafficking of girls became a public rumor when it was charged with new meanings by the local communities. Concerned citizens looked for explanations and found them not only among the sellers of scandalous miniskirts, but especially among *the* Jews. The Jews were accused, among other things, of kidnapping the girls and then killing them as religious human sacrifices. Thus the Orléans rumor was underpinned with an anti-Semitic conspiracy theory. The local communities established themselves in real (and/or virtual) *community spaces* that promised them support and security with new offers of meaning in the face of the things communicated in the rumor (see Chap. 19).

Social groupings of people who have the same or similar views of social problems and processes, i.e. largely inter-individually consistent ideas about the world, move in these community spaces. These can be parties, organizations, interest groups, associations, social networks, sects, media networks, scientific communities, i.e. also communities of people who do not have to know each other, but who have the same or approximately similar ideas, orientations and constructions about reality. Opinion-makers, myth-makers and omnipotent representatives can also be found in the community spaces. They often claim to interpret the world with normative power and to stigmatize and suppress people from other community spaces with their interpretations.

But the Orléans rumor contains another dimension. The political uncertainty in the run-up to the French presidential elections created something like a space of possibility in which gossip, rumors and ultimately conspiracy theories flourish and spread. We therefore also speak of *social spaces of possibility* when referring to the macrosocial framework within which people construct their reality in order to find support and security (see Chap. 21).

Social existence, freedom of movement and individual possibilities of access, e.g. to traditions, undoubtedly belong to the *possibilities* on which people can orient themselves when they try to construct their social reality. But rituals, conventions, myths, social norms, the diversity of social conditions, economic, political, cultural, scientific structures and processes also offer possibilities for individual developments, individual world views, for constructions of the world.

The wider environment may also have had an influence on the Orléans rumor, its spread and eventual containment. *Edgar Morin* and his colleagues (Morin et al., 1969), for example, point to the particular social milieu of a French girls' grammar school in the 1960s, which may well provide a favorable breeding ground for sexualized rumors. The media are also part of the wider environments in which rumor was spread and eventually contained. For example, various regional and national newspapers not only reported the rumor, but also conducted fierce attacks against it (Kapferer, 1996, p. 284). We take these references as an opportunity to draw attention to *environmental spaces* that are capable of influencing the individual and social search for support and security (see Chap. 22).

And finally, in the descriptions of the Rumor of Orleans, there is a seemingly incidental aspect that cannot be neglected. It is the time, the history, the historical background on which the rumor can develop and the corresponding conspiracy theories can only unfold their effect. So we are talking about *time spaces* in which we look for support and security (see also Chap. 22). Not at every time and not at every place people need hold and the security. As reported, the rumor of Orleans died out very soon; the anti-Semitic conspiracy theory had also fulfilled its function as an explanation for the real or only apparent events. Concerned citizens went back to their daily routines.

But time also plays a role in the search for stability and security for another reason. Past events and the memories of them can influence the search. *Jean-Noël Kapferer* (1996, p. 152) mentions such historical events, which could explain why precisely anti-Semitic conspiracy theories played a weighty role in the Orléans rumor: Orléans is the capital of the Loiret department, which also includes the towns of Pithiviers and Beaune-la-Rolande. In 1940, collection camps were set up in both towns, from which some 18000 foreign and French Jews were deported to the Auschwitz extermination camp. It may be that the citizens of Orléans have not forgotten these camps and now interpreted the rumor about the deported girls – in the sense of a perpetrator-victim reversal – as the "revenge" of the Jews against whom one had to defend oneself.

Briefly, succinctly, and to explain why we have told and interpreted the Rumor of Orleans: In our search for the fixed points which might give us support in untenable times, we come across a multitude of possibilities. This requires explanation.

So we have to go further afield. This is done in the following chapters, where we take a closer look at the "spaces" illustrated in Fig. 16.1.

References

Engels, F. (1972). *Herrn Eugen Dührings Umwälzung der Wissenschaft. Marx-Engels Werke* (Bd. 20). Berlin: Dietz (Original: 1894).

Frindte, W. (1998). *Soziale Konstruktionen.* Wiesbaden: Westdeutscher Verlag.

Hofstätter, P. R. (1972). *Individuum und Gesellschaft.* Frankfurt a. M.: Ullstein.

Hewstone, M., Stroebe, W., & Jonas, K. (Eds.). (2015). *An introduction to social psychology.* Oxford: BPS Blackwell.

Kapferer, J. (1996). *Gerüchte. Das älteste Massenmedium der Welt.* Leipzig: Kiepenheuer.

Morin, E., Paillard, B., Burguière, E., Vérone, J., & de Lusignan, S. (1969). *La rumeur d'Orléans.* Paris: Éditions du Seuil.

Rosnow, R. L. (1989). Die Macht des Gerüchts. *Psychologie heute, 16*(5), 20–24.

Watzlawick, P. (1978). *Wie wirklich ist die Wirklichkeit?* München: Piper.

17

Spaces of Meaning, Meaningful Existence, and Cognitive Dissonance

We ourselves, we had stated in Chap. 16, are the first instance which we follow in order to find a foothold in our lives. The knowledge we have of ourselves, the feelings we have about ourselves, the actions we take to gain certainty about ourselves, provide the first foundations on which our lives can be based. *Individual spaces of sense or meaning* we had called this totality of psychic backgrounds. And under the hand the concept of sense emerges, which fits quite well to name the supposedly fixed *individual* points (For orientation we refer to Fig. 17.1 and there to the grey circle in the middle). One more remark: Without going into the numerous philosophical discussions, we treat "sense" and "meaning" as having the same content.

People are born, they live, play, learn, read, write, work, run, drink, drive a car, ride a bicycle, talk, enjoy, cry, are alone, in pairs, suffer, are afraid, are happy, bored, cruel, dance, sing, scream, keep silent, hurt, complain, give birth, become rich, are poor, love, think, win, make music, lose, fight, kill, die, lament, mourn, forget. People do all the things that make up life and that seem meaningful to them or their tormentors. But what is meaningful?

With this question we are on slippery ice. Discussions about the meaning (of life) have been going on since people started thinking aloud about themselves, that is, at least since antiquity. The pre-Socratics, such as *Heraclitus* and *Democritus*, and later *Plato* and *Aristotle* and their disciples, saw the meaning or sense of life as leading a good life. In modern times, modernity and then postmodernity, philosophical discussions mostly revolved around whether the question of the meaning of life was meaningful at all (Grondin, 2006).

W. Frindte, I. Frindte, *Support in Times of No Support*, https://doi.org/10.1007/978-3-658-38637-5_17

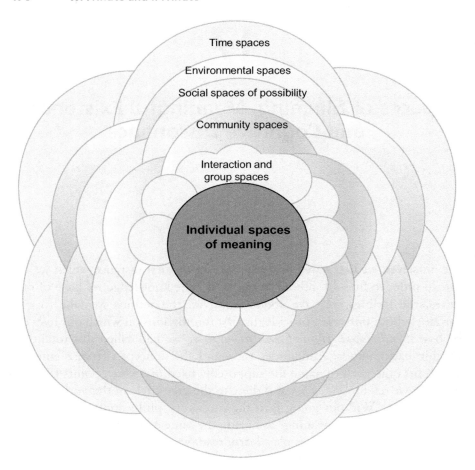

Fig. 17.1 Individual spaces of sense as "fixed points"

If you ask the "world spirit", for example in the form of *Google Scholar,* you will find about 18,500 German-language publications on the "meaning of life". Among them serious ones, such as the works of *Viktor Emil Frankl* (1905–1997), the Austrian neurologist, psychiatrist and founder of logotherapy. Frankl speaks in his books of the "will to sense" (2016, original: 1972) and sees this will as the real motivation of human beings. *Alfred Adler* (1870–1937), another well-known figure from the guild of psychologists and founder of individual psychology, on the other hand, believed that we usually only ask about the sense of life as a result of defeats we have suffered (Adler, 1978, original: 1933). *Paul Watzlawick* wrote the beautiful and readable book "Vom Unsinn des Sinns oder vom Sinn des Unsinns" (2012). *Mihaly*

Csikszentmihalyi, the one who introduced the term *flow* into psychology,[1] connects the concept of sense or meaning with goals, challenges and the ways to master them (2002). And unlike Goethe's Faust, one can exclaim with *Wolfgang Jantzen:* "In the beginning was sense". For him, *sense* is the overarching general, "in which, as a dimension of the subject's lifeline that projects into the future, the subject's engagement with the world refracts" (Jantzen, 2016, p. 82).

It becomes more complicated when one gets involved with Luhmann's systems theory. "Sense," writes *Niklas Luhmann,* "is, in form, not in content, the reproduction of complexity, and specifically a form of reproduction that permits selective access, wherever it begins, but at the same time identifies each such access as selection and, if one may say so, places it under responsibility." (Luhmann, 1988, p. 95).

But perhaps we should first stick to *Carlo Fruttero* and *Franco Lucentini,* who also wrote "The Lover Without a Fixed Address" (1990; L' amante senza fissa dimora, 1986):

> Because life is what it is, it is no wonder that people have always wondered about its possible sense. Basically, there are three common opinions about it: For some, life has a very definite sense; for others, it has no sense at all; for still others, finally, it is not impossible that it has a sense, but everyone must find it out for himself. In any case, it is a 'serious' subject, traditionally reserved for specialists, philosophers, priests, scientific theorists, alpinists, released convicts, oil tanker captains, actresses who have survived the attempt to slit their wrists, etc. (Fruttero & Lucentini, 1995, p. 5)

We're not philosophers, we're not laid-off penitentiaries, and we're not actresses. So we have to be modest.

When someone speaks of the sense of his/her experience and action, then he/she tries to communicate reasons for this experience and action. He or she is not concerned with objective reasons, causes or conditions, etc., nor with purely logical reason-consequence relationships. Rather, these reasons express being motivated, the more or less rational self-affirmation of the respective individual experience and action. By giving these reasons, he or she tries to justify the reasonableness of his or her experience and action (according to his or her respective individual standards) in a given situation and to communicate to us his or her order of things.

---

[1] Flow is the term used to describe a holistic, exhilarating feeling that can arise when one is completely absorbed in an activity.

Therefore, we have used the term *individual space of sense or meaning* to refer to the mental structures and processes with which a person grounds his or her view of his or her own past, present, and future life and of the world at large.

Several years ago, in October 1994, the popular science magazine "Psychologie Heute" devoted itself to the question: "What gives our life sense?" In the introductory article, *Heiko Ernst* (1994, p. 23 f.), the former editor-in-chief of the magazine, puts forward the following theses, for example: "Life is meaningful when there are goals in it." "Life is meaningful when people feel they have control over it." "Life is meaningful when people feel they are valuable and important." "Life is meaningful when it is shaped by fixed values."

The rhetorical figures invoked in the theses refer to categories and concepts with which psychologists try to conceptualize the search for sense (meaning) and support in life. Thus, the talk of *goals* that someone sets out to achieve in order to give meaning to his/her life can refer to "big" or "small" goals. For example, behaving in an environmentally conscious and climate-friendly way is a big and meaningful goal. To meaningfully integrate such a goal into one's life, we can set many small goals. For example, for the trip from Jena to Göttingen to visit children and grandchildren, it can make sense to forego the car and use the through regional train instead. Even the commitment as *Scientists-for-Future* to support the young activists of *Fridays-for-Future* is not a very big goal, but it is subordinate to the big goal of securing a future worth living for our descendants and can thus give our lives support and sense.

In psychology, there are a variety of theories that address the relationship between goal setting and goal achievement on the one hand, and personal well-being and a meaningful life on the other (Brandstätter et al., 2018). Sure, achieving personal goals can be satisfying, but it can also have negative effects on well-being in some circumstances. Do you, dear readers, still remember the advertising classic "My house, my car, my boat" by *Jung von Matt*. Mr. Schröder's house, car or boat are not the goals to strive for, but the investment advisor of the savings bank gives Mr. Schober the security. And Mr. Schröder is pissed off.

In this context, the relationship between "healthy" goals and intrinsic motivation, to which *Julius Kuhl* and *Sander Koole* (2005) draw attention, should not be uninteresting. In contrast to extrinsic motivations ("my house, my dog, my haircut"), intrinsic motivation refers to the drive to perform an activity because one enjoys doing it, because it is fun, meaningful, and not because one is rewarded for it by, for example, money, status, prestige, or other external incentives. Intrinsic motivation now seems to actually help to achieve "healthier" goals and to act in a meaningful way.

The theses cited by *Heiko Ernst* also speak of a life that is meaningful when one can control it. Here, too, implicit reference is made to psychological concepts that are empirically well founded, such as the concept of control beliefs.

This concept, also known in English as the locus of control of reinforcement, was developed by *Julian B. Rotter* (1966). Control beliefs are generalized, i.e. general and lasting, expectations of a person to be able to determine his or her own life to a greater or lesser extent. A distinction is made between internal and external control beliefs. *Internal control beliefs* describe the extent to which a person is convinced that he can control his own life, important life events and their consequences. *External control beliefs* refer to the belief that one's own life and its circumstances are rather controlled and dependent on fate, coincidences or higher powers and thus cannot be controlled by oneself.

However, it is not at all certain who can derive more meaning from life, the internally or the externally convinced. Several studies show that people with strong internal control beliefs are apparently more satisfied with their lives than people with external control beliefs (e.g. Schimmack et al., 2008). Close correlations between the belief in free will, internal locus of control beliefs, and the assessment of leading a meaningful life can also be demonstrated in various studies (e.g., Crescioni et al., 2016). The assumptions supported by meta-analyses[2] that people who are committed to environmental protection and display positive environmental behavior themselves have stronger internal control beliefs than people who are indifferent to the environment and environmental protection should also not be underestimated (e.g. Bamberg & Möser, 2007).

But even for those who believe that their lives are determined by higher powers, i.e. people with external control beliefs, life is by no means less fulfilling or less meaningful. For example, people who believe in God and regularly attend religious services have a larger circle of friends and appear to be more satisfied with their lives than those who describe themselves as non-denominational (Berwian et al., 2017). Attitudes that climate change is man-made and that people should therefore also engage in environmental and climate protection, however, vary depending on religious affiliation. At least for Western Europe and the USA, the finding that younger, less religious women are more likely to be concerned about climate change than older, religious men is not far-fetched (Lewis et al., 2018). We have already mentioned the "conservative white male effect" (McCright & Dunlap, 2013) in this context in Chap. 9. Who can't think of more associations with this?!

However, concepts such as control beliefs help us to further specify our ideas about the search for stability and sense in life. Corresponding antonyms, such as *loss of control* or *disorientation,* also make this clear. Both terms play a central role in the observations of *Wilhelm Heitmeyer* (2018). According to

---

[2] Meta-analyses summarize previous empirical research and attempt to determine an overall effect.

Heitmeyer's argumentation, rapid globalization processes, refugee movements, social disintegration processes and an increasing emptying of democracy are experienced by many people as a loss of control. In search of security and regaining control, some people resort to the political offers that are presented in a marketable way by right-wing populist and conspiracy-theory arguing pied pipers. Also interesting in this context is the experimental observation by *Jennifer Whitson* and *Adam Galinsky* (2008), according to which people who fear losing control over their lives are more willing to believe in conspiracy theories.

In his third, above-mentioned thesis, *Heiko Ernst* links the sense (meaning) of life with the feeling of being important and valuable. It is not at all superficially about always playing the leading roles on the stage of life. No, we want to be taken seriously by what and how we present ourselves. This addresses a basic social need that *Arie Kruglanski* and his colleagues call *Quest of Significance*, the need for a meaningful existence (Kruglanski et al., 2015). People seek recognition, influence, wealth, success. One's place, position, and role in society are also among the values that can constitute a meaningful existence. According to *Kruglanski*, the perception of losing social significance or the loss of significance of important values can be associated with the experience of deprivation, that is, it can lead to a feeling of disadvantage. In order to reduce such feelings, people look for new anchors, for support, in order to be able to achieve recognition and esteem again. Ideologies and religions, but also conspiracy theories or fundamentalist movements can provide support. Identification with such social groups can help to compensate for exclusion or discrimination by other communities and to gain new security and recognition. For *Arie Kruglanski* and his colleagues, the need for a meaningful existence is therefore an important concept in explaining the radicalization of Islamist jihadists.

However, this *need for meaningful existence* is also activated in very everyday situations, such as when people feel they are being ignored by others. *Kipling D. Williams* (2007), a US social psychologist, has done extensive research on *ostracism*. The term has nothing to do with Eastern racism. There is that too. The term *ostracism* is borrowed from the Greek and can be translated as ostracism, ignoring, banishing, shunning someone. It is a form of communication in which communication partners are shunned as communication partners. Numerous studies and meta-analyses (e.g. Gerber & Wheeler, 2009) suggest that the more pronounced ostracism, i.e. social ostracism, is, the more likely the ignored persons are to experience feelings of insignificance, loneliness, helplessness, hurt and a loss of self-worth and support.

Of course, we are also familiar with such forms of ignorance from our everyday computer-mediated communication, such as when our emails go unanswered, no one responds to our discussion posts in science chat, or worse, no one takes note of our latest selfies on Facebook or Instagram.

A theoretical explanation for the consequences of ignoring and ostracism is provided by *Mark Leary's sociometric theory* (Leary, 2005). Leary assumes – like many other psychologists – that people strive for a high self-worth. This striving and the associated, often everyday, small or large attempts to gain recognition, to be praised and admired by others, serves to indicate that one's self plays an important role in social relationships. This is also linked to a fundamental human need, the satisfaction of which can give us support and security: the *need for social belonging*. But we will come to that in the next chapter.

In any case, the sense or meaning of life and our hold in social situations also depends on the extent to which we think we can lead a meaningful life. This is trivial and also a little tautological. But life is also like that.

With *Heiko Ernst's* last thesis about a life that is meaningful when it is shaped by fixed values, we come across further fundamental structures and processes that characterize our space of sense.

The American-Israeli psychologist *Shalom H. Schwartz* has intensively studied, theoretically and empirically, dominant *value orientations* and value concepts of persons in different cultures. For him, *values* are overarching and very general orientations that relate to specific, desirable goals and motivate corresponding actions. They are usually linked to emotions, serve for the (moral) evaluation of actions and can be ranked for individuals and also cultures according to their respective relative importance. A questionnaire survey of teachers and students from 38 countries using the "Schwartz Value Inventory" in the mid-1990s initially revealed seven so-called *cultural values* (Schwartz, 1994). These were later expanded (Schwartz, 2012) to ten values. The values that are more or less significant for each individual and also for all cultures, and the subordinate goals that define them, are:

- *Self-Direction:* Striving for independent thought and action and creative activity.
- *Universalism:* Understanding, tolerance and commitment for all people and for nature.
- *Stimulation:* Need for excitement, novelty and challenges in life.
- *Benevolence:* Preserving and promoting the welfare of others.
- *Hedonism:* Pleasure and satisfaction of sensual needs.
- *Achievement:* Striving for personal success through competence.

- *Power:* Social status and prestige, influence over others, control and access to people and resources.
- *Security:* Striving for security, harmony, stability of society, relationships and oneself.
- *Conformity:* Restriction to actions that do not hurt others and do not violate social norms.
- *Tradition:* Respect for, attachment to, and acceptance of customs, habits, and ideas that traditional cultures and religions have developed for their members.

These universal values can be parsimoniously and descriptively summarized on two dimensions: (1) *openness to change vs. conservatism,* and (2) *self-enhancement vs. self-transcendence* (i.e., values directed toward the well-being of others). Moreover, they are often represented in a circular form, with opposing values and underlying goals being mutually exclusive (e.g., security and stimulation), whereas adjacent values may be mutually reinforcing. In Fig. 17.2, we have depicted this circle in a simplified way.

This structure has been confirmed in numerous international studies, including a large-scale study by *Schwartz* and *Boehnke* (2004) with over 10,000 participants from 27 countries.

Following the model of *Shalom Schwartz,* one can assume that some people find sense and support in their lives when they orientate themselves towards traditional ways. For others, it might be important to strive for success and power in their lives. Still others consider a self-determined life and tolerance as well as empathy towards other people to be important (cf. also Tamir et al., 2016).

A study by *Peter Schmidt* et al. (2007) illustrates that such value orientations can also be reflected in everyday actions and political commitment. The authors examined, among other things, the relationship between the above-mentioned value orientations and aspects of environmentally conscious behavior. Table 17.1 provides an insight into the results.

How should the table be read? The numbers in the columns indicate the strength between the value orientations and (a) environmentally conscious shopping and (b) support for environmental groups. The correlation coefficients range from -1.00 to +1.00. A minus sign in front of the number indicates a negative correlation. A minus sign in front of the number indicates a negative correlation, a plus sign indicates a positive correlation. The asterisks after the numbers mark the significance level, i.e. the level of the statistically significant correlation. In this case, it can be said that people who are more

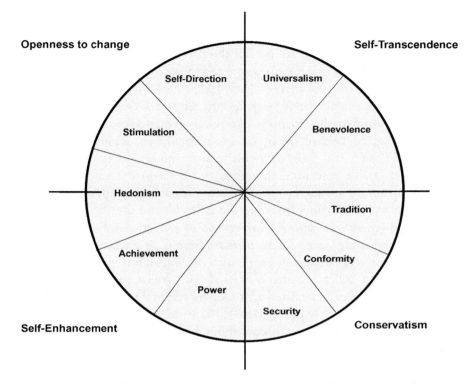

Fig. 17.2 The simplified model of value orientations. (Own illustration after Schwartz, 2012, p. 9)

Table 17.1 Statistical correlations between value orientations and aspects of environmentally conscious behavior

Value orientations	Environmentally conscious shopping	Support for environmental groups
Self-determination	+0.26***	n.s.
Universalism	+0.42***	+0.26***
Stimulation	n.s.	n.s.
Kindness	+0.16**	n.s.
Hedonism	–0.12*	n.s.
Success	–0.17**	n.s.
Power	–0.26***	n.s.
Security	–0.11*	n.s.
Conformity	–0.30***	n.s.
Tradition	n.s.	n.s.

According to Schmidt et al. (2007)
Notes: Only statistically significant relationships are reproduced: n.s. = nonsignificant; * = significant (p < 0.05); ** = very significant (p < 0.01); *** = highly significant (p < 0.001)

likely to strive for self-determination, universalism and goodness are also more likely to make environmentally conscious purchases.

Value orientations, which are part of the psychological foundations of our view of the world, can therefore be expressed in *specific attitudes* and influence our concrete *objectives for action.* They are part of the individual space of meaning, which includes not only specific attitudes (such as the attitude towards environmentally friendly consumer goods), specific and general objectives (e.g. to behave in an environmentally conscious and climate-friendly way) or control beliefs. Cognitive and emotional schemas, ingrained and relatively stable emotions, thoughts, and behaviors (such as smoking a pipe after breakfast) are also facets of the sense space and can provide meaning and support to life. Distinct from specific attitudes and specific objectives are the so-called *generalized attitudes* and *general objectives, which* are also part of the space of meaning. *Generalized attitudes* are not only relatively stable tendencies to perceive, evaluate, and cope with the world in terms of action; they are also complex belief systems associated with social values. In the social psychology literature, generalized attitudes are referred to as *ideological beliefs* (belief systems) (Duckitt & Fisher, 2003). These include national-authoritarian beliefs, which we have already discussed in Chap. 11.

And, of course, the way of seeking and finding sense and support in life also depends on stable *personality traits.* These are individual, relatively time-stable tendencies to experience certain situations in a certain way and to behave in a certain way there. Currently, the most widely used and scientifically recognized model for describing and measuring personality is the *Big Five approach.* This approach, which is very empirically based, emphasizes five key factors or traits that can be used to describe, diagnose, and distinguish personalities. These five factors are *neuroticism, extraversion, openness to experience, social agreeableness,* and *conscientiousness.*[3] The following Fig. 17.3 contains the concise characteristics of the five factors (Rauthmann, 2014, p. 593).

Psychologists also discuss other factors, such as honesty and modesty, sensation seeking (the need for varied, new and complex impressions) and the triad of narcissism, Machiavellianism and psychopathy. *Narcissism* can be expressed as overconfidence, self-centeredness, hypersensitivity to criticism, and a lack of empathy. *Machiavellianism* describes a tendency to exploit and manipulate others, combined with a strong sense of self-interest. Associated

---

[3] The term *Big Five* comes from the US psychologist *Lewis Robert Goldberg* (Goldberg, 1981). In the Anglo-American language area, these five personality factors are referred to with the acronym OCEAN, formed from the English initial letters of the factors. Many psychologists see the *Big Five as the* basic personality factors or traits with which the diversity of human characteristics can be comprehensively described at a high level of abstraction.

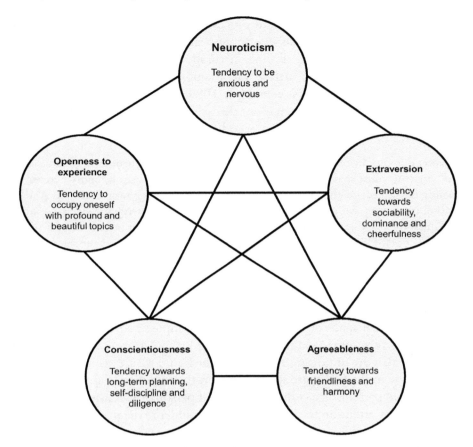

Fig. 17.3 The five basic personality traits (Big Five). (According to Rauthmann, 2014)

with the trait of *psychopathy* are antisocial behavior, selfishness, callousness, and impulsivity. Since narcissism, Machiavellianism and psychopathy often correlate positively with each other and negatively with the personality factor social agreeableness, they are also called the *dark triad of personality* (Externbrink & Keil, 2018).

People with high narcissism scores not only find it exciting to present themselves to others in real or virtual life. Positive self-presentation also has its intrinsic value. I can show others that I am not just clever, but brilliant. Self-promotion can be helpful in appearing in a good light. The person need not worry further about the effectiveness of the light, whether it is a shining candelabra or just an inconspicuous candle. Whether and how the public reacts to the self-promotion as a very consistent genius, the man can not care. The main thing is that he himself believes in his self-promotion and derives from it the meaning of his office and, perhaps, of his life.

The psychological structures and processes that are consciously or unconsciously activated when people seek support and sense in their lives, whether for a short or long period of time, naturally include personal memories, thoughts and expectations, such as our memories of the demonstration on Berlin's Alexanderplatz on November 4, 1989, and the thoughts that recur today about an almost forgotten event that gave us a lot of support back then. *Stefan Heym* said at that time on Alexanderplatz:

> Power does not belong in the hands of an individual or a few or an apparatus or a party. All must share in that power. And whoever exercises it, and wherever, must be subject to the control of the citizens, because power corrupts. And absolute power, we can still see today, corrupts absolutely. Socialism – not Stalin's, the real one – which we want to build at last, for our benefit and for the benefit of all Germany, this socialism is inconceivable without democracy. But democracy, a Greek word, means rule by the people. (Heym, 1989)

Our expectations and desires of the sense of life today are also related to such memories.

The individual space of meaning is thus a complex and elusive imaginary space. We have summarized in the following Fig. 17.4 some of the facets of sense space that are important to us. With the figure we are, as it were, zooming in on the individual sense space drawn in the middle of Fig. 17.1. We are not, however, presenting a complete theory of personality. Rather, we are concerned to draw attention to two processes that underlie the personal search for support and sense.

The processes to which we would like to draw attention have to do, on the *one hand,* with the fact that the psychological facets that tend to be found in the middle of the figure (generalized attitudes, general objectives, value orientations, personality traits, and social needs) are those that prove most stable over the life span. Individual socialization is where these facets are acquired and consolidated. When these central facets of the sense or meaning space are challenged, for example, by information, experiences, communications from third parties, people experience strong cognitive dissonance. *Cognitive dissonance* refers to a state of internal tension that arises when we are confronted with contradictory information in the communication process. Avoiding cognitive dissonance is one of the individual reasons for avoiding or deliberately seeking out communication situations. Humans apparently strive to construct a picture of reality that is as free of contradictions as possible, consistent, and

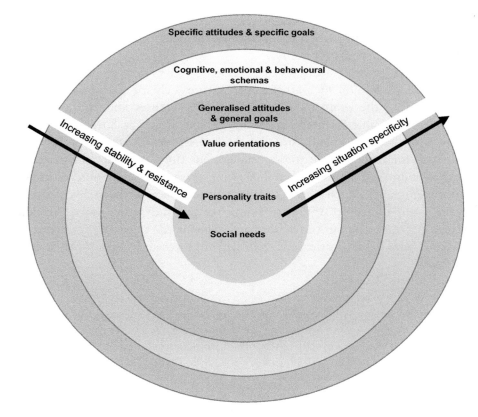

Fig. 17.4   Important facets of the individual space of sense

precisely not dissonant (Festinger, 1957; Frindte & Geschke, 2019).[4] The more strongly mental structures and processes are anchored in the individual sense space, i.e., are located quasi in the middle of Fig. 17.4, the more strongly cognitive dissonance is experienced and the more readily people tend to avoid information, experiences, etc., through which their general objectives, value orientations, or stable personality traits can be called into question.

On the other hand, those mental structures and processes that belong more to the periphery of the sense space, such as specific attitudes or schemata, are more related to concrete situations and are therefore subject to stronger

---

[4] The theory of cognitive dissonance was published in 1957 by *Leon Festinger,* a student of *Kurt Lewin.* Fifty years after its initial publication, US social psychologists *Eddie Harmon-Jones* and *Cindy Harmon-Jones* (2007, p. 14) write that despite its age, cognitive dissonance theory still has great integrative and generative power. Now and then, the theory is also referred to as the most important theory in social psychology because it has stimulated more research than "any other theory in the field" (Peus et al., 2011, p. 63).

learning and adaptation processes. One thinks, for example, of attitudes towards special foods and drinks or towards the neighbor who has no car but can make an excellent cappuccino.

The crux of specific attitudes or specific objectives now seems to be that people like to develop such attitudes or pursue such specific objectives that correspond to the more basic psychological structures and processes, for example, their value orientations or their personality traits. Specific attitudes or specific objectives, but also situational schemata, in fact provide the "empirical" basis for generalized attitudes, value orientations, or personality traits.

That sounds a bit esoteric. Here is an example: xenophobic attitudes towards migrants can be seen as specific attitudes because they refer to a very special group of people. At the same time, such attitudes can be an expression of national-authoritarian convictions and generalized images of the enemy, or they can refer to value orientations in which power and security play a central role.

As Umberto Eco said:

> Having an enemy is important not only to define one's identity, but also to build an obstacle against which one can demonstrate one's value system and by fighting it prove one's worth. Therefore, if one does not have an enemy, one must fabricate one. (Eco, 2014, p. 9)

To affirm our nationalist beliefs or our power orientations, we develop dismissive attitudes toward supposed strangers, and we seek information with which to affirm our rejections and our central facets of sense space.

But even supposedly unprejudiced people are not immune to such tendencies. We have already pointed this out in Chap. 11 in connection with media preferences. People with universalistic value orientations, in which appreciation, tolerance and the well-being of other people are significant, may have a positive attitude towards migrants. This is a good thing. It only becomes difficult when positive people close their eyes to the actual intercultural problems that exist in an immigrant society. The German language is difficult for some adult migrants. Crime by migrants has increased significantly since 2014; however, so has hate crime against people who are perceived as immigrants or migrants. Unemployment, low education, own experience as a victim of violence are problems that are particularly pronounced among migrants and that can encourage criminal behavior (cf. Pfeiffer et al., 2018). There is no question that these factors can also pave the way for Germans to enter criminal milieus. It should be equally obvious that many immigrants come to Germany with experiences and value orientations (e.g. on gender relations) that stand in stark contrast to everyday German culture. Many of the immigrants come from societies that are Muslim and patriarchal in structure. These and similar problems must be taken seriously and discussed openly, without immediately discrediting those who draw attention to these problems as anti-Muslim racists.

At the beginning of May 2019, a conference was held at Frankfurt's Goethe University on the topic of "The Islamic headscarf – symbol of dignity or of oppression?" The occasion for the conference was an exhibition at Frankfurt's Museum of Applied Arts, which featured fashion from the Islamic world. *Susanne Schröter,* the organizer of the conference and director of the Frankfurt Research Center *Global Islam,* wanted the conference to initiate a scientific and interdisciplinary debate on fashion in Islam. In the run-up to the conference, however, Susanne Schröter found herself exposed to a smear campaign, which was probably launched and pushed predominantly by students at the university. On social media, Susanne Schröter was called an anti-Muslim racist and her dismissal from the university was demanded. Critics, in this case Muslims and pro-Muslim individuals, were disturbed by a scholarly and critical discussion about religiously motivated garments (Eimermacher, 2019).

Sometimes even the seemingly politically correct and hyper-moralists are bothered by free speech, free thought and the freedom of science. From time to time they tend to ignore information or experiences that contradict their fundamental value orientations. This tendency we had earlier referred to as *confirmation bias* (Chap. 11). It is the tendency to search for, interpret or remember information that corresponds to one's own opinion on a certain topic or confirms this opinion (Peter & Brosius, 2013, p. 467).

> In a nutshell: avoidance of *cognitive dissonance* and *confirmation bias* are indications that the individual space of sense is not only the first anchor to which we hold on and find support with ourselves, but is also a first important space in which we like to mirror ourselves and our attitudes, beliefs and orientations. In our search for support and sense, we are independent subjects who like to refer to ourselves, that is, we are self-reflective. We usually feel comfortable in our own subjective world of sense, which can also become an echo chamber.

Man is a true narcissist; he likes to reflect himself everywhere, he puts himself as a foil under the whole world. (Goethe, 1981, original: 1809, p. 270)

References

Adler, A. (1978). *Der Sinn des Lebens*. Frankfurt a. M.: Fischer Taschenbuch (Original: 1933).

Bamberg, S., & Möser, G. (2007). Twenty years after Hines, Hungerford, and Tomera: A new meta-analysis of psycho-social determinants of pro-environmental behaviour. *Journal of Environmental Psychology, 27*(1), 14–25.

Berwian, T., van Doorn, A., & Runkel, A. (2017). *Wer glaubt, wird selig*. Quelle. https://www.zeit.de/gesellschaft/2017-10/religion-glaube-zufriedenheit-glueck-studien. Accessed 21 Nov 2018.

Brandstätter, V., Schüler, J., Puca, R. M., & Lozo, L. (2018). *Motivation und emotion*. Berlin: Springer.

Crescioni, A. W., Baumeister, R. F., Ainsworth, S. E., Ent, M., & Lambert, N. M. (2016). Subjective correlates and consequences of belief in free will. *Philosophical Psychology, 29*(1), 41–63.

Csikszentmihalyi, M. (2002). *Flow: The psychology of happiness: The classic work on how to achieve happiness*. London: Rider.

Duckitt, J., & Fisher, K. (2003). The impact of social threat on worldview and ideological attitudes. *Political Psychology, 24*(1), 199–222.

Eco, U. (2014). *Die Fabrikation des Feindes*. München: Hanser.

Eimermacher, M. (2019). *Auf Tuchfühlung*. Quelle: https://www.zeit.de/2019/19/kopftuchkonferenz-universitaet-frankfurt-susanne-schroeter-protest-islam. Accessed 8 Mai 2019.

Ernst, H. (1994). Die unstillbare Neugier auf Sinn. *Psychologie heute, Oktober, 1994*, 22–25.

Externbrink, K., & Keil, M. (2018). *Narzissmus, Machiavellismus und Psychopathie in Organisationen: Theorien, Methoden und Befunde zur dunklen Triade*. Wiesbaden: Springer-Fachmedien.

Festinger, L. (1957). *A theory of cognitive dissonance*. Stanford: University Press.

Frankl, V. E. (2016). *Der Wille zum Sinn*. Göttingen: Hogrefe (Original: 1972).

Frindte, W., & Geschke, D. (2019). *Lehrbuch Kommunikationspsychologie*. Weinheim: Beltz.

Fruttero, C., & Lucentini, F. (1990). *Der Liebhaber ohne festen Wohnsitz*. München: Piper.

Fruttero, C., & Lucentini, F. (1995). *Der rätselhafte Sinn des Lebens*. München: Piper.

Gerber, J., & Wheeler, L. (2009). On being rejected: A meta-analysis of experimental research on rejection. *Perspectives on Psychological Science, 4*(5), 468–488.

Goethe, J. W. (1981). *Die Wahlverwandtschaften Werke, Hamburger Ausgabe* (Bd. 6). München: dtv (Original: 1809).

Goldberg, L. R. (1981). Language and individual differences: The search for universals in personality lexicons. *Review of Personality and Social Psychology, 2*, 141–165.

Grondin, J. (2006). *Vom Sinn des Lebens*. Göttingen: Vandenhoeck & Ruprecht.

Harmon-Jones, E., & Harmon-Jones, C. (2007). Cognitive dissonance theory after 50 years of development. *Zeitschrift für Sozialpsychologie, 38*(1), 7–16.

Heitmeyer, W. (2018). *Autoritäre Versuchungen: Signaturen der Bedrohung I*. Berlin: Suhrkamp.

Heym, S. (1989). Rede am 4. November 1989 in Berlin. Quelle: https://www.dhm. de/archiv/ausstellungen/4november1989/heym.html. Accessed 8 Mai 2019.

Jantzen, W. (2016). *Am Anfang war der Sinn: Zur Naturgeschichte, Psychologie und Philosophie von Tätigkeit, Sinn und Dialog*. Berlin: Lehmanns Media.

Kruglanski, A. W., Gelfand, M. J., Bélanger, J. J., Hetiarachchi, M., & Gunaratna, R. (2015). Significance quest theory as the driver of radicalization towards terrorism. In J. Jerard & S. M. Nasir (Hrsg.), *Resilience and resolve: Communities against terrorism* (S. 17–30). London: Imperial College Press.

Kuhl, J., & Koole, S. (2005). Wie gesund sind Ziele? Intrinsische Motivation, Affektregulation and das Selbst. In R. Vollmeijer & J. Brunstein (Hrsg.), *Motivationspsychologie und ihre Anwendung* (S. 109–127). Stuttgart: Kohlhammer.

Leary, M. R. (2005). Sociometer theory and the pursuit of relational value: Getting to the root of self-esteem. *European Review of Social Psychology, 16*(1), 75–111.

Lewis, G. B., Palm, R., & Feng, B. (2018). Cross-national variation in determinants of climate change concern. *Environmental Politics, 28*, 1–29.

Luhmann, N. (1988). *Soziale Systeme*. Frankfurt a. M.: Suhrkamp Taschenbuch (Erstveröffentlichung: 1984). English version: Social systems. Stanford: Stanford University Press (1996).

McCright, A. M., & Dunlap, R. E. (2013). Bringing ideology in: The conservative white male effect on worry about environmental problems in the USA. *Journal of Risk Research, 16*(2), 211–226.

Peter, C., & Brosius, H. (2013). Wahrnehmungsphänomene. In H. Medienwirkungsforschung (Hrsg.), *Wolfgang Schweiger & Andreas Fahr* (S. 463–480). Wiesbaden: Springer VS.

Peus, C., Frey, D., & Braun, S. (2011). Konsistentheorien. In D. Frey & H. W. Bierhoff (Hrsg.), *Sozialpsychologie – Individuum und soziale Welt* (S. 61–84). Göttingen: Hogrefe.

Pfeiffer, C., Baier, D., & Kliem, S. (2018). *Zur Entwicklung der Gewalt in Deutschland*. Jugendliche und Flüchtlinge als Täter und Opfer. Zürich: Hochschule für Angewandte Wissenschaften. Quelle: https://www.zhaw.ch/storage/shared/sozialearbeit/News/gutachten-entwicklung-gewalt-deutschland.pdf.   Accessed 07 Mai 2019.

Rauthmann, J. (2014). Fünf-Faktoren-Modell. In M. A. Wirtz (Hrsg.), *Dorsch – Lexikon der Psychologie* (18. Aufl.). Bern: Hogrefe.

Rotter, J. B. (1966). Generalized expectations for internal versus external control of reinforcement. *Psychological Monographs, 80*, 1–28.

Schimmack, U., Schupp, J., & Wagner, G. G. (2008). The influence of environment and personality on the affective and cognitive component of subjective Well-being. *Social Indicators Research, 89*(1), 41–60.

Schmidt, P., Bamberg, S., Davidov, E., Herrmann, J., & Schwartz, S. H. (2007). Die Messung von Werten mit dem "Portraits Value Questionnaire". *Zeitschrift für Sozialpsychologie, 38*(4), 261–275.

Schwartz, S. H. (1994). Are there universal aspects in the content and structure of values? *Journal of Social Issues, 50*, 19–45.

Schwartz, S. H. (2012). An overview of the Schwartz theory of basic values. *Online readings in Psychology and Culture, 2*(1), 11.

Schwartz, S. H., & Boehnke, K. (2004). Evaluating the structure of human values with confirmatory factor analysis. *Journal of Research in Personality, 38*(3), 230–255.

Tamir, M., Schwartz, S. H., Cieciuch, J., Riediger, M., Torres, C., Scollon, C., Dzokoto, V., Zhou, X., & Vishkin, A. (2016). Desired emotions across cultures: A value-based account. *Journal of Personality and Social Psychology, 111*(1), 67.

Watzlawick, P. (2012). *Vom Unsinn des Sinns oder vom Sinn des Unsinns*. Wien: Picus Verlag.

Whitson, J. A., & Galinsky, A. D. (2008). Lacking control increases illusory pattern perception. *Science, 322*(5898), 115–117.

Williams, K. D. (2007). Ostracism. *Annual Review of Psychology, 58*, 425–452.

18

Interaction and Group Spaces: Of Love and Groupthink

This chapter, as the title suggests, is about the interaction and group spaces, i.e., the dark circles in Fig. 18.1. But to go into medias res, we refer immediately to the next figure (Fig. 18.2).

We want to have good friends, be there for our family, strive for happiness and harmony in our social relationships, but also want to be independent and enjoy life, have children, of course help people in need, be successful in our jobs and live in material prosperity, but also get to know other countries and cultures. Questions about the sense of life, one's own religion or active participation in political events are not entirely unimportant, but on average they rank far down the list of desirable things in life.

As is well known, there are many forms of human interaction that belong to the infinite lightnesses and difficulties of being: two people loving each other in the same bed; the Trabbi driver[1] with raised middle finger who overtakes the bird-pointing BMW driver without catching up; S.L. and his virtual Facebook group; our daughters and us; the conversation with the postman; the discussions in the reading circle; the conversation with E.S. about the potentials of S4F; the old lady and the fare dodger in the tram; the lie that H. tells about S. to K.; the students and the university lecturer in lecture hall E20; the call from M., that he'd be on TV tonight.

In 2018, the Allensbach Institute for Public Opinion Research asked around 23,000 people aged 14 and over what they consider important and worthwhile in their lives. Figure 18.2 provides an insight into the results.

---

[1] "Trabbi" refers to the Trabant, the most driven passenger car in the former GDR.

© The Author(s), under exclusive license to Springer Fachmedien Wiesbaden GmbH, part of Springer Nature 2022
W. Frindte, I. Frindte, *Support in Times of No Support*,
https://doi.org/10.1007/978-3-658-38637-5_18

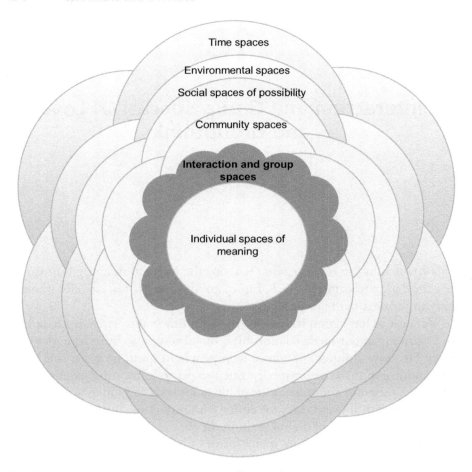

Time spaces

Environmental spaces

Social spaces of possibility

Community spaces

**Interaction and group
spaces**

Individual spaces of
meaning

Fig. 18.1 Interaction and group rooms as "fixed points"

The most exciting forms of human relationships are still those in which the actors meet face to face. This is where people live and love, kill and die. We call these immediate forms of human interaction *space*. Interaction space includes all those social forms in which we meet and communicate with other people directly (face to face).

Here is the people's paradise, contented, great and small shout joyfully: Here I am man, here dare it to bebe! (Goethe, 1973, p. 179).[2]

---

[2] After the translation by Edgar Alfred Bowring (1883).

What do you personally consider to be particularly important and worthwhile in life?

(according to Allensbacher Markt- und Werbeträgeranalyse, 2018, **N** = 23,000
respondents aged 14 and over, agreement in percent)

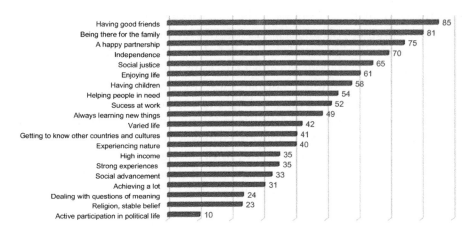

Fig. 18.2 What is important and worthwhile in life?. (According to Allensbach Institute for Public Opinion Research, 2018)

It is difficult for us to find other, more appropriate words for what is going on in the interaction space. The interactions can be *formal*, as between boss and employee; they can also be *informal*, as in friend and love relationships.

Relationships with friends and family are important and meaningful. In research on the role and function of real social networks, a distinction is often made between intimate ties, core ties and routine ties (Wellman et al., 2008).

Intimate relationships are close, regular and strongly emotional relationships between two and more people who support and help each other. The love relationship between two people is probably the most intimate relationship in the interaction space.

Psychologists, when speaking scientifically about love, like to talk about a complex, multi-layered phenomenon that is experienced in a variety of different relationships. Love can describe the relationships between lovers, parents and their children, between friends, with a neighbor or with God. Many other forms of love are equally conceivable. Especially that form of love which – again from a scientific point of view – is called "romantic love" or a special form of "close relationships" (Berscheid & Reis, 1998).

"By Love are blest the Gods on high, frail man becomes a deity, when love to him is given…" (Schiller, "The Triumph of Love", 1830, p. 23).[3]

Don't tell us you haven't experienced this yet!? Love connects two people directly, without there seeming to be any reasons for it. In their love, two people can find support and sense in life. But love is also an emotion that can hardly be controlled at will. It is closely linked to the affective subsystem, so that fluctuations in feelings can affect love (Simmel, 1923). This is why love is usually a less stable emotion, a "normal chaos" (Beck & Beck-Gernsheim, 1990).

Core ties are those close relationships and regular contacts with friends or family members who are very familiar to us and from whom we can get support and assistance and to whom we are happy to lend our help. We maintain *regular relationships* (routine ties) with work colleagues, for example, in order to receive information and advice in certain situations. The closeness between the persons is usually not very pronounced; the contact takes place, but is not very close (Kneidinger, 2010).

William Chopik (2017) surveyed 271,053 adults from 97 countries about happiness, family, and friendships. In addition, 7481 older people were interviewed about their social relationships and any illnesses. Younger people up to the age of 30 emphasize that family *and* friends are equally important to them for their own health and well-being. From the age of 30, this changes. Now friends become more important when it comes to one's happiness, health and well-being. According to the results, good and stable friendships provide support and security. In this respect, it is not surprising if people, the older they get, renounce superficial friendships and above all cultivate deep friendships that can make them happy.

This may vary from culture to culture, but it doesn't change the fact that we rely on our close friends, often more than members of our own family.

In the space of interpersonal interactions, the individual can try out his/her ideas of reality, test them for fit but also construct them anew. In the interaction space it will become apparent whether it was meaningful to let oneself be moved for these or those reasons in order to find sense and support in life.

When the social relations of the people in the interaction space have a certain stability in space and time, they begin to form a social group. In social psychology there is no consensus on how to define a social group. This makes it easier for us to offer our own conceptual construction: We like to speak of a social group when we are dealing with a number of people who interact with each other, construct social ideas about reality together in this way, with which

---

[3] After the translation by Edgar Alfred Bowing (1851).

they are able to stabilize and structure their ongoing interactions independently, develop a certain sense of belonging ("we-feeling") and support the social identity of the involved interaction partners (the group members).

The stable intimate relationship between two people who love each other can also easily be considered a small group from this point of view.

Through the ongoing interactions, the more or less coinciding ideas about the world and reality, through the sense of belonging and the identity-forming function of their common interactions, etc., the interaction partners increasingly distinguish themselves as a group from other groups. Groups are distinguished from other groups by a group-specific knowledge that they use to establish certain in-group norms and standards by which they interpret reality. Group relationships do not function without emotional involvement. High feelings after successful group performance, but also negative moods and emotions in groups are not infrequently shared interindividually and can influence group communication.

In social psychology, we speak of *primary groups.* These include the family, groups of friends, residential communities, i.e. groups to which one feels particularly attached and in which the feeling of belonging is very pronounced. These are often distinguished from *secondary groups,* groups in which cohesion is less strongly developed and which play a lesser role as social reference systems. There is also talk of formal and informal groups, of open and closed groups, of homogeneous and heterogeneous groups, or of real and virtual groups.

Primary groups in particular can provide support and security. Membership in these groups satisfies the basic *need for social belonging,* which we have already written about in Chap. 17. People want to be recognized and appreciated by the members of their reference groups. From recognition and appreciation they can draw social capital. This refers to the "vitamin B" which, according to Pierre Bourdieu (1983), is an important individual resource for achieving individual goals and which is based on belonging to a stable network of social relationships.

Add me, add me. Would you like to add me as a friend? (Chumbawamba, 2008).

The fact that the social networks that can be established in and by means of social media are also suitable for accumulating social capital should be a commonplace by now. Social media, such as Facebook, Instagram, Twitter, YouTube or WhatsApp, are used to entertain, to inform, to present oneself or to gain friends, recognition and support.

The first version of Facebook went online in January 2004. Currently, the network has more than two billion users per month. Facebook, Twitter, YouTube, Instagram, etc. are among the social media that are shaping our current epoch. In this new epoch, the boundaries between what used to be called the real reality and the virtual reality are blurring. But it also blurs the real and virtual possibilities to find support and security in life.

Communication in social networks can strengthen social relationships in the real world (Utz, 2015). It may change the way people view and interact with the real world. For example, during the Arab Spring in 2011, Facebook served as a platform to mobilize and organize people politically (Wilson et al., 2012). Communication on social media can lead to *shitstorms* (an avalanche-like wave of outrage that takes place on social media) that make people feel bullied (Steinke, 2014). *Cyberbullying* is the new word to describe bullying in the digitalized world (Whittaker & Kowalski, 2015). *Trolls* (provocateurs) can hang out in social media, which, in order to attract attention, are capable of stirring up conflicts between communicating media users out of revenge, anger or just for fun (Hardaker, 2010). The role of social media in spreading conspiracy theories should also not be forgotten (see Chap. 15).

The virtual world of social media is no better or worse than the world we still call the real one.

Several years ago, *Howard Rheingold*, one of the early net activists, described this very consensus:

> People in virtual communities use words on screens to exchange pleasantries and argue, engage in intellectual discourse, conduct commerce, exchange knowledge, share emotional support, make plans, brainstorm, gossip, feud, fall in love, find friends and lose them, play games, flirt, create a little high art and a lot if idle talk. People in virtual communities do just about everything people do in real life, but we leave our bodies behind. You can't kiss anybody and nobody can punch you in the nose, but a lot can happen within those boundaries. … (Rheingold, 2000, p. xvii, Original: 1993).

Vriens and van Ingen (2018) have wondered whether social media are capable of destroying our important core social relationships in the real world, as some social scientists have suspected (e.g. Turkle, 2011). Vries and van Ingen's findings, while not quite as surprising, are somewhat reassuring. The representative study with 5312 adult Dutch people shows that intensive users of social media communicate primarily with people from their intimate and core relationships.

One could say that social media expand the real interaction space and the possibilities to accumulate social capital and to search for new social anchors.

Like the individual *space of meaning*, however, the *interaction and group space* as a way of seeking security, support and sense is not without problems. The problems, simply put, have to do with the nature or dynamics of interactions and group processes.

The interaction partners who have become group members, whether as a couple in boundless love or as a group of friends without ifs and buts, demarcate themselves from their environments. Internally, in the group, this boundary formation functions in the sense of setting norms, sanctions, conformity requirements, etc.; externally, the boundary formation manifests itself as symbolic demarcation from other groups, through devaluation, stigmatization, etc. Group-specific language games, group codes and symbols are observable features of boundary formation (Frindte & Geschke, 2019). We can refer to this demarcation as *communication compression.* The term *cohesion* also refers to what happens within groups. *Cohesion* refers to that in-group phenomenon that we colloquially refer to as a "we-feeling". The greater the sense of belonging, which in the case of lovers – as we all know, even if we otherwise know little about love – often manifests itself as a tingling in the stomach, the greater the satisfaction with the social relationships and the stronger the commitment to the interaction partners or other group members.

And this is where it can become problematic. When the *tendency towards communication compression or cohesion* is at a very high level, social groups function as systems that are relatively closed off from their external worlds. Group-specific communication takes place predominantly in the interaction space of one's own group. There is hardly any communications between group and environment. This sounds more abstract than it actually is.

Let us first dwell on the most intimate form of social relationship, love between two people. *Erich Fromm,* the famous psychologist, philosopher and colleague of *Theodor W. Adorno, Max Horkheimer* and *Leo Löwenthal* at the Frankfurt Institute for Social Research until the National Socialists came to power, published his well-known little book *The Art of Loving in* 1956 in exile in the USA. There you will find, among other things, the following thought-provoking sentences:

> Love is possible only if two persons communicate with each other from the center of their existence, hence if each one of them experiences himself from the center of his existence. Only in this 'central experience' is human reality, only here is aliveness, only here is the basis for love. Love, experienced thus, is a constant challenge; it is not a resting place, but a moving, growing, working together; even whether there is harmony or conflict, joy or sadness, is secondary to the fundamental fact that two people experience themselves from the essence

of their existence, that they are one with each other by being one with themselves, rather than by fleeing from themselves (Fromm, 1956, p. 103).

"Love is: work, work, work!", as *Evje van Dampen*, aka *Hape Kerkeling*, says. Work, in order to be one with each other and to have the feeling that the world outside is quite unimportant for a certain time. That's what the intimacy of a love relationship is all about – the temporary isolation from the world. In *Robert* Sternberg's (1986) model of love, intimacy is one of the three points of the *Triangle of Love*, along with passion and commitment. In the intimate relationship it can happen that the partner is seen predominantly in a positive light. Which is not necessarily a bad thing. Psychological studies show, among other things, that a positively distorted image of the partner can certainly benefit happiness in the love relationship (Fletcher, 2015; Kunkel, 2017; Woods et al., 2015).

In other words, it does no harm to the love relationship if the lovers shut themselves off from their environments now and then, are alone with themselves and look at reality through their own rose-colored glasses. This is true for older couples, too. We know what we are writing about.

> The real point, though, is that love is isolating. If I love a woman madly, I expect her to love me alone and not others (in the same sense, anyway). A mother loves her children passionately (we think a father can too, WF/IF) and wishes to be loved back by them just as preferentially (mommy only exists once), and to other people's children she would never feel an equal love. Love, then, is in its own way selfish, possessive, and selective (Eco, 2016, p. 127 f.).

If we now turn our gaze away from the intimate love relationship and direct it to the disdainful everyday life, however, we come across a disadvantage of extreme communication isolation, which *Irving* Janis (1972) described years ago as groupthink. Irving evaluated the minutes of the meetings of the staff of the American President *John F. Kennedy* during the so-called Cuban Missile Crisis in 1962 and came to a surprising and disturbing conclusion. At that time, the American administration had decided to overthrow the Cuban government of *Fidel Castro* with the help of Cuban exiles. At the same time, the Soviet Union began deploying intermediate-range nuclear missiles in Cuba. The venture nearly led to nuclear war between the US and the USSR. Thirteen days the world was on the brink of World War III in no small part because Kennedy's staff discussed possible courses of action that would have involved serious missteps. They discussed, for example, setting up a naval blockade against Cuba; air attacks on Soviet ships and an invasion of Cuba were also considered options, as was a nuclear first strike against the Soviet Union. The GDR, by the way, was also involved. The GDR holiday ship, the *MS Völkerfreundschaft*, broke through the American blockade ring and was almost sunk. Only after intensive secret diplomacy could the crisis be ended.

Ten years later, in 1972, *Irvin Janis* was able to analyze important meeting minutes of the Kennedy staff and came across group-specific interaction and communication patterns that could explain the possible and fortunately not realized wrong decisions. An extreme condensation of communication, i.e. groupthink, in the Kennedy staff and an unreal *sense of* "we" *were* demonstrated, among other things, by the fact that the members of the staff were subject to an illusion of invulnerability, ignored moral concerns when discussing possible decisions, overestimated the group-internal consensus of opinion and simply did not take note of external information and other conflict solutions.

The phenomenon of groupthink as an expression of extreme communication compression and an unreal *we-feeling* can ultimately lead to strong distortions of reality and wrong decisions. Similar distortions of reality have become apparent in political decisions in later years, for example in the run-up to the Iraq war in 2002/2003. In 2004, an investigative committee of the US Senate came to the conclusion that the CIA had exaggerated and possibly falsified indications of weapons of mass destruction in Iraq. The CIA's assessments had been characterized by a false groupthink (Der Spiegel, 2004).

But it is not only in the political arena that *groupthink* can be observed. Consider, for example, the serious distortions of reality that guided the managers of the German automotive industry when they installed their cheating software in diesel cars in order to circumvent legally prescribed limits for car emissions. Did the perpetrators really think that nothing could come to light?

Similar phenomena to groupthink are described by the risky *shift phenomenon* or *ingroup bias*. The risky shift phenomenon refers to the empirically well-founded observation that groups often make riskier decisions than individuals. Ingroup bias is a cognitive and social bias that leads us to find members of our own groups more likeable, to judge them better, and to prefer them when making decisions (Fritsche, 2018). On the sociopolitical stage, ingroup bias manifests itself as ethnocentrism, nationalism, or patriotism. This, and the connection between ingroup bias and the need for a positive social identity, will concern us in the next chapter.

At this point, however, we would like to remind you once again of the *confirmation bias*, which we have already mentioned in Chap. 17. The tendency described with it to hold as true above all that information which corresponds to our previous opinion is closely connected with the ingroup bias. We seek and accept above all that information (from the classical media or the Internet) which corresponds to the views of the groups to which we feel ourselves to belong.

> Social groups are social realities and they construct social realities in a self-dynamic way. This is probably what *Kurt Lewin* had in mind when he spoke of the "self-regulating processes within the group" in 1943 (Lewin, 1982, p. 230, original: 1943). However, momentum and self-regulation do not protect against folly. If the members of social groups do not succeed in opening up the self-created group boundaries and interacting and communicating with the group environments (persons outside the group, other groups and institutions), the danger of extreme groupthink and increasing group egoisms grows. In this way, one's own group becomes an echo chamber in which the group members are mirrored and the real reality is no longer taken note of.

References

Beck, U., & Beck-Gernsheim, E. (1990). *Das ganz normale Chaos der Liebe*. Frankfurt a. M.: Suhrkamp.

Berscheid, E., & Reis, H. T. (1998). Attraction and close relationships. In D. T. Gilbert, S. T. Fiske, & G. Lindzey (Eds.), *The handbook of social psychology*. New York: Oxford University Press.

Bourdieu, P. (1983). Ökonomisches Kapital, kulturelles Kapital, soziales Kapital. In R. Kreckel (Ed.), *Soziale Ungleichheiten, Soziale Welt* (pp. 183–198). Göttingen: Schwarz.

Bowing, E. A. (1851). *The poems of schiller*. London: John W. Parker and Sons.

Bowring, E. A. (1883). *The poems of Goethe translated in the original metres second edition revised and enlarged*. London: George Bell and Sons.

Chopik, W. J. (2017). Associations among relational values, support, health, and Well-being across the adult lifespan. *Personal Relationships, 24*(2), 408–422.

Chumbawamba. (2008). Add me. Songtext aus dem Album *"The Boy Bands Have Won"*, Songwriter: Allan Whalley, Judith Abbott, Louise Watts & Neil Ferguson. Add Me © Sony/ATV Music Publishing LLC.

Eco, U. (2016). *Pape Satàn*. München: Hanser.

Fletcher, G. J. (2015). Accuracy and bias of judgments in romantic relationships. *Current Directions in Psychological Science, 24*(4), 292–297.

Frindte, W., & Geschke, D. (2019). *Lehrbuch Kommunikationspsychologie*. Weinheim: Beltz.

Fritsche, I. (2018). Soziale Kognition. In O. Decker (Ed.), *Sozialpsychologie und Sozialtheorie* (pp. 173–188). Wiesbaden: Springer VS.

Fromm, E. (1956). *The art of loving*. New York: Harper & Row.

Goethe, J. W. (1973). *Faust. Der Tragödie erster Teil*. Berliner Ausgabe (Bd. 8). Berlin: Aufbau Verlag (Original: 1808).

Hardaker, C. (2010). Trolling in asynchronous computer-mediated communication: From user discussions to academic definitions. *Journal of Politeness Research, 6*(2), 215–242.

Institut für Demoskopie Allensbach. (2018). *Allensbacher Markt- und Werbeträgeranalyse.* https://www.ifd-allensbach.de/awa/inhalte/uebersicht/uebersicht.html. Accessed: 16. Feb. 2019.

Janis, I. (1972). *Victims of groupthink: A psychological study of foreign policy decisions and fiascoes.* Boston: Houghton Mifflin.

Kneidinger, B. (2010). *Facebook und co. – Eine soziologische analyse von Interaktionsformen in online social networks.* Wiesbaden: VS Verlag.

Kunkel, J. M. (2017). Die rosarote Brille. Idealisierung des Partners in Liebesbeziehungen. *360°–Das studentische. Journal für Politik und Gesellschaft, 12*(1), 8–19.

Lewin, K. (1982). Forschungsprobleme der Sozialpsychologie I: Theorie, Beobachtung und Experiment. In C-F. Graumann (Hrsg.), *Kurt-Lewin-Werkausgabe,* (Bd. 4). Bern: Huber (Original: 1943).

Rheingold, H. (2000; Original: 1993). *The Virtual Community.* Cambridge, Massachusetts, London, England: The MIT Press. German Version: Virtuelle Gemeinschaft. Bonn: Addisson Wesley (Deutschland).

Schiller, F. (1830). *Sämtliche Werke in einem Band.* Haag: Gebrüder Hartmann.

Simmel, G. (1923). Über die Liebe (Fragment). In G. Simmel (Ed.), *Fragmente und Aufsätze (aus dem Nachlass und Veröffentlichungen der letzten Jahre).* München: Drei Masken Verlag.

Der Spiegel. (2004). Wir hätten diesen Krieg nicht autorisiert. https://www.spiegel.de/politik/ausland/vernichtendes-senatsurteil-wir-haetten-diesen-krieg-nicht-autorisiert-a-307968.html. Accessed: 20. Apr. 2019.

Steinke, L. (2014). *Bedienungsanleitung für den Shitstorm: Wie gute Kommunikation die Wut der Masse bricht.* Wiesbaden: Springer Gabler.

Sternberg, R. J. (1986). The triangular theory of love. *Psychological Review, 93,* 119–135.

Turkle, S. (2011). *Alone together: Why we expect more from technology and less from each other.* New York: Basic Books.

Utz, S. (2015). The function of self-disclosure on social network sites: Not only intimate, but also positive and entertaining self-disclosures increase the feeling of connection. *Computers in Human Behavior, 45,* 1–10.

Vriens, E., & van Ingen, E. (2018). Does the rise of the internet bring erosion of strong ties? Analyses of social media use and changes in core discussion networks. *New Media & Society, 20*(7), 2432–2449.

Wellman, B., Carrinton, P. J., & Hall, A. (2008). Networks as personal communities. In B. Wellman & S. D. Berkowitz (Eds.), *Social structures a network approach* (pp. 130–184). New York: Cambridge.

Whittaker, E., & Kowalski, R. M. (2015). Cyberbullying via social media. *Journal of School Violence, 14*(1), 11–29.

Wilson, R. E., Gosling, S. D., & Graham, L. T. (2012). A review of facebook research in the social sciences. *Perspectives on Psychological Science, 7*(3), 203–220.

Woods, S., Lambert, N., Brown, P., Fincham, F., & May, R. (2015). "I'm so excited for you!" how an enthusiastic responding intervention enhances close relationships. *Journal of Social and Personal Relationships, 32*(1), 24–40.

19

Community Spaces: Of Rabbits, Wolves, Social Identities and Foreign Groups

The Rabbits Are to Blame for Everything

In order not to lose the thread, we refer to Fig. 19.1 and there to the dark circles. And by way of introduction, we begin with a story by *James Thurber*, a US writer whom we learned to appreciate years ago for his fables.

> **Overview**
>
> "Within the memory of the youngest child there was a family of rabbits who lived near a pack of wolves. The wolves announced that they did not like the way the rabbits were living. (The wolves were crazy about the way they themselves were living, because it was the only way to live.) One night several wolves were killed in an earthquake and this was blamed on the rabbits, for it is well known that rabbits pound on the ground with their hind legs and cause earthquakes. On another night one of the wolves was killed by a bolt of lightning and this was also blamed on the rabbits, for it is well known that lettuce-eaters cause lightning. The wolves threatened to civilize the rabbits if they didn't behave, and the rabbits decided to run away to a desert island. But the other animals, who lived at a great distance, shamed them, saying, 'You must stay where you are and be brave. This is no world for escapists. If the wolves attack you, we will come to your aid, in all probability'. So the rabbits continued to live near the wolves and one day there was a terrible flood which drowned a great many wolves. This was blamed on the rabbits, for it is well known that carrot-nibblers with long ears cause floods. The wolves descended on the rabbits, for their own good, and imprisoned them in a dark cave, for their own protection. When nothing was heard about the rabbits for some

(continued)

W. Frindte, I. Frindte, *Support in Times of No Support*,
https://doi.org/10.1007/978-3-658-38637-5_19

(continued)

weeks, the other animals demanded to know what had happened to them. The wolves replied that the rabbits had been eaten and since they had been eaten the affair was a purely internal matter. But the other animals warned that they might possibly unite against the wolves unless some reason was given for the destruction of the rabbits. So the wolves gave them one. 'They were trying to escape', said the wolves, 'and, as you know, this is no world for escapists'" (Thurber, 1972, p. 267f.; Original: 1940).

Moral: Run, don't walk, to the nearest desert island.

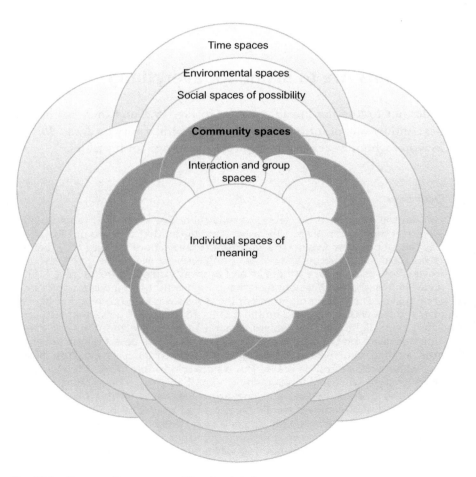

Fig. 19.1 Community spaces as "fixed points"

Fables by *James Thurber* are usually politically incorrect; especially when you think of the current debates about the protection status of wolves in Germany, but more on that later.

Thurber's fable points to several aspects that are not uninteresting in our context.

Ingroups and Social Identities

In Chap. 18 we mentioned the *ingroup* bias. Social groups and communities with which people identify and compare themselves can provide support. No question about it. By no means does it have to be just the immediate reference groups, one's family, close group of friends, or highly valued work team. People can also identify with social communities whose members they do not need to know all.

That's how we, the authors, felt at one with all fans of the *Carl Zeiss Jena* football club on 19 May 2019. On that day, the Jena team won its home match against *1860 Munich* and thus secured its place in the third division. WE had won, cheered and were part of a large community in which we felt safe and secure, no matter how the European election would turn out a week later.

Please don't take the example too seriously; we are more interested in handball.

> I don't like the football fan because he has a strange peculiarity: He does not understand that you are not one, and insists on talking to you as if you were one (Eco, 1993, p. 87).

However, the example is not so completely indifferent to us then again. It's true, we don't know most of the fans of *Carl Zeiss Jena*. But on this said Sunday in May 2019, we shared the view of the football world with many Jena people. We were part of a football-savvy Jena community space. For a short time, we belonged to a *interpretive community* whose members looked at the football world in a similar way as we did. We as football-interested "wolves" saw the Jena football world in the same way as the other Jena "football wolves".

Interpretive communities are social communities of people who have the same or similar views of social problems and processes, i.e. largely inter-individually consistent social constructions.

In the social science literature, one finds a number of terms that are meant to denote similar social realities as we are trying to do with the term *interpretive community. Tilman* Reitz (2014), following *Ludwig Wittgenstein,* speaks of "language communities", *Zygmunt Bauman* (1991) occasionally of "community of meaning", and *Ludwik Fleck* of "thought collectives" (Fleck, 1979, original: 1935).[1]

With these and similar terms, the various authors attempt to describe the reality of social groupings and communities whose members use concordant forms for dealing with their reality; e.g. a concordant use of language, concordant stores of knowledge, or concordant identifications with regional and/or cultural characteristics.

Interpretive communities can be parties, organizations, interest groups, associations, social networks, sects, media networks, scientific communities. They are of social value to those who identify with them. People compare themselves with the members of relevant interpretive communities, are themselves members of these communities, use and change the community-specific codes in order to find and determine the sense and identity of their own existence.

The function of interpretive communities is nicely described in the *Social Identity Theory* developed by *Henri Tajfel* and *John C. Turner* (1986). For Tajfel (1978, p. 28), a group is a number of people who feel or perceive that they are a group, categorize themselves as belonging to a group, and are categorized in the same way by other groups. This relatively minimalist definition, which departs from traditional social psychological group definitions, has an essential criterion that is very similar to what we use to describe interpretive communities: the interindividually consistent ways in which each group member views the world. For this reason, we are very sympathetic to *Tajfel's* explanations (and those of his successors) about the meaning and processes of social identity (cf. Frindte & Geschke, 2019): People *categorize* their social world (persons, objects, and events) to reduce the complexity of reality. Through social categorizations, people assign themselves to certain

---

[1] In our opinion, *Ludwik Fleck's* concept of the *thought collective is* one of the most interesting: In 1935, the physician Ludwik Fleck wrote the book "Entstehung und Entwicklung einer wissenschaftlichen Tatsache" (Genesis and Development of a Scientific Fact), which should actually belong to the classics of the philosophy of science. However, Fleck, a Polish Jew, did not find a large audience with his German-language book in Nazi Germany. After a stay in the Lwów Ghetto and a fight for survival in Auschwitz and Buchenwald, Fleck died almost forgotten in Israel in 1961. It was only through a brief reference by *Thomas S. Kuhn* in the preface to his book "The Structure of Scientific Revolutions" (1962) that attentive readers again came across Fleck's book and its exciting ideas. A sample: "If we define 'thought collective' as a community of persons mutually exchanging ideas or maintaining intellectual interaction, we will find by implication that it also provides the special carrier for the historical development of any field of thought, as well as for the given stock of knowledge and level of culture. This we have designated thought style" (Fleck, 1979, p. 39).

interpretive communities, to the "wolves", to the people of Jena, to football fans, or to men and women only.

Social categorization of the world has an important function for the individual. He or she perceives himself or herself as a member of *social categories* (interpretive communities), identifies with these categories, and defines his or her social place within social communities. The sum of these social self-assignments and identifications is a person's *social identity.* People strive for a positive social identity. To do so, they need to establish a positive relationship with relevant communities.

One could exclaim with Goethe:

Man cannot exist well alone, therefore he gladly joins a party, because there he finds, if not peace, at least reassurance and security (Goethe, 1972, p. 539; original: 1823).

In order to assess the value or prestige of the relevant communities, *social comparisons* with one's own and with significant foreign communities are important. Since social identity is a central component of the self-concept and people generally have a need for a positive social identity, the said social comparisons must lead to positive results in each case. Therefore, a so-called *positive distinctiveness,* i.e. a better performance of one's own group or community in comparison to foreign groups, is strived for.

As Jena "wolves" we have to be better than the "rabbits" from Bavaria. That makes sense and conveys a sense of stability in the chaos of football and other things, even if the football results may show otherwise.

Foreign Groups and Dealing with Threats

People resort to social categories (in their definitions of themselves and others) when they see sense in them in order to secure themselves and their social identity. The social psychologist *Michael Hogg* (2000) assumes exactly this when he says that in order to reduce general insecurity, people use social categories, identify with them and devalue those who do not fit into their own social category.

Certainly, *Ingroup Love* is not the same as *Outgroup Hate,* as *Marilynn Brewer* (1999) stated years ago. That is, belonging to and identifying with relevant deute communities does not necessarily lead to rejection and discrimination against other, foreign communities (cf. also Chap. 14). As victorious "wolves" we do not have to despise and hate the defeated "rabbits" as well.

Unless they, the "rabbits", threaten us, for example, when they disguise themselves as "wolves" or as migrants. Please do not overlook our irony.

An interesting social psychological theory – the *Integrated Threat Theory* by *Walter Stephan* and *Cookie Stephan* (2000) – draws attention to the connection between the experience of threat and the devaluation of and discrimination against foreign groups and communities. We illustrate the basic statements of this theory in Fig. 19.2.

The authors distinguish between four types of *perceived* threats: realistic threats, symbolic threats, intergroup anxiety and negative stereotypes. *Realistic threats* include existential dangers (e.g. being struck by lightning as a "wolf", to recall Thurber's story), economic, political, social or physical risks faced by one's community or group. Perceived or suspected attacks on one's own group's system of values, norms, and beliefs are among the *symbolic threats* ("rabbits" threaten civilization, "Muslims" threaten Western culture, "Jews" threaten the purity of the nation). *Intergroup anxiety* is the fear of contact with members of foreign groups, as these are experienced as unpleasant, negative, precisely as threatening (the fear of the "wolves" to meet the rabbits in the open; the AfD's fear of "Umvolkung"; the fear of Islam…). The fear of foreign groups is often linked to *negative stereotypes* towards foreign groups ("rabbits"

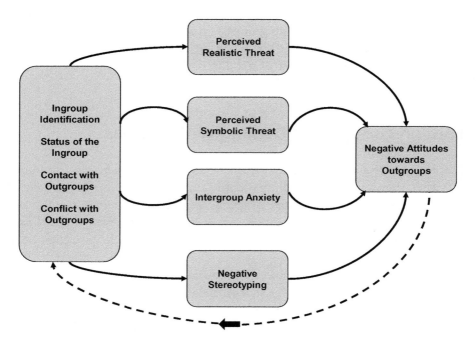

Fig. 19.2 The Integrated Threat Theory according to Stephan and Stephan (2000)

are lettuce eaters; "Muslims" are knifemen and "Jews" are money-grubbing). Because of these negative stereotypes, members of the self-group assume that the foreign groups will behave negatively and inappropriately towards them.

Whether the said threats actually exist is completely irrelevant. If they are perceived and interpreted as threatening by one's own group, one's own interpretive community, then they are also threatening and lead to perceiving the foreign groups as dangerous and rejecting them.

Following the theory further and looking at the left part of the figure, the quality and extent of perceived threats from foreign groups depend on a number of factors (the so-called antecedents):

- of the strength with which people *identify* with their own groups: The stronger we as "wolves" howl with the "wolves", the greater the threats we see ourselves exposed to by the "rabbits"; the more important the "purity" of the German people is to us Germans, the more threatened we see ourselves by migrants and refugees;
- from the *status* and *importance of* our own group: we are "wolves" and not mice. That is why we feel threatened by the "rabbits". We are an economic world power. Therefore … etc.
- from the actual or only virtual *contact* with the foreign groups and
- from previous experiences in dealing with foreign groups and any *conflicts* that the members of the own group have already experienced with foreign groups and communities. We will spare ourselves examples.

There are now a number of studies that have confirmed the empirical relevance of Integrated Threat Theory (e.g. Riek et al., 2006). The role that the media can play in the portrayal of perceived threats posed by migrants and in the dissemination of prejudices has also been examined in various other studies (e.g. Joyce & Harwood, 2014; Stephan et al., 2005).

In Fig. 19.2, one discovers – at the very bottom – another dashed arrow running from the negative attitudes towards outgroups *back* to these initial factors. This is to illustrate that we are dealing with a circular process that takes place between the initial factors, the perceived threats and the negative attitudes towards outgroups. What does this mean?

According to *Integrated Threat Theory*, negative attitudes towards "the Muslims" and "Islam", for example, can be interpreted as consequences of perceived threats. People, groups and communities try to justify their attitudes in general and their prejudices in particular. They look for anchors to which they can attach their attitudes and prejudices. Following *Integrated Threat Theory*, these anchors are negative stereotypes, fear of foreign groups, and most importantly, symbolic or realistic threat perceptions that exist regardless of whether or not there is "objective" evidence for these perceptions. It is quite enough if reasons are available on which people can *meaningfully* base their attitudes and prejudices. Such reasons gain weight when we strongly identify with our own groups ("We as the German people"), consider our relevant German communities to be particularly important (and demand the "rights of the German people"), avoid contacts with foreign groups (because "refugees" behave like "wolves" and "live at the expense of the welfare state"), and the conspiracy theories about the conflicts between our relevant communities and the "refugees" or "wolves" are promoted by the media.

But meaningful invocation here does not mean pointing to objective reasons, causes, or conditions, etc. It is enough to draw on our own negative attitudes towards foreign groups, attitudes that are also shared by the other members of our interpretive community.

> In times of manifold threats, some people – not only the "wolves" and not only the Germans – spin in a circle between perceived threats, negative attitudes towards foreign groups and nationalistic superelevations of their own group and community (see Chap. 14). We therefore venture a guess: not only in small groups (Chap. 18), but also in larger communities, the interpretive communities, the danger of group egoisms seems to grow and the community space becomes an echo chamber of self-affirmation. Regional, national, and international threats do not diminish as a result. On the contrary.

One element of confusion is that it is often impossible to tell the difference between identifying with one's own roots, understanding those who have other roots, and judging what is good and what is bad (Eco, 2012, p. 202).

References

Bauman, Z. (1991). *Modernity and ambivalence*. Cambridge, UK: Polity Press.

Brewer, M. B. (1999). The psychology of prejudice: Ingroup love and outgroup hate? *Journal of Social Issues, 55*(3), 429–444.

Eco, U. (1993). *Wie man mit einem Lachs verreist*. München: Hanser.

Eco, U. (2012). *Im Krebsgang voran*. München: Deutscher Taschenbuch Verlag.

Fleck, L. (1979). Genesis and development of a scientific fact. Edited by T. T. Trenn and R. K. Merton. Chicago and London: University of Chicago Press. (Original: 1935).

Frindte, W., & Geschke, D. (2019). *Lehrbuch Kommunikationspsychologie*. Weinheim: Beltz.

Goethe, J. W. (1972). *Aus den Heften „Zur Naturwissenschaft“*. Berliner Ausgabe (Bd. 18). Berlin: Aufbau Verlag (Original: 1823).

Hogg, M. A. (2000). Subjective uncertainty reduction through self-categorization: A motivational theory of social identity processes. *European Review of Social Psychology, 11*, 223–255.

Joyce, N., & Harwood, J. (2014). Improving intergroup attitudes through televised vicarious intergroup cognition: Social cognitive processing of ingroup and out-group information. *Communication Research, 41*(5), 627–643.

Reitz, T. (2014). *Sprachgemeinschaft im Streit Philosophische Analysen zum politischen Sprachgebrauch*. Bielefeld: Transcript.

Riek, B. M., Mania, E. W., & Gaertner, S. L. (2006). Intergroup threat and outgroup attitudes: A meta-analytic review. *Personality and Social Psychology Review, 10*(4), 336–353.

Stephan, W. G., & Stephan, C. W. (2000). An integrated threat theory of prejudice. In S. Oskamp (Ed.), *Reducing prejudice and discrimination* (pp. 23–46). Hillsdale: Erlbaum.

Stephan, W. G., Renfro, C. L., Esses, V. M., Stephan, C. W., & Martin, T. (2005). The effects of feeling threatened on attitudes toward immigrants. *International Journal of Intercultural Relations, 29*(1), 1–19.

Tajfel, H. (Ed.). (1978). *Differentiation between social groups*. London: Academic.

Tajfel, H., & Turner, J. (1986). The social identity theory of intergroup behavior. In S. Worchel & W. G. Austin (Hrsg.), Psychology of intergroup relations (2. Aufl., S. 7–24). Chicago: Nelson-Hall.

Thurber, J. (1972). *Lachen mit Thurber*. Berlin: Volk und Welt. Original: Thurber, J. (1940). Fables for our time and famous poems illustrated. New York and Evanston: Harper and Row publishers.

20

Social Spaces of Possibilities: Bright Moments, Dark Times, Ideologies and Religions

But the times are dark, the mores are corrupt, and even the right to criticize, if not stifled with censorship measures, is thrown to the fury of the people (Eco, 2012, p. 15, original Italian edition: 2006).

Figure 20.1 serves as an orientation and we ask: Do we really have to worry or is *Umberto Eco* exaggerating? It is already a few years ago when he wrote down this sentence – ostensibly referring to his Italian homeland, which at that time once again had to put up with *Silvio Berlusconi, a* Milanese prime minister who had been "rejuvenated" with facial surgery, was well versed in the Italian national song, and had been accused and convicted of tax evasion and many other crimes.

On the other hand, things don't seem to be quite so bleak in Germany in 2019.

Germany Mid 2019 – Bright Moments, Dark Times

In April 2019, 2.2 million people were officially unemployed. The unemployment rate was 4.9%. This is the lowest figure since 1990 (Zeit Online, 2019a). In 2005, the unemployment rate had peaked at 11.7% in Germany as a whole and at 18.7% in eastern Germany (see Chap. 4).

In 2018, approximately 100,000 refugees or migrants came to Germany; in 2015, there were still over one million. Since the Russian war against Ukraine, however, the number of refugees to Germany has risen sharply again. More than one million people from Ukraine have sought protection in Germany

W. Frindte, I. Frindte, *Support in Times of No Support*, https://doi.org/10.1007/978-3-658-38637-5_20

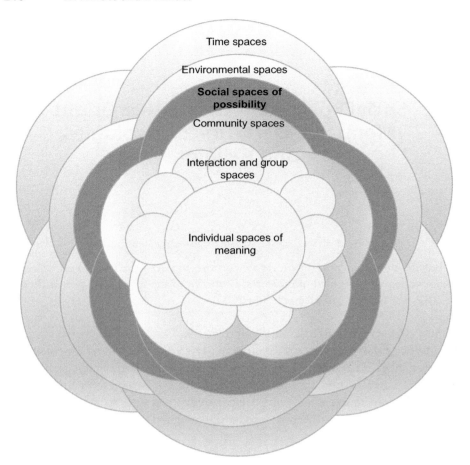

Fig. 20.1 Social spaces of possibilities as "fixed points"

since the war began. The AfD fears that the "political elites and institutions of the EU" are pursuing an asylum and immigration policy "which puts European civilization in existential danger" (AfD, 2019). The other, major parties, of course, see it quite differently. For Bündnis 90/Die Grünen, the SPD and Die LINKE, the right to asylum is a human right. CDU and CSU are also committed to the right of asylum, but want to limit the number of refugees. In the meantime they are stranded in Libya or drowning in the Mediterranean.

In a study published in April 2019 by the *Friedrich Ebert Foundation,* which is not without controversy, the authors of the study state, among other things, that 54.1% of the adults surveyed in 2005 agreed with negative statements against asylum-seeking people. Xenophobia as a whole is widespread among Germans, but not among all and not in all regions, they say:

Xenophobia is high in the new federal states, among formally low educated, conservative-oriented respondents as well as trade union members. It is particularly conspicuous among AfD voters, who overall show high values in all devaluations of groups with regard to party preference (Zick et al., 2019, p. 111).

The study of the Friedrich-Ebert-Stiftung also showed that 86.3% of the interviewees think it is important that Germany is governed democratically, every second person expresses confidence in the functioning of democracy, far more than 50% are in favor of civil commitment and the greater the confidence in democracy, the lower the level of group-focused enmity.

Incidentally, in a separate 2018 study of 2112 young people aged 14 to 18 or 19, over 60% of respondents said it was important to be more politically active so they could help influence political decisions. Almost 80% expressed positive attitudes towards foreigners (For example: "Foreigners should have exactly the same rights as everyone else in Germany."; "Foreigners should be allowed to vote in the Bundestag in Germany" (Frindte et al., 2019).

Germany is one of the safest countries in the world, according to *Horst Seehofer*, the former Federal Minister of the Interior, presenting the latest crime statistics in April 2019, with the number of criminal offences falling by 3.6%. This means that crime in Germany reached its lowest level since 1992 (Tagesschau.de, 2019). Crime by immigrants also appears to be on the decline. However, in 2018, the number of anti-Jewish crimes increased by ten percent overall: the police registered 1646 crimes nationwide in 2018. In 2017, there were still 1504.[1]

Economically, Germany is not doing badly at the moment (in 2019). To highlight just one example, in 2017, all German-based companies that make cars or car parts combined for around 426 billion Euro in revenue. Despite the diesel scandal, which cyclists don't even want to talk about anymore, car companies in Germany made record profits in 2018. Volkswagen reported selling more than 10.8 million vehicles worldwide in 2018, nearly 1% more than in 2017, while Daimler and BMW increased their car sales by about 1%. However, this changed in 2019. Sales of German cars are falling, especially in China. The US is threatening punitive tariffs on cars from Europe. In Germany, more driving bans are imposed on diesel cars in major cities. Hard times are ahead for car drivers and car manufacturers.

Although economic experts puzzled over whether overall economic growth would decline in 2019 and whether it would be a crisis year, wages and salaries increased significantly. Certainly, workers in the West still have more in their

---

[1] In 2021, the number of anti-Semitic offenses rose to 3027.

wallets than in the East. For example, workers in Ingolstadt earn twice as much as their colleagues in Görlitz (Zeit Online, 2019b). Productivity is also lower in the East than in the West. This is not only because 464 of the 500 largest German companies are based in the West. The *Leibnitz Institute for Economic Research* in Halle (IWH) attributes the lower economic performance of eastern companies to an incorrect subsidy policy. If these were linked to conditions to maintain or create jobs, then this could stand in the way of an increase in labor productivity (IWH, 2019). It was also somewhat difficult to understand the IWH's recommendation that eastern German cities should receive more support than rural areas. One can imagine that politicians in the East were loudly annoyed by such a formulation. The left-wing Prime Minister of Thuringia, *Bodo Ramelow,* and his colleague from Saxony-Anhalt, *Reiner Haseloff* (CDU), were outraged in rare unity about the unworldliness of the economists from Halle.

There are not only differences between East and West Germany. The gap between rich and poor is also widening. The most recent data comes from 2016. In that year, income differences in Germany were higher than at any time since 1990. Above all, the incomes of the highest and highest earners rose by an enormous 35%; in the lowest income groups, real income actually fell. Nevertheless, Germans are satisfied with their incomes. In 2016, satisfaction reached an all-time high compared with previous years.

However, the majority of Germans (property dealers and owners perhaps excluded) are hardly satisfied with "living in Germany". Property prices in Germany have been rising significantly for several years. In the third quarter of 2018, single-family and multi-family houses became 7.6% more expensive across Germany compared to 2017. Condominiums became 8.2% more expensive in the same period. In Berlin, for example, the price per square meter for new rentals is more than ten Euro, in Munich even 17 Euro (Süddeutsche.de, 2018). Who can pay that, who has so much money?

At the beginning of May 2019, *Kevin Kühnert*, then chairman of the Jusos, the SPD's junior organization, also asked himself this question. In an interview with "Die Zeit" he said, among other things, that he did not think "that it is a legitimate business model to make a living from other people's living space" (Zeit Online, 2019c). Everyone should own, at most, the living space in which they live themselves. He, Kevin Kühnert, advocates a collectivization of large companies "by democratic means": "It is less important to me whether in the end BMW's doorbell says 'state-owned car company' or 'cooperative car company' or whether the collective decides that it no longer needs BMW in this form".

Kevin Kühnert's statement in the aforementioned *Zeit* interview met with a broad, but predominantly negative response in Germany. Kühnert was heavily criticized by the CDU/CSU, the AfD, business associations and the SPD's own ranks. The CDU and the FDP saw Kühnert's statements as a serious declaration of war on the social market economy. The SPD member of parliament *Johannes Kahrs* asked via Twitter: "What has he been smoking?". The "Bild" newspaper called Kühnert's statement a "crazy advance" and asked how much GDR was in the SPD (Bild.de., 2019). The cabaret artist *Dieter Nuhr* described the Juso leader in his ARD program "Nuhr im Ersten" as a "chubby college dropout, …who knows nothing of the world except his party apparatus" (Stern.de, 2019).

It seems as if all the critics haven't read the SPD's manifesto from 2007. Well, maybe they don't have to, but it would have been good. There it says among other things (and there you must times through):

> Globalization, the opening of borders and of markets, is the result not only of technical innovations but also of political decisions. It offers the chance to overcome hunger, poverty and epidemics. World trade brings new jobs and prosperity to many people. At the same time, however, global capitalism is characterized by a lack of democracy and justice. It thus stands in the way of the goal of a free world based on solidarity. It exacerbates old injustices and creates new ones. That is why we are fighting for a policy that formulates a social response to global capitalism in our own country, in Europe and in the world. Our history […] demands an order of economy, state and society, in which the civil, political, social and economic basic rights are guaranteed for all people, all people can lead a life without exploitation, oppression and violence, i.e. in social and human security (Basic Program of the SPD, 2007, p. 7 and p. 16).

We, the authors of this book, are not SPD members, but we think that the Juso leader is standing firmly on the ground of the program of his own party. The SPD would do well to recognize that and thus blow a little more wind into the ideological debates of this, our country. But we'll get to those debates later.

First of all, let us pause briefly for a moment on the German population and their views of the social spaces of possibility.

In February 2019, the *Centrum für Strategie und Höhere Führung,* a company based at Lake Constance, published a study conducted by the Institut für Demoskopie in Allensbach (Security Report, 2019). 1219 German adults were asked about their worries and fears. Figure 20.2 provides a summary of the findings.

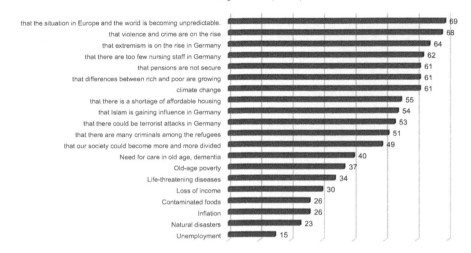

Fig. 20.2 Personal concerns and worries about safety. (Safety Report 2019)

The political situation in Germany and the world, as well as the current and future private situation, are not perceived and assessed as particularly rosy by the respondents. They are worried about the unpredictable political situation in Europe and the world, about violence and crime, the possible increase in extremism in Germany, the care and pension situation, the gap between rich and poor, climate change, unaffordable housing. The possible influence of Islam in Germany, the terrorist dangers, the refugee problem, the divisions in society, poverty in old age, the fear of life-threatening diseases, etc. also mark the perceptions in untenable times.

Some of the concerns expressed by Germans can only be vaguely substantiated. Crime, according to the Federal Minister of the Interior, is on the decline. The refugee problem has eased over the past year. Terror threats are also not as evident in Germany at present. Extremism, on the other hand, is still a problem, especially when it expresses itself in right-wing populist terms. Likewise, the nursing situation in Germany is in crisis. Not to mention climate change. The gap between rich and poor continues to widen. Globally, the fortunes of billionaires rose by 12% in 2018. In contrast, the poorer half of the world's population suffered losses of 11% (Deutschlandfunk, 2019).

Who offers support and security at the societal level in such times – the state, the parties, the church or other institutions? And what can the state, parties, church, business associations and other social institutions offer?

The tasks of the state are, as is well known, in the German Basic Law. One of the best and most famous sentences is undoubtedly found in Article 1: "Human dignity is inviolable. It is the duty of all state authority to respect and protect it. (2) The German people therefore profess inviolable and inalienable human rights as the basis of every human community, peace and justice in the world".

Holding on to it can provide support and security. No question about it.

Parties have the task of representing the political interests of the people. Churches are to bring God's word among the people. Trade associations represent the economic interests of their members, draw up technical and legal rules for the industry they represent and engage in lobbying.

All well and good. But what is – from a social psychological point of view – the bond that unites the members and supporters of a party, the faithful of a church or the members of associations?

It is – from our point of view – an *ideology*. That may be irritating at first, perhaps also wrong, but in any case simplistic. But we are, after all, followers of *William von Ockham* (c. 1288–1347) and his principle of parsimony, Ockham's Razor: "Entia non sunt multiplicanda praeter necessitatem", in English: "Entities should not be multiplied beyond necessity" (cf. Hübener, 1983). It is a rule of economy. The application of the rule means that in the explanation of reality one should use terms sparingly and avoid such assumptions that might prove superfluous for the explanation.

Ideologies

Ideologies cannot be killed, even if the accusation of ideology is often used as a killer argument and their end has been proclaimed time and again. *Raymond Aron*, the French philosopher and sociologist, held out the prospect of the end of ideologies as early as 1955 (Aron, 1955), as did his American colleague *Daniel Bell* five years later (Bell, 1960). Both said goodbye to class struggle-oriented dreams of social life in a rosy future. In future, the focus would no longer be on utopian dreams of the future, but on practicable and technically efficient solutions to social problems (Lütjen, 2008).

But, as we said, ideologies are alive and well. The accusation of being ideological, for example, is perfectly suited to accuse the opposing interlocutors of political fallacy in talk shows or feature articles. To speak once again of Kevin Kühnert, the Juso chairman: In a guest article for the conservative magazine *Cicero* entitled "Socialism is not an opinion, but a crime", the SPD member

Stefan Hasenclever accuses the Juso chairman of having fallen for a "dangerous ideology" (Hasenclever, 2019).

The fact that accusations of ideology can be used as argumentation tools has to do with the history of the concept of ideology. The term *ideology* was coined by the philosopher *Antoine Louis Claude Destutt de Tracy* during the Great French Revolution. De Tracy and his colleagues intended it to give a new impetus to the Enlightenment and, within the framework of a "doctrine of ideas" (ideology), to analyze and disseminate those ideas through which social processes could be advanced. *Napoleon,* the first emperor of the French, saw in these endeavors a threat to his claim to power and contemptuously called the group of philosophers "ideologists" (Mannheim, 1969, p. 66; original: 1929). Thus the term ideology acquired the disparaging meaning that still attaches to it today: Ideologies are not infrequently regarded as doctrinaire, irrational ideas.

In a letter from *Friedrich Engels* to *Franz Mehring of* 14 July 1893, we find the designation of ideologies as "false consciousness" (Engels, 1968, p. 97, original: 1893). And with this false consciousness Marxists and opponents of Marx have had plenty to contend with. What has emerged in the meantime is an ambiguous and controversial term.

Karl Mannheim (1969, p. 53 ff.) was probably the person who most aptly explained the concept of ideology. He distinguished between a *particular* and a *total* concept of ideology. The *particular concept of* ideology refers to ideas and conceptions of opposing groups which one does not want to believe and which one consciously accuses of concealment and falsification.

That is to say, it is always the *other* groups and communities that are ideologically screwy. Recently, for example, members of the AfD or the party-organized liberals in Germany have been saying that the "green" ideology is endangering the liberal foundations of economic activity through its climate and environmental policies (Grossbarth, 2019).

The *total* concept of ideology, on the other hand, refers to the central guiding idea or worldview of an epoch or of a historically and socially concrete grouping. Such a guiding idea or worldview, however, cannot simply be described as lies and deception; rather, it characterizes a system of conventions and traditions that are typical for an epoch or grouping.

> When we attribute to one historical era one intellectual world and to ourselves another one, or if a certain historically determined social stratum thinks in categories other than our own, we refer not to the isolated cases of thought-content, but to fundamentally divergent thought-systems and to widely differing modes of experience and interpretation (Mannheim, 1969, p. 55; 1936, p. 51).

Terry Eagleton (1995) has gathered even more ways to define ideologies: Ideologies can be the ideas of a social group or class; (false) ideas to legitimize political power; illusions about the social; socially motivated ways of thinking, etc. In a society, ideologies can be used to deceive, to unify the ideas of members of society, to present social conditions as natural, to rationally justify political decisions, etc..

Ideologies are still being produced and constructed. They owe their vitality to the current relevance of the global and the many-voiced talk about globalization. In the age of globalization, there are political and cultural ideologies in the plural, competing with each other, sometimes peacefully coexisting (Herkommer, 1999).

Ideologies in the post-ideological age have at least the following characteristics: they are important *social frames of reference* by which members of interpretive communities (Chap. 19) interpret their history, explain the present, envision the future, and attempt to persuade other interpretive communities how the world should be viewed and managed. Such ideologies include neo-conservatism and neoliberalism as well as feminism, the ecology movement, the ideologies of self-help groups in the health and social sectors, of gay and lesbian groups, of squatters and militant "autonomous" groups, of political parties and social movements.

We can call ideologies *meta-narratives* (Chap. 13). They, the ideologies, are not as great as the grand narratives of whose end *Jean-François Lyotard* (1986, 1979) spoke, but the contemporary ideologies already have the claim to be great and better than other narratives.

In this respect, ideologies are certainly suitable as fixed points, as overarching reference systems for orientation in a complex world. *John T. Jost's* (2006) plea can also be understood in this sense when he states that ideologies are an important factor in everyday life:

> That is, ideology helps to explain why people do what they do; it organizes their values and beliefs and leads to political behavior (Jost, 2006, p. 653).

Social movements, political parties, business associations and other interest groups are interpretive communities (see Chap. 19) and have their respective ideological views of the social spaces of possibility. These views are neither true nor false, but interest-led, and the interests have to do with convictions and value attitudes, which in turn are used to justify the uniqueness and "correctness" of their own ideologies.

Flavio Azevedo et al. (2019) recently conducted an extensive study of nearly 11,000 adults from the United States and the United Kingdom to determine, among other things, whether and to what extent individuals who subscribe to neoliberal ideologies hold authoritarian and socially dominant beliefs, i.e., beliefs about the superiority of one's own group or community. The results are not particularly surprising: people who endorse neoliberal ideas and ideologies are more authoritarian, hold clearly socially dominant views, and believe that the current economic structures in the US and the UK, as well as the current status relations between men and women, are good and right.

> We are dealing, the results could be interpreted, again – as mentioned at the end of Chap. 19 – with a gyroscope or an echo chamber in which members of certain interpretive communities move when they interpret social conditions: People rely on prominent ideologies (here, neoliberalism) to find social anchors for their individual attitudes and beliefs (authoritarian and socially dominant views); and the individual beliefs are the reasons why the ideological anchors are sought and found to be good.

People are sometimes like cats and like to bite each other's tails (only proverbially, of course).

Religions

To speak of religion in the same breath as ideology, as we do at this point, is presumptuous. Therefore, in order not to cause more trouble, we do not want to refer here to *Karl Marx* and *Friedrich Engels,* who write in the "German Ideology" – so to speak in one go – of "morality, religion, metaphysics and other ideology" (Marx & Engels, 1969, p. 26; original: 1845–1846). And we mention Marx's famous quotation from the "Critique of Hegel's Philosophy of Right" only to show that we know it without having to interpret it further:

"Religion is the sigh of the oppressed creature, the mind of a heartless world, as it is the mind of mindless conditions. It is the opium of the people" (Marx, 1972, p. 378; original: 1844).

As a religious person one will clearly see the great differences between the values and rituals of one's own religion and those profane ideologies and consider them important. The less religious are of course also aware of the differences that exist, for example, between the proceedings of a CDU or SPD party conference on the one hand and the rituals of an Easter service on the other. Religions can also do this, namely provide orientation, support and security for those who identify with the respective religion (Fromm, 1930; Fischer et al., 2018).

Religious and ideological doctrines of faith remain distinctly attractive in our scientific age precisely because they offer us a safe haven in the face of the frustrating complexity of reality (Harari, 2018, p. 305).

Gordon Allport (1966) distinguishes between intrinsic and extrinsic religiosity. *Intrinsically* oriented people, according to Allport, practice their religion for its own sake and out of conviction, whereas for *extrinsically* oriented people the social factor is in the foreground, such as social relationships, the experience of security and comfort, or social prestige. Linked to the extrinsic function of religiosity are those processes which we have mentioned under the aspect of social identity (Chap. 19). Identification with one's own religious community can, under these aspects, be connected with fear of and devaluation of those who are not counted among one's own religious community.

Perhaps people of religious faith, whether they are Christians, Jews, Muslims or members of another religion, will come to terms with the formulation that we have already used in a similar way to describe ideologies: Religions are important social reference systems with which members of religious communities interpret their history and present and design the future.

Religions, like ideologies, provide fixed points. Erich Fromm defines in this sense:

Religion in this broad sense of the definition – as need for a system of orientation – is something peculiar to all humans in one form or another. I should like to add, the choice is not at all between religion or no religion, provided we use the term in this general sense. The choice is only between a good religion and a bad religion, or a better religion or a worse (Fromm, 2010, p. 29, Original: 1953).

If we have not generated any major contradictions up to this point, then the Gretchen question could be asked at this point: "Now tell me, how do you feel about religion?"

A study conducted by the *Pew Research Center* in October 2018, which has already been mentioned several times in this book, shows that people from European countries differ greatly in their religiosity. Especially in Greece (55%), in Bosnia (54%) and in Romania (50%) religion plays an important role in the lives of more than half of the people. In Germany, only 11% say so, in Sweden 10% and in the Czech Republic 7% (*Pew Research Center*, 2018a).

However, 24% of Germans say they attend a church service at least once a month, 9% pray daily and ten percent believe in God with absolute certainty. That's not much, but it's not so bad either; belief in God can possibly not only provide support, but also be of manifold benefit. We do not want to think about the witch burnings or the ban on the use of condoms at this point.

Indeed, another (global) study from the *Pew Research Center* (2018b) shows that people who are involved in religious communities are happier than less religious people. Religious people drink less alcohol and smoke less often. In some, not all countries, but tending also to Germany, religious people rate their health better than the less religious. At the very least, regular church attendance or regular attendance at other religious events is closely related to life satisfaction, as we have already pointed out earlier (Chap. 17) (Berwian et al., 2017). The more often such visits take place, the more satisfied the visitors are with their lives.

However, it is hard to overlook the fact that European countries are not among the centers of religious attachment. These are more likely to be found in Brazil, India and among Christian fundamentalists in the USA. Worldwide, however, the importance of religion in everyday life seems to be declining (Pickel, 2013), even if esoteric and spiritual offers try to open up new spaces for finding sense. This is by no means about clairvoyance or magic. The offer of the new esotericism includes seminars for life help, yoga for the stressed, Reiki (laying on of hands) for life energy or homeopathy. All this in order to find new ways to one's own self (Barth, 2014).

If we broaden our view a little more, we notice that numerous studies point to the stronger prejudices of religious people. The more often respondents go to church, the more likely they are to reject ethnic diversity in their society and to want more distance from non-believers or those of a different faith. This is suggested by an analysis within the framework of the *European Social Survey* with respondents from more than 20 European countries (Coenders et al., 2005). Such results are by no means uncontroversial. Indeed, other studies find close positive correlations between religious orientation and pro-social engagement, but almost exclusively in economically less affluent countries (Guo et al., 2018).

Religiosity, i.e. the extent and quality of individual religious belief, is shown in many empirical studies to be not the only, but nevertheless an important predictor of Islamist fundamentalist beliefs. In addition to religiosity, other psychologically relevant factors influence Islamist fundamentalist beliefs (e.g., authoritarian beliefs, perceived group-based discrimination, or – in some circumstances – preference for and use of certain media; Schaafsma and Williams, 2012). We have already reported on this in Chap. 14.

Especially for Muslims and Muslim communities that experience their religion as threatened by the various consequences of the globalization of capitalism (dominance of Western values, individualism and dissolution of traditional communities, competition in economic, political and cultural fields, discrimination by non-Muslim communities, etc.), the return to the traditional, religious foundations seems to be a possibility to restore the threatened social identity or to protect the community from further attacks (see Fox, 2007).

Religions provide their believers with usable reference systems for individual interpretation of the world, social identification with their own social communities, and categorization of foreign communities. At the same time, religion serves to submit those people and institution that administer the proper use of religious rituals. With such submission, believers seek to align their actions with an imagined cosmic order. This, too, can provide support and security.

Religious fundamentalism is based on religion and religiosity. Every religion has the potential for fundamentalism. But not every religion tends towards fundamentalism. Religions or their interpretations become fundamentalist when they appear with a claim to sole representation (cf. Segady, 2006).

> **Overview**
>
> In a nutshell: everything is possible in the social spaces of possibility, many things are feasible, many things can happen. The factual can be interpreted in many ways and the interpretations, whether through ideologies, religions or on the basis of other social reference systems, can be a support and anchor in times of no support. The ideas, perspectives and interpretations floating in the social spaces of possibility can also – as in the spaces of sense, groups and communities – become echo chambers in which people and interpretive communities confirm themselves.
> Or: *"Too much confusion here,"* said William. *"Non in commotione, non in commotione Dominus"* (Eco, 1985, p. 598).

References

AfD. (2019). Quelle: https://www.afd.de/migrationspolitik/. Accessed: 20. Mai 2019.
Allport, G. W. (1966). The religious context of prejudice. *Journal for the Scientific Study of Religion, 5*, 447–457.
Aron, R. (1955). *L'opium des intellectuels*. Paris: Calmann-Lévy.
Azevedo, F., Jost, J. T., Rothmund, T., & Sterling, J. (2019). Neoliberal ideology and the justification of inequality in capitalist societies: Why social and economic dimensions of ideology are intertwined. *Journal of Social Issues, 75*(1), 49–88.
Barth, C. (2014). *Esoterik – Die Suche nach dem Selbst: sozialpsychologische Studien zu einer Form moderner Religiosität*. Bielefeld: Transcript.
Bell, D. (1960). *The end of ideology*. Cambridge: Harvard University Press.

Berwian, T., van Doorn, A., & Runkel, A. (2017). Wer glaubt, wird selig. Quelle: https://www.zeit.de/gesellschaft/2017-10/religion-glaube-zufriedenheit-glueck-studien. Accessed: 21. Nov. 2018.

Bild.de. (2019). Kühnert will BMW enteignen. Quelle: https://www.bild.de/politik/inland/politik-inland/kevin-kuehnert-fuer-kollektivierung-juso-chef-will-enteignung-z-b-von-bmw-61602026.bild.html. Accessed: 20. Mai 2019.

Coenders, M., Lubbers, M., & Scheepers, P. (2005). Majorities' attitudes toward minorities in western and eastern European societies. Results from the European social survey 2002–2003. Report 4, Vienna, Austria: *European Monitoring Center on Racism and Xenophobia.*

Deutschlandfunk. (2019). Schere zwischen Arm und Reich wird größer: Quelle: https://www.deutschlandfunk.de/ungleichheitsbericht-von-oxfam-schere-zwischen-arm-und.769.de.html?dram:article_id=438921. Accessed: 20. Mai 2019.

Eagleton, T. (1995). *Ideology.* London: Routledge.

Eco, U. (1985). *Der Name der Rose.* Berlin: Volk und Welt.

Eco, U. (2012). *Im Krebsgang voran.* München: Deutscher Taschenbuch Verlag.

Engels, F. (1968). Brief Engels an Franz Mehring vom 14. Juli 1893. Marx-Engels Werke (Bd. 39). Berlin: Dietz.

Fischer, P., Jander, K., & Krueger, J. (2018). Sozialpsychologie der menschlichen Existenz: Positive Psychologie und Psychologie der Religion. In P. Fischer, K. Jander, & J. Krueger (Eds.), *Sozialpsychologie für Bachelor* (pp. 179–201). Berlin: Springer.

Frindte, W., Richter, K., & Wohl, S. (2019). Studie Interkulturelle Erziehung im Projekt ViDem – Vielfalt zusammen leben, miteinander Demokratie lernen. Quelle: https://www.ifkw.uni-jena.de/studie_interkulturelle_erziehung.html.

Fromm, E. (1930). Die Entwicklung des Christusdogmas: Eine psychoanalytische Studie zur sozialpsychologischen Funktion der Religion. *Imago, 16*(3–4), 305–373.

Fromm, E. (2010). *The pathology of normalcy.* New York: American mental Health Foundation Inc. (Erstveröffentlichung 1953).

Fox, J. (2007). The increasing role of religion in state failure: 1960 to 2004. *Terrorism and Political Violence, 19*(3), 395–414.

Grundsatzprogramm der SPD. (2007). Quelle: https://www.spd.de/fileadmin/Dokumente/Beschluesse/Grundsatzprogramme/hamburger_programm.pdf. Accessed: 20. Mai 2019.

Grossbarth, J. (2019). Die anti-ökologische Hysterie. *Süddeutsche Zeitung vom* 31. Mai 2019, S. 9.

Guo, Q., Liu, Z., & Tian, Q. (2018). Religiosity and prosocial behavior at national level. *Psychology of religion and spirituality,* march 8, Online Publication: https://doi.org/10.1037/rel0000171. Accessed: 18. Juni 2019.

Harari, Y. N. (2018). *21 Lektionen für das 21. Jahrhundert. München: Beck. English Version: 21 Lessons for the 21st Century.* London: Jonathan Cape - Random House.

Hasenclever, S. (2019). „Sozialismus ist keine Meinung, sondern ein Verbrechen". Quelle: https://www.cicero.de/innenpolitik/kevin-kuehnert-sozialismus-verstaatlichung-spd-godesberger-programm. Accessed: 21. Mai 2019.

Herkommer, S. (1999). Ideologie und Ideologien im nachideologischen Zeitalter. Quelle: http://www.rote-ruhr-uni.com/cms/IMG/pdf/Herkommer_Ideologie.pdf. Accessed: 21. Mai 2019.

Hübener, W. (1983). Ockham's razor not mysterious. *Archiv für Begriffsgeschichte, 27*, 73–92.

IWH. (2019). „Vereintes Land – drei Jahrzehnte nach dem Mauerfall". Halle: Leibnitz-Institut für Wirtschaftsforschung. Quelle: https://www.iwh-halle.de/nc/presse/pressemitteilungen/detail/neue-iwh-publikation-zieht-bilanz-vereintes-land-drei-jahrzehnte-nach-dem-mauerfall/. Accessed: 23. Apr 2019.

Jost, J. T. (2006). The end of the end of ideology. *American Psychologist, 61*(7), 651.

Lütjen, T. (2008). Das Ende der Ideologien und der amerikanische Sonderweg. *Zeitschrift für Politik, 55*(3), 292–314.

Lyotard, J.-F. (1986). *Das postmoderne Wissen.* Graz: Böhlau.

Mannheim, K. (1969, Original: 1929). *Ideologie und Utopie.* Frankfurt a. M.: Verlag G. Schulte-Bulmke. English Version: Ideology and Utopia (1936). London: Routledge.

Marx, K. (1972). *Zur Kritik der Hegelschen Rechtsphilosophie Marx-Engels Werke* (Bd. 1). Berlin: Dietz. (Original: 1844).

Marx, K., & Engels, F. (1969). *Die deutsche Ideologie. Marx-Engels Werke* (Bd. 1). Berlin: Dietz. (geschrieben: 1845–1846).

Pew Research. (2018a). Eastern and western Europeans differ on importance of religion. Quelle: https://www.pewforum.org/2018/10/29/eastern-and-western-europeans-differ-on-importance-of-religion-views-of-minorities-and-key-social-issues/. Accessed: 16. Mai 2019.

Pew Research. (2018b). Religion's relationship to happiness, civic engagement and health around the world. Quelle: https://www.pewforum.org/2019/01/31/religions-relationship-to-happiness-civic-engagement-and-health-around-the-world/. Accessed: 21. Mai 2019.

Pickel, G. (2013). *Religionsmonitor.* Gütersloh: Bertelsmann Stiftung.

Schaafsma, J., & Williams, K. D. (2012). Exclusion, intergroup hostility, and religious fundamentalism. *Journal of Experimental Social Psychology, 48*(4), 829–837.

Segady, T. W. (2006). Traditional religion, fundamentalism, and institutional transition in the 20th century. *The Social Science Journal, 43*(2), 197–209.

Sicherheitsreport. (2019). Quelle: https://www.sicherheitsreport.net/sicherheitsreport-2019/. Accessed: 20. Mai 2019.

Stern.de (2019). Dieter Nuhr macht sich über Kühnert im Fernsehen lustig – der reagiert schlagfertig. Quelle: https://www.stern.de/politik/deutschland/dieter-nuhr-macht-sich-ueber-kevin-kuehnert-lustig—der-reagiert-schlagfertig-8705852.html; aufgerufen: 20.05.2019.

Süddeutsche.de. (2018). Deutschlands Mietmarkt ist kaputt. Quelle: https://projekte.sueddeutsche.de/artikel/wirtschaft/miete-wohnen-in-der-krise-e687627/. Accessed: 20. Mai 2019.

Tagesschau.de. (2019). Eines der sichersten Länder der Welt. Quelle: https://www.tagesschau.de/inland/kriminalstatistik-125.html. Accessed: 20. Mai 2019.

Zeit Online. (2019a). Arbeitslosigkeit im April auf Tiefstand. Quelle: https://www.zeit.de/wirtschaft/2019-04/arbeitsmarkt-arbeitslosigkeit-bundesagentur-fuer-arbeit-arbeitslosenquote-gesunken. Accessed: 20. Mai 2019.

Zeit Online. (2019b). Löhne hängen stark vom Wohnort ab. Quelle: https://www.zeit.de/gesellschaft/zeitgeschehen/2018-08/gehalt-lohn-verdienst-einkommen-regionale-unterschiede. Accessed: 20. Mai 2019.

Zeit Online. (2019c). Was heißt Sozialismus für Sie, Kevin Kühnert? Quelle: https://www.zeit.de/2019/19/kevin-kuehnert-spd-jugendorganisation-sozialismus. Accessed: 20. Mai 2019.

Zick, A., Küpper, B., & Berghan, W. (2019). *Verlorene Mitte – Feindselige Zustände. Rechtsextreme Einstellungen in Deutschland* 2018/19. Herausgegeben für die Friedrich-Ebert- Stiftung von Franziska Schröter. Bonn: Dietz.

21

Environment and Time: Of Extended Bodies and Other Relativities

Environment is a broad field. It can be viewed from biological, geographical, anthropological, economic, ecological, technical, political or media perspectives and many more. We are now in the "outer" spaces (see Fig. 21.1) and will have to limit ourselves.

From a psychological point of view, and not only from this one, we can consider the environment first of all as the totality of a person's living space. Social psychologists therefore like to speak of the environment as a *subject-centered behavioral space* (Graumann & Kruse, 2003). This may sound somewhat esoteric, but it is easy to explain: What is psychologically interesting about the environment is not what is standing, lying, walking, falling, rising, crawling and flitting "out there", but only this and that which has an influence on people and can be influenced by them.

Even this restriction is still too broad for our concerns. We would then also have to include the spaces of interaction, group, community and social possibility we have described in the environment, and that would be quite appropriate. But, as I said, we want to limit ourselves.

We do this by once again referring to *Karl Marx* and interpreting him a little further. In the "Grundrisse der Kritik der politischen Ökonomie", the preparatory work for "Capital", we find the following thought-provoking sentence:

Through the hunting of the tribes, a region of the earth first becomes a hunting ground; through agriculture, the earth, the land first set as the extended body of the individual (Marx, 1983, p. 401; original: 1857–1858).

W. Frindte, I. Frindte, *Support in Times of No Support*,
https://doi.org/10.1007/978-3-658-38637-5_21

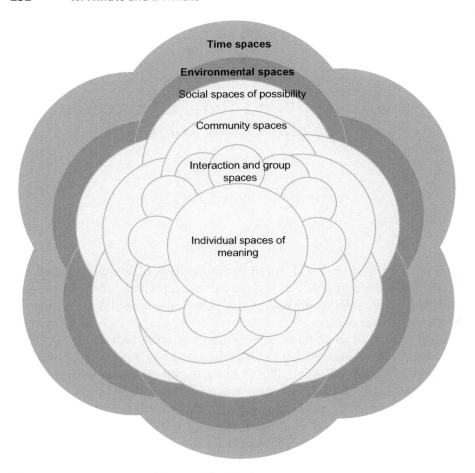

Fig. 21.1 Environment and time as "fixed points"

We are concerned in this sentence with the metaphor of the "extended body," which we like to take up to describe our limited view of environmental spaces. Marxist and non-Marxist exegetes have interpreted the Marxian metaphor differently. We want to change it a little.

In general, it is the natural, external conditions of production and reproduction that are described by the extended body (Müller, 2016). For the farmer, the soil on which he sows and harvests (as long as this is still possible) is part of his extended body. The tools necessary for this are equally part of it. The professional driver experiences his truck now and then as an extended body. We ourselves extend our body with glasses in order to be able to see better. A bicycle can become an extended body by improving the natural speed of our legs. The computer on which we write the manuscript for this book extends and improves not only our natural writing tools, but also our memory. The tablet or a smartphone can lengthen or atrophy our natural senses to look, hear, and talk to the world. Our own apartment, for which there are still loans to be paid or for which we have to pay an increased rent again, is also part of our extended corporeality. Likewise, the garden with its roses and peppermint plants can become an extended corporeality, provided we regard it, the garden, as an important life resource.

As *Jim Morrison* and the *Doors* said many years ago (Morrison, 1968):

"She has a house and garden
I would like to see what happens…"
(Jim Morrison, 1968)

Nature as a whole, with its fauna and flora, is also part of the extended human body. And when the report of the World Biodiversity Council (IPBES) reports that one million to eight million animal and plant species are threatened with extinction due to climate change, then our extended body is also at risk (Süddeutsche.de, 2019). We know this. We had already reported that more than 70% of Germans see climate change as the greatest threat to their own security (Chap. 9).

If we take the metaphor of the extended body seriously, then we are still dealing, despite the intended restriction, with diverse, complex and contradictory environmental spaces. This includes our immediate environment (house, apartment, garden, bicycle, computer, smartphone, etc.), which we can influence directly, and the more or less indirect environment (fauna, flora, climate, media in general), without which we could not live, but which we are only able to influence indirectly.

The immediate as well as the indirect environments are important conditions for our aliveness, insofar as they are fixed points for support and security. Growing roses or parsley in the garden makes sense for those who like it, who see gardening as a distraction and enrichment of their lives. Riding a bicycle to save money or to reduce one's own CO_2 emissions is also meaningful and substantial, even if one's own individual influence on climate change does not seem very great.

With increasing age, the willingness to take measures to live more sustainably apparently increases – according to a study by *YouGov*. More than 2000 people in Germany were surveyed. Of the over-55 s, two-thirds (66%) are willing to do without plastic. This willingness is lower in the other age groups. Regional foods are preferred more often by older people (62%) than by younger people. 54% of the over-55 s are willing to save energy and electricity through responsible behavior (e.g. by using energy-saving light bulbs). Among 18–24 year olds, 43% express this willingness. Among 25- to 34-year-olds, the figure is only 34% (YouGov, 2019). Does this show the alliance of the young of *Fridays-for-Future* and *Parents-* or *Grandparents-for-Future?*

However, the immediate as well as the indirect environments are ambivalent fixed points for our support and our security. The indirect environments certainly even more so than the immediate ones; the threats to our climate, fauna and flora that are not always visible and immediately apparent make this clear. The rising rents in our immediate environment or the parched garden soil in the hot summer months of 2018 and 2019 are also examples of how the immediate environments are not only capable of providing security, but can be perceived as threats.

And this is where the *time spaces* come into play, which help to determine our search for fixed points that could give us support in times of no support. It is initially reassuring if it is true that the elderly also think about the future and see in the future of their children and grandchildren an anchor to worry about and to commit themselves – for example – to environmental protection. In the stereotypes that are not infrequently encountered in everyday life, the elderly and old are nevertheless more likely to be attributed a primary view of the past and present and less future orientation (cf. Pichler, 2010).

Kurt Lewin was one of the first to draw attention to the psychological importance of time and time perspectives (Lewin, 1969, original: 1936, 1982, original: 1942). The US psychologist *Lawrence K.* Frank (1939) draws on Lewin and argues that people not only live in the present, but in order to gain certainty they also need to think about the past and the future. Frank writes of "quest for certainty," that is, a search or need for certainty, a term, incidentally, that he may have borrowed from the title of a book by *John Dewey* (Dewey, 1929). In order to gain certainty and a foothold in the present, people orient themselves to the past and the future. These orientations are called *time perspectives* in psychology. Current psychological thinking about time perspectives is closely associated with the name *Philip Zimbardo*. This is the one who conducted the infamous, social psychological prison experiment at Stanford (e.g., Zimbardo, 2005). In the late 1990s, Zimbardo and his colleague *John Boyd* put forward a theory of individual perspectives on time (Zimbardo & Boyd, 1999). We will discuss this theory further in Chap. 24. For now, just this: people develop dominant time perspectives. They orient themselves either to present things and events or to past or future things. These orientations influence perception, emotions and behavior.

From a psychological point of view, *time spaces* are primarily connected with orientations in time. We seek and find support and security in the past, in the present or in the future. The time periods that are significant for our search can be short (example: "I need a break now to get back into balance.") or longer (example: "In order to be able to deal with national and global risks, I find support in God.").

But similar to the *environmental spaces*, the *time spaces* in which we search for support and fixed points are ambivalent and only relative anchors. What gives us support and security today (e.g. the meta-narrative of the socially oriented party with which we identify ourselves) can "vanish into thin air" tomorrow (e.g. after the next election).

Or, to quote *Tom* Waits (1985):

"… and it's time time time time
and it's time time time time, and it's time time time time time
and it's time time time that you love
and it's time time time time".
(Tom Waits, 1985)

References

Dewey, J. (1929). *The quest for certainty: A study of the relation of knowledge and action*. New York: Minton, Balch & Co.

Frank, L. K. (1939). Time perspective. *Journal of Social Philosophy, 4*, 293–312.

Graumann, C. F., & Kruse, L. (2003). Räumliche Umwelt. Die Perspektive der humanökologisch orientierten Umweltpsychologie. In P. Meusburger & T. Schwan (Eds.), *Humanökologie. Ansätze zur Überwindung der Natur-Kultur-Dichotomie* (pp. 239–257). Wiesbaden: Fritz Steiner Verlag.

Lewin, K. (1969). Grundzüge der topologischen Psychologie. In *Bern, Stuttgart: Huber (original: Principles of topological psychology, 1936)*. New York & London: McGraw-Hill.

Lewin, K. (1982). Feldtheorie des Lernens. In von Carl-Friedrich Graumann (Hrsg.), *Kurt-Lewin-Werkausgabe* (Bd. 4). Bern: Hans Huber (original: Field theory of learning, yearbook of the National Society for the study of education, 1942, 41, 215-242).

Marx, K. (1983). In M-E. Werke (Hrsg.), Grundrisse der Kritik der politischen Ökonomie, (Bd. 42). Berlin: Dietz (Original: 1857–1858).

Morrison, J. (1968). Love street. Songtext von the doors aus dem album „waiting for the sun", Songwriter: Jim Morrison, John Densmore, Ray Manzarek & Robby Krieger. TTG Studios, Hollywood, California.

Müller, H. (2016). Marx, Bloch und das Praxiskonzept in der Transformationsepoche. In H.-E. Schiller (Ed.), *Staat und Politik bei Ernst Bloch* (pp. 187–210). Baden-Baden: Nomos.

Pichler, B. (2010). Aktuelle Altersbilder: junge Alte und alte Alte. In K. Aner & U. Karl (Eds.), *Handbuch Soziale Arbeit und Alter* (pp. 415–425). Wiesbaden: VS Verlag.

Süddeutsche.de. (2019). Der Mensch verdrängt eine Million Tier- und Pflanzenarten. https://www.sueddeutsche.de/wissen/artensterben-ipbes-bericht-1.4434207. Accessed: 26. Mai 2019.

Waits, T. (1985). Time. Songtext aus dem Album Rain Dogs, Songwriter: Tom Waits. © Island Records.

YouGov. (2019). Nachhaltigkeit: Die Ältesten leben besonders verantwortlich. https://yougov.de/news/2019/05/23/nachhaltigkeit-die-altesten-leben-besonders-verant/. Accessed: 26. Mai 2019.

Zimbardo, P. G. (2005). Das Stanford Gefängnis Experiment. Eine Simulationsstudie über die Sozialpsychologie der Haft (3. Aufl.). Goch: Santiago Verlag.

Zimbardo, P. G., & Boyd, J. N. (1999). Putting time in perspective: A valid, reliable individual-differences metric. *Journal of Personality and Social Psychology, 77*(6), 1271–1288.

Part V

From the Search for the Island

22

Interlude (To Take a Breath)

The author would have to pass away after he had written. So that he does not
disturb the text's own movement (Eco, 1986, p. 14).

But we are still alive. Not that we dare compare ourselves to *Umberto Eco* and
try to rely entirely on the inherent movement of the text so far. What we have
written in the chapters of *Part IV of* this book is not easy fare, since we have
allowed ourselves to be driven by the variety of socio-psychological offers to
find support and fixed points in life. And we have not even striven for
completeness.

Therefore, we use the following short passages to recapitulate our view of
the multiple possibilities of a search for fixed points.

There was talk of (a) individual spaces of meaning, (b) interaction and
group spaces, (c) community spaces, (d) social spaces of possibility, (e) environmental spaces and (f) time spaces. In this way we wanted to draw attention to the fact that *(a)* we find support in ourselves. "Cogito ergo sum", I
think, therefore I am, is the first principle in the epistemology of *René Descartes*
(1994, original: 1641). But we also mean (b) that our relationships with loved
ones, with friends, colleagues or sports comrades can give us a foothold.
Therefore, the phrase "communicamus ergo sum", we communicate, therefore I am, is not inappropriate. The groups we care about, *(c)* the communities
whose ideas we follow, *(d)* the social opportunities we are exposed to, as well
as *(e)* the environment and *(f)* the temporal circumstances and historical
events we remember – all this is part of the bouquet of stories to hold on to,
even if they rarely grew on the tree of knowledge.

© The Author(s), under exclusive license to Springer Fachmedien Wiesbaden GmbH, part
of Springer Nature 2022
W. Frindte, I. Frindte, *Support in Times of No Support*,
https://doi.org/10.1007/978-3-658-38637-5_22

The *fixed points* are ourselves and our concatenation with the social groups, communities, societal, natural, and temporal circumstances with which we identify in our supposed search for footing. However, these fixed points can quickly become echo chambers or filter bubbles in which we feel comfortable and validated because we don't have to fear cognitive dissonance, are allowed to nurture our group egoisms, can ignore facts and real dangers, and don't have to think about tomorrow.

Whether such an effort to find a foothold in one's own *ego,* in the collective *we,* or in the *here and now* can be relevant, successful, or harmful to others,

> …we always know after the fact, and even then it often takes a long time for the effects to show. So we can do no more than listen to our friends (if we have any), read, play music, watch TV series (if we find pleasure in them), think about everything that is happening around us, and draw our conclusions from it. Personally, I would add that, in any case, we should not recommend or encourage actions that are dictated by hatred and that might feed hatred. I write this not because I have a theory about the effect of hatred, but because I personally have no intention of being guided by hatred. That is all I can say (Feyerabend, 1992, p. 209 f.).[1]

Paul Feyerabend (1924–1994) created turmoil with his publications, especially where scientists believed themselves to be guardians of the only truth, experts of knowledge, advocates of the pure method. Some resented the mirror he held up to them, others recognized themselves and their neighbors in his brilliant analyses of the history of science, seeing that boundaries must be crossed if we are to know and live.

Sometimes rules have to be broken and boundaries crossed so that we can leave our echo chambers and filter pales to search for new fixed points.

That is what the last, the fifth part of our book will be about. At least we try to.

---

[1] The quotation is taken from the German publication "Über Erkenntnis - Zwei Dialoge" by Paul Feyerabend. This book was first published in Italian under the title "Dialogo sul metodo" (1989). An English version entitled "Three Dialogues on Knowledge" was published in 1991 (Oxford: Basil Blackwell). However, the English version does not contain the passages from which the quotation is taken. Therefore, we have translated the German quote into English.

References

Descartes, R. (1994). *Meditationen über die Grundlagen der Philosophie mit den säm-tlichen Einwänden und Erwiderungen*. Hamburg: Felix Meiner Verlag (Original: Meditationes de prima philosophia, in qua Dei existentia et animae immortalitas demonstratur, 1641).

Eco, U. (1986). *Nachschrift zum "Namen der Rose"*. München: Deutscher Taschenbuch Verlag.

Feyerabend, P. (1992). *Über Erkenntnis zwei Dialoge*. Frankfurt a. M./New York: Campus.

23

A Touch of Philosophy of Science Theory and Vipassana Meditation

You surely know, dear readers, *Maurits Cornelis Escher* (1898–1972), the Dutch graphic artist known for his "impossible" depictions of figures, buildings and gestures. There is a print by Escher entitled "Ascending – Descending". In the picture, which is a lithograph from 1960, one sees a large building with a never-ending staircase on its roof, on which people are moving in rows of two. The people are climbing the stairs, always moving in circles, so they never reach the end of the stairs. One floor below, another person stands watching the endless activity. While the people on the stairs are obviously moving in a seemingly senseless circle, the observer on the lower floor can actually only see the heads of the people moving on the endless stairs. The observer can observe, but will hardly be able to find and express a sufficient explanation for what is observed.

It seems to us that the people on the stairs are those who keep going in circles in the accelerated world without thinking about the futility of their own actions. Whether it is the right-wing populist, nationalist, anti-Semitic, Islamist circles or the echo chambers of the "do-gooders". They, we, move in the hamster wheel of our own spaces and no longer see the sense of our movements.

So we turn to independent observers, called experts or scientists, or they turn to us for advice. The experts, however, tend from time to time to want to view what they observe and explain in a value-free way. They do not participate in the meaningless hustle and bustle of the hamster wheel and like to invoke the value-free nature of science. *Max Weber* (1973) is often cited as a

W. Frindte, I. Frindte, *Support in Times of No Support*, https://doi.org/10.1007/978-3-658-38637-5_23

guarantor, although the thesis of value freedom actually goes back to the Scotsman *David Hume* (1973; original: 1739/40).

But in order not to digress even further, we return to *Escher*'s graphic. No matter how the observer tries to turn and turn below the people walking upstairs in the circle above, he is standing one floor lower than his "objects of observation". And he only sees something, but never everything that happens in the upper room of the hamster wheel. He, the observer, is blinded in two ways: on the one hand, he excludes the possibility of observing something completely different, for example, what happens or could happen outside the big building on whose roof people run in endless circles. On the other hand, the distinction the observer has made to observe something is always obscured.. The decision to observe something, once made, is no longer present in the process of observation and investigation, because no observer can observe his observation while he is observing, as the wise *Niklas Luhmann* noted (cf. Luhmann, 1991, p. 63 ff.).

However: another observer could observe what distinctions our observer uses, and thus see what this observer cannot see. With such an observation of observation, it might be possible to uncover the blind spots of our observer. And indeed, there is another person in *Escher*'s graphic. This person is now sitting one floor lower than our observer, on a staircase leading out of the building. This person is either looking away from the building into the distance or is lost in thought. He is probably the most interesting person in the graphic.

What role could this person play in the concert of others in the picture? It could be someone who is taking a break from running up and down the stairs. Or it could be a colleague of the observer who is trying to think through what his colleague has just observed, a pausing empiricist or a reviewer with a penchant for theorizing and criticizing. It would also be possible that this person has taken note of the stair run in the circle, but judges the hamster wheel as not very human-friendly and prefers to occupy himself with himself, a self-observer, so to speak. Also conceivable would be a person who has no interest at all in what is happening on the roof of the building and prefers to look into the distance in order to conceive or discover other worlds, a utopian under circumstances.

Many roles are conceivable and many interpretations of Escher's graphic are possible. We find the two most recently considered roles, that of the self-observer and that of the utopian, particularly exciting.

The fact that we now consider these two roles to be particularly interesting has to do with our conception of what it means to be human. We claim that humans differ from other living beings at least by the following qualities: (a) by their competence to locate themselves in the world structure as human subjects and to reflect on their individual and historical development, (b) by their knowledge that they will have to die at some point[1] and (c) by their ability to anticipate the future with hope. It is this last ability that we are interested in, since it is related to a central need that we like to call the *need for continued life.* In order to satisfy this need, we can hope for life after death, plant an apple tree today (von Ditfurth, 1985), take care of climate change so that our grandchildren will still find a livable earth in 30 years' time, or…

Before we turn to the utopian, however, let us first dwell on the self-observer. As is well known, self-observation is an exciting field. We make ourselves the object of our attention. We observe our appearance and/or our mental processes and states. It cannot be ruled out that we may be subject to some self-deceptions in the process. Self-observation does not always lead to self-knowledge.

Yuval Noah Harari, the Israeli historian, points out an important aspect of introspection that we are happy to take up at this point. In his book "21 Lessons for the 21st Century", *Harari* deals with the global and individual challenges of our time and formulates recommendations on how to deal with these demands in the future. In a world in which threats have multiplied and globalized, but handy explanations and instructions for dealing with them are lacking, he argues, a "clear idea about what life is all about" (Harari, 2018, p. 17) is urgently needed. It is to the twenty-first century that Harari dedicates his lessons. The term *lesson,* as we know, comes from Latin ("lectio"), meaning "that which is read" or "the lecture," and in church worship referred to the reading aloud of a significant section of the Bible, usually apostles' or martyrs' stories, grand narratives, that is, intended to instruct those listening. Great stories and narratives as well as teachings Harari also provides. He writes about disillusionment, about work and missing jobs, about freedom in digital times, about equality, nationalism, about God and religion, immigration, terrorism and war, about post-factuals and conspiracy theories, and about the future that is not in the cinema. His penultimate chapter ends with the following remarkable sentence:

> So if you want to know the truth about the universe, about the meaning of life, and about your own identity, the best place to start is by observing suffering and exploring what suffering really is (Harari, 2018, p. 404).

---

[1] This is one of the core theses of the exciting *Terror Management Theory* (TMT), which, mind you, is *not* concerned with explaining terrorism, but assumes that, unlike other living beings, we humans know about our mortality, have to deal with this knowledge, and manage the fear (terror) it causes (Greenberg et al., 2009).

Implicitly, Harari pleads for more empathy in dealing with the world, people and ourselves. Harari sees one way to develop empathy – at least for himself – in focused, i.e. conscious self-awareness or self-observation. A friend suggested to him that he should try attending a *Vipassana meditation course.* A meditation teacher taught him this method, which originated in Buddhism. Since then, he has been meditating for two hours a day. Meditation is an instrument for directly observing one's (own) mind. In *Vipassana meditation,* you learn to be more aware of your sensations and your body and to be more mindful of yourself. One realizes, says Harari, that the deepest source of one's own suffering lies in the patterns of one's own mind.

Neurobiological and neurophysiological studies now prove the actual effects of mindfulness meditation as it is taught in the Vipassana courses offered worldwide. In brain areas related to attention and sensory processing, significant changes apparently occur after meditation. The release of neurotransmitters, substances responsible for the excitation of nerve cells (e.g. dopamine and serotonin), seems to change after meditation. People who have successfully completed Vipassana meditation courses are apparently better able to regulate their attention and emotions, memory performance improves, self-perception becomes more differentiated, and they become more aware of their own body (Esch, 2014; Fox et al., 2014).

This is not much, but it may help you to recognize your own strength and to be prepared for the big challenges.

Perhaps our person on the stairs leading out of the building in *Escher's* graphic is just that person who takes the time, like *Yuval Noah Harari,* to meditate two hours a day in order to be able to deal more empathetically and mindfully with himself, the world and the possible human hamster wheels in the other 22 h of the day.

That would be nice. And we would like to take this lesson of greater mindfulness towards ourselves to heart. But we doubt whether the dictators of this world, the far-right or Islamist terrorists, the right-wing populists and new-right nationalists are ready to do so. Surely it would be good if the Trumps, Höckes, Gaulands, Orbáns and whatever their names may be would take a meditation course more often. Back pain, depression and various signs of old age could also be alleviated by this. Perhaps these people would also better understand the suffering in this world. But it would hardly alleviate the suffering of others.

However, we dare to doubt whether those people who seek their salvation and the sense of life in post-factualism, nationalism, fundamentalism or other screwed-up world views will understand *Harari's* lesson. The serious climate

changes, the worldwide refugee movements, the terrorist threats or the murders with right-wing extremist backgrounds, can hardly be prevented by
meditation.

So we need to rethink.

References

Esch, T. (2014). Die neuronale Basis von Meditation und Achtsamkeit. *Sucht,*
60(1), 21–28.

Fox, K. C., Nijeboer, S., Dixon, M. L., Floman, J. L., Ellamil, M., Rumak, S. P.,
Sedlmeier, P., & Christoff, K. (2014). Is meditation associated with altered brain
structure? A systematic review and meta-analysis of morphometric neuroimaging
in meditation practitioners. *Neuroscience and Biobehavioral Reviews, 43*, 48–73.

Greenberg, J., Landau, M., Kosloff, S., & Solomon, S. (2009). How our dreams of
death transcendence breed prejudice, stereotyping, and conflict: Terror management theory. In T. D. Nelson (Hrsg.), Handbook of prejudice, stereotyping, and
discrimination (S. 309–332). New York: Psychology Press.

Harari, Y. N. (2018). *21 Lektionen für das 21. Jahrhundert.* München: Beck. English
version: 21 lessons for the 21st century. London: Jonathan Cape - Random House.

Hume, D. (1973). *Ein Traktat über die menschliche Natur.* Hamburg: Felix Meiner
Verlag (Original: 1739/40).

Luhmann, N. (1991). Wie lassen sich latente Strukturen beobachten? In P. Watzlawick
& P. Krieg (Eds.), *Das Auge des Betrachters.* München: Piper.

Von Ditfurth, H. (1985). *So lasst uns denn ein Apfelbäumchen pflanzen.* Hamburg:
Rasch.

Weber, M. (1973). *Gesammelte Aufsätze zur Wissenschaftslehre.* Tübingen: Mohr.

24

Visionaries Do Not Need to See a Doctor

We look once again at the person in *Escher's* graphic, sitting on the outside steps of the building and looking into the distance. Perhaps, we had suspected, it could be a person who wants to discover other worlds. Possibly it is a utopian and visionary who imagines a future after the pointless stair climbing on the hamster wheel.

"Anyone with visions should see a doctor." With this legendary sentence, *Helmut Schmidt* commented on the visions that *Willy Brandt* tried to formulate in the 1980 Bundestag election campaign. Our man in Escher's graphic simply remains seated. Whether he has the intention of going to the doctor, we doubt. So what could his motives be?

Philip Zimbardo and *John Boyd* (2009, p. 262) report the following study conducted by *Walter Mischel* and colleagues in 1990 (Shoda et al., 1990): Children averaging four years of age from a kindergarten at Stanford University in California were offered either one piece of candy, which they were allowed to eat immediately, or two pieces of candy if they were willing to wait 15 min for it. As expected, most of the children (two-thirds) wanted the one candy so they could snack on it right away. The remaining third wanted to wait to get two candies later. Fourteen years later, the now adults were studied again. Now it turned out that those who 14 years earlier were willing to wait a while in order to get two sweets then, differed significantly from the others (the two thirds who wanted to have and eat the one sweet right away). The people who waited then had better school records; they were more confident and determined.

W. Frindte, I. Frindte, *Support in Times of No Support*,
https://doi.org/10.1007/978-3-658-38637-5_24

Philip Zimbardo and *John Boyd* derived from these and several other findings the hypothesis that people a) differ with regard to their, often unconscious, attitudes towards time and b) order and give sense to their lives on the basis of their attitudes towards time. The authors (Zimbardo & Boyd, 1999) speak of time perspectives and also refer to *Kurt Lewin* (1942, German: 1982). According to Lewin, a person's ideas and behavior depend not only on his or her present situation. Hopes and desires as well as intentions are always influenced by one's past. However, a person's attitudes towards life and happiness are primarily shaped by future expectations. Lewin calls the totality of a person's views about his future and his past time *perspectives.* Zimbardo and Boyd differentiate Lewin's view of time and highlight six time perspectives in particular: positive past orientation, negative past orientation, hedonistic present orientation, fatalistic present orientation, transcendental future orientation and open future orientation .

While people with a *positive past orientation* remember mostly the good things about their life so far, people with *negative past orientations* cannot detach themselves from bad experiences and memories, no matter how positive the present moment might look (Zimbardo et al., 2013). People who turn to *the present in* a predominantly *hedonistic way* love pleasure and fun in the here and now. They find it difficult to postpone rewards or gratifications. People who are *fatalistic* about *the present* believe that plans for the future are pointless because their lives are determined by others, by chance, or by higher powers anyway. The belief in higher powers also plays an important role for people who have a more *transcendental view of the future.* They believe in life after death and are usually very religious. *People with an open future orientation* are guided in their actions by desires, fears, hopes and expectations for the future. They prefer long-term rewards to short-term satisfaction of their desires and expectations. Future-oriented people are more willing to commit to causes that may have a later payoff. Their interest in the common good is greater than the urge to advance their own interests exclusively. Overall, they seem to be more successful, less aggressive, more empathic, and less depressed than people with other time perspectives.

Zimbardo and Boyd developed a questionnaire to capture interindividual differences in time perspectives, which has been tested in numerous studies and has proven to be valid and reliable in national studies (in the USA, Brazil, Greece, Italy, Sweden or Germany; e.g. Stolarski et al., 2011) and in international comparisons (Sircova et al., 2014).

For example, *Allyson Brothers* et al. (2014) examined associations between future orientation (as a positive perspective on an open future), optimistic life attitudes, and self-rated health in a smaller sample of 625 adults. Table 24.1 provides an excerpt from the findings.

Here again, a brief reading guide: The numbers in the columns indicate the correlations between the future orientations and the selected psychological variables (attitudes, opinions, assessments, etc.). In the column headers, the numbers indicate the variables that are named in the first column. The other numbers in the cells are so-called correlation coefficients, which can take on values from -1.00 to +1.00. A minus sign in front of the number indicates a negative correlation, a plus sign indicates a positive correlation. The asterisks after the numbers again mark the significance level, i.e. the level of the statistically significant correlation.

The message from the table is that people with a positive future orientation, i.e. who are convinced that the future is open and that many things are possible in the future, are more optimistic, more satisfied with their lives, more socially open-minded (extraverted), report fewer depressive symptoms and have a more positive assessment of their state of health.

Monika Buhl and *Daniela Lindner* (2009) present similar findings. The authors asked 1700 German adolescents about their time perspectives using a German version of Zimbardo and Boyd's questionnaire. Those who have optimistic ideas about their future are more satisfied with their lives than adolescents with other time perspectives; those who are optimistic about the future rate their relationship with their teachers and classmates more positively and like to assume responsibility in their living environment.

Environmental awareness and concern for the biosphere are also positively related to an open perspective on the future (Milfont & Gouveia, 2006). Meta-analyses comparing and summarizing several studies show that people who are future-oriented not only have a strong environmental awareness, but also behave in a more environmentally friendly way (e.g. Milfont et al., 2012).

Table 24.1 Statistical relationships between future orientation and selected psychological variables

	1	2	3	4	5	6
1. Future Orientation (Future is open)	–					
2. Optimistic Attitude to life	+.59*	–				
3. Life satisfaction	+.28*	+.37*	–			
4. Extraversion as a Personality trait	+.57*	+.46*	+.31*	–		
5 Depressive symptoms	−.25*	−.50*	−.43*	−.17*	–	
6. Self-assessed health status	+.28*	+.35*	+.22*	+.29*	−.24*	–

Note: * = significant ($p < .05$)
According to (Brothers et al., 2014)

In a study project conducted in Jena (Brecht et al., 2016),[1] 209 German adults were a) also asked about their time perspectives and b) asked to fill out a questionnaire about their own civil courageous behavior. The central finding of this small study can be summarized as follows: Not those people who are positively or negatively oriented towards the past and also not those who look at the present in a fatalistic way are willing to show civil courage. The people who show moral courage are mainly those who either turn to the present in a hedonistic way or who are guided in their expectations, desires and actions by an optimistic view of the future. Hedonists like to get involved spontaneously in situations where moral courage is required. The future-oriented plan more their engagement and commitment.

Zimbardo and Boyd (2009, p. 135ff.) come to similar conclusions: Future people take care of their health, they are diligent, planful, active problem solvers, successful, aware of their mortality, and a realistic hope dies last for them.

Perhaps, one could speculate, the future-oriented first develop a plan, a project, or a vision of a desired future, and then commit themselves with full dedication, great commitment, and courage to the realization of this vision.

This would then be the positive interpretation with which we once again look at the individual person in *Escher's* graphic, sitting on the outside steps of the building and looking into the distance. We see in this person a future-oriented person. Sure, that may or may not be the case. But since we are optimists, we consider this interpretation more likely than one that could impute fatalism or a negative view of the past to said individual.

However, we do not want to overinterpret *Escher's* graphic and leave it at the statement: To orient oneself towards a positive future, to have a vision of a peaceful, people- and climate-friendly world, can give life meaning and support. However, in order to also bring along the past-oriented and present-centered and not only future-focused people, there must be offers, visions or – let us simply say – utopias for a people-friendly future to orient oneself by.

> Looking into the future and developing positive visions of the future is not only healthy, but vital and of social relevance and urgency. Visionaries and optimists for the future do not need to see a doctor, they need to be in power.

[1] We would like to take this opportunity to thank Maria Brecht, Dorothea Gröninger, Tobias Husung, Lisa de Koster and Franziskus Kuhnt, who have taken up Zimbardo and Boyd's research approach in a nice project work to investigate the influence of diverse perspectives on time on civility (Brecht et al., 2016).

References

Brecht, M., Gröninger, D., Husung, T., de Koster, L., & Kuhnt, F. (2016). *Zeitperspektive und Zivilcourage. Der Einfluss der individuellen Zeitperspektive auf zivilcouragiertes Verhalten. Ein Studienprojekt.* Friedrich-Schiller-Universität (unveröffentlicht).

Brothers, A., Chui, H., Diehl, M., & Pruchno, R. (2014). Measuring future time perspective across adulthood: Development and evaluation of a brief multidimensional questionnaire. *The Gerontologist, 54*(6), 1075–1088.

Buhl, M., & Lindner, D. (2009). Zeitperspektiven im Jugendalter. Messung, Profile und Zusammenhänge mit Persönlichkeitsmerkmalen und schulischem Erleben. *Diskurs Kindheits-und Jugendforschung, 4*(2), 197–216.

Lewin, K. (1982). Feldtheorie des Lernens. In C.-F. Graumann (Hrsg.), *Kurt-Lewin-Werkausgabe* (Bd. 4). Bern: Huber (Original: 1942).

Milfont, T. L., & Gouveia, V. V. (2006). Time perspective and values: An exploratory study of their relations to environmental attitudes. *Journal of Environmental Psychology, 26*(1), 72–82.

Milfont, T. L., Wilson, J., & Diniz, P. (2012). Time perspective and environmental engagement: A meta-analysis. *International Journal of Psychology, 47*(5), 325–334.

Shoda, Y., Mischel, W., & Peake, P. K. (1990). Predicting adolescent cognitive and self-regulatory competencies from preschool delay of gratification: Identifying diagnostic conditions. *Developmental Psychology, 26*(6), 978.

Sircova, A., Van De Vijver, F. J., Osin, E., Milfont, T., Fieulaine, N., Kislali-Erginbilgic, A., Zimbardo, P. G., et al. (2014). A global look at time: A 24-country study of the equivalence of the Zimbardo time perspective inventory. *SAGE Open, 4*(1), 1–12.

Stolarski, M., Bitner, J., & Zimbardo, P. G. (2011). Time perspective, emotional intelligence and discounting of delayed awards. *Time & Society, 20*(3), 346–363.

Zimbardo, P. G., & Boyd, J. N. (1999). Putting time in perspective: A valid, reliable individual-differences metric. *Journal of Personality and Social Psychology, 77*(6), 1271–1288.

Zimbardo, P. G., & Boyd, J. N. (2009). *The time paradox – The new psychology of time.* New York, London, Toronto: Free Press.

Zimbardo, P. G., Sword, R., & Sword, R. (2013). *Die Zeitperspektiven-Therapie: Posttraumatische Belastungsstörungen behandeln.* Bern: Huber.

25

Stop at Utopia

Utopia? Yes, but as reason teaches, a utopia made indispensable by the new arrangement of balances in the world. It is either this or nothing. To survive, Europe is *doomed*, if you will, to develop instruments of a common foreign and security policy. Otherwise it will become – without wishing to offend anyone – Guatemala (Eco, 2012, p. 52; emphasis in the original).

In 2012, the Viennese publisher Paul Zsolnay published the book "Der europäische Landbote" (The European Courier) by *Robert Menasse*. The title of the book is an obvious allusion to *Georg Büchner's* pamphlet "Der Hessische Landbote" (The Hessian Courier), in which, after a concise introduction, the famous call "Peace to the huts! War on the palaces!" (Büchner, 1979, original: 1834) appears. Büchner intended his pamphlet to spark a revolution against those "up there." The final paragraph of the text reads:

You stirred up the earth for a long life, then you dig a grave for your tyrants. You built the castles of constraint, then you overthrow them, and build the house of liberty. Then ye may baptize your children freely with the water of life. And until the Lord calls you by his messengers and signs, watch and prepare yourselves in the spirit, and pray yourselves, and teach your children to pray, »Lord, break the rod of our drivers, and let your kingdom come to us-the kingdom of righteousness. Amen (Büchner, 1979, p. 186 f.).

A utopia is formulated, a vision that promises freedom and peace to those in the cottages after the revolution against those in the palaces.

W. Frindte, I. Frindte, *Support in Times of No Support*, https://doi.org/10.1007/978-3-658-38637-5_25

Robert Menasse aims at something similar with his book: he pleads for the abolition of national democracies and for a democratic new beginning for Europe:

> National democracy blocks post-national development, post-national development destroys democracy. Is this contradiction irreconcilable? If so, then one would have to decide against Europe … and for nationality conflicts, with all their consequences, which are eternally possible because they have historically already been real? No, the contradiction can of course be abolished – one just has to become aware of it first, then one has to make decisions that in the 21st century we finally really want to overcome the 19th century, then one has to become comfortable with the idea of forgetting democracy for the time being, of abolishing its institutions insofar as they are national institutions, and of dooming this model of a democracy that seems so sacred and precious to us because it is familiar to us. We must overthrow what will fall anyway if the European project succeeds. We must break this last taboo of enlightened society: that our democracy is a sacred good. And we must invent a new democracy (Menasse, 2012, p. 98).

We have quoted this long passage at such length because Menasse can also be misunderstood. *Heinrich August Winkler* used excerpts from the end of this passage, though without mentioning the last sentence, in an article in Die Zeit entitled "Schluss mit den Träumen" (Winkler, 2019, p. 8) to expose – we assume – *Robert Menasse*'s supposedly anti-democratic view. Winkler argues for strengthening the European role of national parliaments in order to combat the opponents of European integration in the long term. Menasse wants to do the same, only by other means, namely by strengthening *democratic* institutions at the *European* level. So please, read Menasse in full and quote the relevant passages exactly!

> Either Europe will once again, but this time peacefully, become the avant-garde of the world, or Europe will definitely prove to the world that lasting lessons cannot be learned from history, and that there is no humane way to put beautiful utopias into the law of reality (Menasse, 2012, p. 107).

A similar idea was developed by *Ulrike Guérot,* who in 2016 published a book entitled "Warum Europa eine Republik werden muss! Eine politische Utopie" (English version: Why Europe Should Become a Republic!: A Political Utopia, 2019).

Both Menasse and Guérot see the end of the European nation states and call for a constitution for a free, peaceful Europe of the regions and not a

Europe of nations or peoples. A European republic could comprise 50 to 60 regions. Such regions could be, for example, the Lower Rhine region, the Ore Mountains or the Elbe region. Catalonia or Scotland would perhaps also form their own regions. Each region would have the right to elect two representatives to the European Parliament by direct vote. Visions and ideas for so-called Euro-regions are already well developed. One can look at the possible maps of a Europe of regions on *Google*, for example (Regions of Europe, 2019). In a European Republic of Regions, the respective regions would have a great deal of autonomy. The cultural diversity of the regions could be preserved and political and economic cooperation could be promoted beyond the former national borders. The European Parliament would have the right of initiative, i.e. it could form a European government, pass laws, etc. And if, for example, two AfD members were elected to the European Parliament from the region of Saxony, they would be judged – by their voters – not by how much they support a Germany of Germans, but by whether and how they are committed to strengthening their Saxon region in a European republic.

The idea behind the idea of a European republic is simple. It is not the nations that emerged or were bloodily fought for in Europe, especially in the nineteenth century, that are the salt in our native soup. The regions in which we live are home to us. That's where the bread tastes special, that's where the football club we like plays, that's where we argue with our neighbors, that's where we feel at home. "Regional identity is the root of European identity" (Menasse, 2012, p. 88).

Such a plea or demand is obviously at odds with current political developments in Europe. In France, Germany, the Netherlands, Poland, Hungary and elsewhere in Europe, right-wing populist movements are not only gaining ground, but are on the verge of taking over government power or have already done so.

In this respect, one could rightly claim that *Robert Menasse* and *Ulrike Guérot* are in the good, highly respected, but ultimately failed ranks of the social utopians.[1] Nor is it only about the future of Europe and the visions of its democratic and regional shaping. It is about more.

---

[1] The term social utopians is used here in a broader sense than is usual in political philosophy. There, as a rule, those persons are called social utopians who designed and published ideas of a humane society, especially in France, the United Kingdom and Germany at the beginning of the nineteenth century. Among the most important representatives are Claude Henri de Saint-Simon, Charles Fourier, Pierre-Joseph Proudhon, Louis-Auguste Blanqui and Louis Blanc, the Scottish-born Robert Dale Owen and the German Wilhelm Weitling.

That is why Europe, left alone by the course of events (by a quasi-Hegelian decree according to which things must go as reality, which is rational, dictates), must either become Europe or disintegrate (Eco, 2012, p. 51).

As is well known, social utopias are more or less scientifically elaborated wish or fear images of future times. *Richard Saage* (1990), to whom we owe the redefinition of political utopia in scientific discourse, starts from the premise, following *Norbert Elias,* "…that political utopias are fictions of inner-worldly communities that condense into either a wish-image or a fear-image. Further, they are inextricably linked to social critique: Without the antithetical confrontation with what appears worthy of criticism in socio-political conditions, political utopia would lose its identity" (Saage 1990, p. 14).

The line of social utopians is long: it begins with the prophet *Yeshayahu* (known as *Isaiah*) and the utopia of the kingdom of peace: "They will turn their swords into plowshares and their spears into pruning hooks. For no nation shall lift up a sword against another, and they shall learn war no more" (Isaiah, 2:4–5). A similarly formulated vision is found in the prophet *Micah* (Micah, 4, 3–5). It stands as a bronze sculpture in front of the UN headquarters. This sculpture was created by the Soviet sculptor *Yevgeny Viktorovich Vuchetich*. In the 1980s, young peace-moving GDR citizens wore patches with the image of this sculpture. In doing so, they wanted to express their longing for peace and their criticism of the arms race, even if they had to reckon with repression by the GDR state power. But this vision is still fruitful and that is a good thing.

Plato's "Politeia" (380 B.C.) and his ideas about an ideal state or *Thomas Morus* and his novel "On the Best State of a Republic and on the New Island of Utopia" (Morus, 1970, original: 1516) are also worth remembering when it comes to philanthropic utopias and visions. One year before Luther slammed his theses on the church door in Wittenberg, Morus developed a utopia of a society in which money is abolished, a philanthropic work culture, universal care for the sick and elderly, and an equal education system determine how people live together (cf. Saage, 1997).[2] *Francis Bacon's* fragment "Nova Atlantis" (Bacon, 1984, original: 1627) should not be forgotten, which was published one year after its author's death and in which an ideal-typical, scientifically and technically developed society is described.

The small writing "Zum ewigen Frieden. Ein philosophischer Entwurf" (Perpetual Peace: A Philosophical Sketch) by *Immanuel Kant* (1795) can also

---

[2] Dieter Kraft (2013), however, points out that in *Utopia*, Morus does not sketch an ideal possibility, but a real-practical way to deal with the consequences of early capitalist developments in England.

easily be counted among the great visions. In six preliminary articles, Kant develops his idea of how lasting peace can be established in and between states. Preliminary Article 5, for example, states, "No state shall interfere violently in the constitution and government of another state" (Kant, 1977, p. 199). Kant's little writing was not without effect. International law, the founding of the united nations and today's bilateral dealings between states are likely to have been influenced by Kant's philosophical blueprint, even if his preliminaries are repeatedly and more often violated.

Six years before Kant's *Eternal Peace*, *Friedrich Schiller* also had a vision. In his inaugural lecture in Jena on 26 May 1789, the following remarkable sentence is found:

> "The barriers are broken which segregated states and nations in hostile egoism. All thinking minds are now linked by a cosmopolitan bond, and all the light of his century can now shine on the spirit of a newer Galileo and Erasmus" (Schiller, 1953, p. 21, original 1789). And the society that *Faust* envisages at the end of the tragedy is certainly also one of the great, often disputed and misinterpreted social utopias: "Such a throng I would like to see, Standing on free ground with free people" (Goethe, Faust. Der Tragödie zweiter Teil, 1973, p. 528).[3]

With a small historical leap and the neglect of important other utopians, *Karl Marx* and *Friedrich Engels* come into the game of utopias in the nineteenth century. In 1875, for example, Karl Marx formulates the following vision, among others, in his "Critique of the Gotha Program":

> In a higher phase of communist society, after the enslaving subordination of the individual to the division of labor, and therewith also the antithesis between mental and physical labor, has vanished; after labor has become not only a means of life but life's prime want; after the productive forces have also increased with the all-around development of the individual, and all the springs of cooperative wealth flow more abundantly – only then can the narrow horizon of bourgeois right be crossed in its entirety and society inscribe on its banners: From each according to his ability, to each according to his needs! (Marx, 1973, p. 21, original: 1875).

Crucial is the last sentence. It is often interpreted as Marx's idea of equality, justice and principles of distribution in a communist society (Busch, 2005) and would thus supposedly be dead. However, the idea is apparently not dead.

---

[3] Herfried Münkler (2011), among others, reports on how Faust's vision of a free people on free soil was repeatedly instrumentalized for political purposes, whether during the Nazi era or under socialism.

It pops up every now and then as a description or as a metaphor, for example, when pondering a just social policy in a social market economy (e.g., Opielka, 2003), when philosophers reflect on the moral survival of humanity (e.g., Schmied-Kowarzik, 1995), or when sociologists analyze post-growth societies (e.g., Mayert, 2018). We like this sentence. But it would be better if it could also be realized.

In 1918 *Ernst Bloch* published "Der Geist der Utopie" (The Spirit of Utopia) and years later "Das Prinzip Hoffnung" (The Principle of Hope) (1954–1959). *Theodor W. Adorno* considered Bloch's book "Principle of Hope" not a good book, it was poor in intellectual content (Schiller, 2019). Yet it is Bloch's main work, in which he seeks to answer such crucial questions as: Who are we? Where do we come from and where are we going? Bloch, for whom, incidentally, *Faust* is the supreme exemplar of a utopian man, wrote *The Principle of Hope* between 1938 and 1947 in exile in the United States. His point was to show that the open social systems of the (then) present require a new way of thinking and feeling in order to anticipate the future possibilities of present realities. Hoping, according to Bloch, is an active activity and can be taught. Every human being is capable of learning to hope and to work towards future goals.

"As long as," writes Bloch (1985, p. 3), "man lies in trouble, private as well as public existence are permeated by daydreams; by daydreams of a better life than the one he has had so far."

Quasi as a reaction or answer to Bloch's Principle of Hope, *Hans Jonas* publishes "Das Prinzip Verantwortung" (The Imperative of Responsibility" in 1979, a plea for ethical action in the technological age, the age in which humanity is capable of destroying itself and the whole earth. And in 1975, the American *Ernest Callenbach* published his far-sighted work *Ecotopia,* in which he develops an ecological vision that could today be the guideline for our dealings with nature and ourselves (German translation: Callenbach, 1978). The list of well-known social visions and utopias could be continued and enriched with many a fiction example. Among the dark utopias, the dystopias, are certainly the novels "The War of the Worlds" and the "The Time Machine" by *Herbert George Wells,* "The Iron Heel" by *Jack London* or "Brave New World" by *Aldous Huxley.*

Volker Braun is also worth thinking about. He turned 80 in 2019 and has lost nothing of his dialectical thinking. Suhrkamp Verlag published a collection of selected speeches and writings to mark his 80th birthday (Braun, 2019). One, a *speech on the future,* delivered on 3 November 2010 at the Ernst-Bloch-Zentrum Ludwigsfelde, is particularly worth reading. After criticizing the cart we humans have driven into the muck of the financial and climate crises, Braun searches for the future and finds future spaces. He peers into a museum of the future, where the "ideological junk of the put-offs" is on display. He enters a dungeon of the future filled with melted glaciers, nuclear repositories, and the debts that will have to be paid in the future. He is staying in a workshop of the future that not everyone is allowed into. Here, "crude realities" are experimented with to create the dreamed-of. And then there is a future into which one can only catch a narrow glimpse. But one sees nothing, at least "nothing real as in the other chambers, only what can be." The future is open. Futures need to be rethought because the thing "calls for turmoil."

Yes, turmoil, revolution or just reform? In 2017, a book caused a stir in academic circles that explored *real utopias* and ways out of capitalism. *Erik Olin Wright*, a US sociologist who died in January 2019, developed alternative conceptions to capitalism and the design of post-capitalist societies. He was a campaigner for the introduction of an unconditional basic income and advocated for political justice, radical democracy and for real, feasible utopias.

> Rather than taming capitalism through reforms "from above" or smashing it by means of a revolutionary rupture, the core idea is that capitalism should be eroded by building emancipatory alternatives in the spaces and fissures within capitalist economies while struggling to defend and expand those spaces (Wright, 2017, p. 11).[4]

According to *Erik Olin Wright,* two global trends could intensify the spaces and cracks in capitalism: climate change and the information revolution. Both trends challenge capitalist states. Public goods must be provided to respond to climate change, and new policies are needed to address the impending marginalization of workers engaged in traditional labor activities. In this context, Wright argues, popular mobilization in the struggle for democratic-egalitarian forms of life could be promising. The transformation of capitalism into a democratic-egalitarian society would indeed take place within capitalism, primarily and initially in marginal areas and free spaces that are withdrawn from the profit interest of capital but protected by the state. Such free spaces can be found, for example, in many parts of civil society, in non-capitalist economic organizations or in democratic cooperative associations of trade unions and civic groups.

Such ideas and visions about the ways out of capitalism and about the feasibility of social change also exist in Germany. A well-known example is the

---

[4] The original edition was published in 2010 with the title "Envisioning Real Utopias", Brooklyn: Verso Books. The quotation reproduced here is a translation from the preface to the German edition of 2017.

Futurzwei Foundation for *Future Sustainability*, which is committed to a "grandchild-friendly, open society" and is headed by *Harald Welzer* (e.g. Welzer, 2019). Addressing grandchildren and their future is also *Dieter Klein*[5] with his book "Das Morgen tanzt im Heute. Transformation in Capitalism and Beyond it" (Klein, 2013), when he pleads for a "democratic green socialism".

Ulrich Beck, whom we have already quoted in several places, also developed such ideas. Although he repeatedly insisted (Beck, 2002) that the question of who will emerge as the winner from the Second Modernity is open in principle, he sees in the "counter-power of the cosmopolitan left" an essential force for the success of a cosmopolitanism worth striving for.

> Cosmopolitanism is, in other words, the next big idea to come after the historically worn-out ideas of nationalism, communism, socialism, neoliberalism, and this idea *could* make possible the improbable that humanity, without reverting to barbarism, will survive the 21st century" (Beck, 2002, p. 16; emphasis in original). At its core, cosmopolitanism means "the recognition of the otherness of others (ibid., p. 412).

That is utopian and sounds very abstract. *Slavoj Žižek,* who likes to claim to be a pessimist and considers global capitalism to be the real threat to our civilization (Žižek, 2018; original: 2017), is more concrete. We take the liberty of quoting him at length:

> The basic gesture of the West should not be the witnessing of some highly dubious and patronizing 'respect' for the Other; rather, we should struggle for the emancipatory dimensions within our own tradition (the heritage of equality, social justice, and so on) that provide strong arguments against colonialism and racism. Moreover, to establish the link between the left in the West and the poor and displaced of the Third World, it is crucial to overcome the tensions between Western modernity and Third World anti-modernity (even if the latter appears in the guise of anti-imperialism). This link can only come about through a double self-criticism: One side (that of the protesting left in the West) must abandon its obsession with middle-class cultural and sexual problems, and the other (that of the Third World) must recognize cultural and sexual modernization as the only way to escape neocolonialist exploitation-in other words, it

---

[5] Dieter Klein was Professor of Economic Foundations of Politics at Humboldt University in Berlin until his retirement. He was one of the founders of the "Modern Socialism Theory" project, which advocated alternative paths of development even before the end of the GDR in 1989.

must learn the hard lesson that antimodernism ultimately promotes new forms of imperialism (Žižek, 2018, p. 59 f.).[6]

> Real utopias could be feasible and successful if they transcend the limits of what has been done so far, start from the free spaces of the present, formulate alternatives for a better future and are put into perspective by innovative minorities.

Serge Moscovici, whose theory of social change through minorities we have already mentioned once in Chap. 13 (Moscovici, 1979), assumes that under certain conditions a social minority can trigger fundamental changes in attitudes and opinions among the members of a social majority and thus important processes of social change: A minority wishing to exert social influence must first adopt a recognizably alternative standpoint to that of the majority. This alternative point of view must be held by the minority in a united manner and over a longer period of time. It must therefore be united, reckon with the time factor and be patient in the process. By consistently presenting new information and alternative world views, the minority creates individual cognitive conflicts (cognitive dissonance) on the side of the majority individuals. Indeed, they might wonder why the minority, in its socially weak position, holds opinions that differ from those of the majority and creates dissent with the majority. Maybe there could be something to what the minority keeps putting forward? And so not only will the majority members be unsettled and stimulated to think about the dissent between minority and majority opinions, but over time more and more majority members may switch to the minority position. Especially when the minorities, with their alternative views, anticipate developments and trends that correspond to the current zeitgeist, the willingness of the majority to perceive and take seriously the arguments of the minority increases. The Greens, for example, succeeded in this in the 1970s and 1980s by vehemently, consistently and persistently drawing attention to the need for an ecological turnaround – even before the other political parties and movements.

Who could be the innovative, visionary minorities of today? To find a vague answer to this question, let us return to *Robert Menasse* and *Ulrike Guérot* and enrich our return with an example: In the spirit of the earlier social utopians, both criticize the existing conditions (here in the EU and in Europe) and postulate (in the sense of a wishful thinking) the disappearance of the nation-state and a Europe without borders. Menasse and Guérot have identified the

---

[6] The quote is a translation from the German publication.

citizens in the European states as the actors or subjects of these social changes. This means that the disappearance of the nation-state will, from their (utopian point of view), not be a change from "above", but one from "below".

Even if such changes are not to be expected in the near future, one could speculate by means of an empirical example and develop visions without immediately being sent to the doctor. We draw on the results of a study we conducted in summer 2015 to analyze attitudes towards Muslims and Islam (Frindte & Dietrich, 2017). Using a standardized questionnaire, 975 German adults were interviewed. This was a non-representative sample. The questionnaire contained various subscales that captured authoritarian beliefs (see Chap. 11), positive attitudes towards Muslims, identification with Europe, educational attainment, and the use of classical and digital media for political information.

The findings of the 975 respondents were evaluated by means of a cluster analysis, among other things, in order to identify statistically relevant groupings that differ with regard to the significant variables.

Cluster analysis yielded four homogeneous clusters that were readily interpretable.[7]

Figure 25.1 illustrates the results.

We interpret this figure in the announced speculative mode: in our total sample there is a not small grouping (grouping 4), which includes 24.7% of the persons from the non-representative (!) total sample and which is characterized by the following features, especially in relation to grouping 1 (grouping 1 with 17.6%): The respondents from grouping 4 have the lowest values in authoritarian beliefs and they have a higher level of education than the persons from the other groupings; they inform themselves mainly via the websites of traditional print media (Der Spiegel, Die Zeit) and not via classic television or social media; they have very positive attitudes towards Muslims and they identify relatively strongly with Europe.

The last finding makes us optimistic, since we interpret it in the sense of the utopia of the disappearance of the nation state and a Europe without borders

---

[7] We have already briefly introduced cluster analysis in Chap. 14. It is a statistical method for data reduction by forming groups or clusters. The members of a cluster should be as homogeneous as possible with regard to their characteristic values and the members of different clusters should be as heterogeneous as possible. A subsequent discriminant analysis shows that the grouping variables are significantly suitable to distinguish the – in our case – found four clusters. The classification result showed that in the first cluster all cases can be classified correctly, in the second cluster 92.3%, in the third cluster 94.3% and in the fourth cluster again all cases. Discriminant analysis, like cluster analysis, is a multivariate method for analyzing group or class differences. With this method, it is possible to examine two or more groups, taking into account several variables, and determine how these groups differ. Unlike cluster analysis, however, discriminant analysis is not an exploratory (search) procedure, but a confirmatory procedure (test).

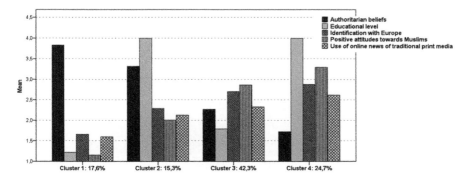

Fig. 25.1 Statistical groupings of Europe-oriented and less Europe-oriented people. (After Frindte & Dietrich, 2017)

advocated by *Menasse* and *Guérot*. There are still educated and politically informed people who have a positive view of ethnic minorities, refugees in general and Muslims in particular, reject authoritarian and power-oriented social structures and identify with Europe. This group of people does not appear to be particularly large – measured against the total population; it comprises just under a quarter of the total sample. But that is not what matters. Social change is initiated and realized by minorities. Here we fully agree with *Serge Moscovici* (1979). But it should not and must not be the right-wing populist minorities who are currently striving for social change in their own interests.

Perhaps the innovative, visionary minorities are precisely those who stand up for tolerance, openness, cultural diversity, foreigners and refugees, who know how to defend themselves against xenophobia and democratic hostility, and who hold fast to a Europe without borders. It is about them, it must be about them. They are the actors of the future and the future shapers of a peaceful and humane European continent. It is their personal commitment, their determination, their cohesion over time and their future orientation that count. The young people of *Fridays-for-Future* have what it takes to be innovative minorities who can initiate a positive future.

> You don't have to be called a "chubby college dropout" if you criticize capitalism and demand a life without exploitation, oppression, and violence. You don't have to apologize for your own Asperger's syndrome if you think climate change is an existential crisis. One is not anti-democratic if one demands the end of national democracies in Europe and a European-constituted democracy. The times of the great real utopias of a humane and peaceful future are not over. They are only just beginning.

Or, as John Lennon sang years ago:
"Imagine all the people
Living life in peace…"
(John Lennon, 1971).

References

Bacon, F. (1984). *Neu-Atlantis*. Berlin: Akademie (Original: 1627).

Beck, U. (2002). *Macht und Gegenmacht im globalen Zeitalter*. Frankfurt a. M.: Suhrkamp. In *English version: Power in the global age: A new global political economy*. Cambridge, Oxford: Polity.

Bloch, E. (1985). *Das Prinzip Hoffnung*. Bloch Gesamtausgabe, (Bd. 5). Frankfurt a. M.: Suhrkamp (Original: 1954–1959).

Braun, V. (2019). *Die Verlagerung des geheimen Punkts*. Berlin: Suhrkamp.

Büchner, G. (1979). *Dichtungen*. Leipzig: Reclam (Original: 1834).

Busch, U. (2005). Schlaraffenland – Eine linke Utopie? *Utopie kreativ, 181*, 978–991.

Callenbach, E. (1978). *Ökotopia – Notizen und Reportagen von William Weston aus dem Jahre 1999*. Berlin: Rotbuch (original: 1975, Ecotopia : The notebooks and reports of William Weston).

Eco, U. (2012). *Im Krebsgang voran*. München: Deutscher Taschenbuch Verlag.

Frindte, W., & Dietrich, N. (Eds.). (2017). *Muslime, Flüchtlinge und Pegida. Sozialpsychologische und kommunikationswissenschaftliche Studien in Zeiten globaler Bedrohungen*. Wiesbaden: Springer VS.

Goethe, J. W. (1973). Faust. Der Tragödie erster Teil. *Berliner Ausgabe,* (Bd. 8). Berlin: Aufbau Verlag (Original: 1808).

Guérot, U. (2016). *Warum Europa eine Republik werden muss! Eine politische Utopie*. Bonn: Dietz.

Guérot, U. (2019). *Why Europe should become a republic!: A political utopia*. Dietz.

Kant, I. (1977). *Zum ewigen Frieden. Ein philosophischer Entwurf*. Werke in zwölf Bänden. Frankfurt a. M.: Suhrkamp (Original: 1795).

Klein, D. (2013). *Das Morgen tanzt im Heute Transformation im Kapitalismus und über ihn hinaus*. Hamburg: VSA Verlag.

Kraft, D. (2013). Über den Begriff der Utopie. Verständnis und Missverständnis einer verbogenen Kategorie. In H. Kopp (Hrsg.), *Wovon wir träumen müssen … Marxismus und Utopie* (S. 83–106). Hamburg: Laika.

Lennon, J. (1971). Imagine. Songtext aus dem Album „*Imagine*", Songwriter: John Lennon. © Apple Records, EMI Group, Universal Music.

Marx, K. (1973). Randglossen zum Programm der deutschen Arbeiterpartei. *Marx-Engels Werke,* (Bd. 19). Berlin: Dietz (Original: 1975).

Mayert, A. (2018). Marx, Ökomarxismus und Postwachstumstheorie. *Ethik und Gesellschaft*, (1). Quelle: http://ethik-und-gesellschaft.de/ojs/index.php/eug/article/view/1-2018-art-7. Accessed: 12. Juni 2019.

Menasse, R. (2012). *Der Europäische Landbote: Die Wut der Bürger und der Friede Europas oder Warum die geschenkte Demokratie einer erkämpften weichen muss.* Wien: Paul Zsolnay.

Morus, T. (1970). *Der utopische Staat.* Übersetzt und herausgegeben von K. J. Heinisch. Reinbek: Rowohlt.

Moscovici, S. (1979). *Sozialer Wandel durch Minoritäten.* München: Urban und Schwarzenberg. . English Version: Social Influence and Social Change. London: Academic.

Münkler, H. (2011). *Die Deutschen und ihre Mythen* (2. Aufl.). Reinbeck bei Hamburg: Rowohlt Taschenbuch.

Opielka, M. (2003). Was spricht gegen die Idee eines aktivierenden Sozialstaats. *neue praxis, 6,* 543–557.

Regionen Europas. (2019). *Eurotopia – Visionen für eine Organisation mit 60 Regionen.* https://regionen-europas.work/eurotopia.html. Accessed: 26. Juni 2019.

Saage, R. (1990). *Das Ende der politischen Utopie?* Frankfurt a. M.: Suhrkamp.

Saage, R. (1997). Zum Verhältnis von Individuum und Staat in Thomas Morus Utopia. *Utopie kreativ, 85*(86), 134–145.

Schiller, F. (1953). *Was heißt und zu welchem Ende studiert man Universalgeschichte? Die Jenaer Antrittsvorlesung von Friedrich Schiller.* Jena: Jenaer Reden und Schriften (Original: 1789), Heft 1.

Schiller, H.-E. (2019). Tod und Utopie: Ernst Bloch, Georg Lukács. In R. Klein, J. Kreuzer, & S. Müller-Doohm (Hrsg.), *Adorno-Handbuch.* Stuttgart: Metzler.

Schmied-Kowarzik, W. (1995). Unsere gesellschaftliche Wirklichkeit und die Utopie sittlichen Überlebens der Menschheit. In H. Lenk & H. Poser (Hrsg.), *Neue Realitäten. Herausforderung der Philosophie: XVI. Deutscher Kongress für Philosophie Berlin 20–24. September 1993* (S. 339–353). Berlin: de Gruyter.

Welzer, H. (2019). Alles könnte anders sein. Eine Gesellschaftsutopie für freie Menschen. Frankfurt a. M.: Fischer.

Winkler, H. A. (19. Juni 2019). Schluss mit den Träumen. Die Zeit, Nr. 26.

Wright, E. O. (2017). *Reale Utopien. Wege aus dem Kapitalismus.* Berlin: Suhrkamp.

Žižek, S. (2018). *Der Mut der Hoffnungslosigkeit.* Frankfurt a. M.: Fischer. English original: The courage of hopelessness - a year of acting dangerously (2017). London: Allen Lane.

26

Look Up Eco – A Virtual Conversation

WF/IF: Buongiorno, Signor Eco. Or do you wish us to address you Professore or cher Commandeur de la Légion d'Honneur?

UE: It has always impressed me "how the French, when interviewing a writer, an artist, a politician, avoid the use of reductive forms of address such as professor, eminence or minister. There are people whose intellectual capital is indicated by the name with which they sign their ideas" (Eco, in: Martini & Eco, 1999, p. 21).

WF/IF: Thank you. We like to stay with "Signor Eco". We are of course very pleased that you have agreed to be taken at our word.

UE: "Certainly, but I have decided that the best way to express my approval is precisely not to censure" (Eco, 2016, p. 16).

WF/IF: Signor Eco, we have taken the liberty of using your novel *the Foucault pendulum,* and in particular said pendulum, as a metaphor to search for social psychological traces that can help us to learn more about people's need for meaning and support. Have we understood your novel in your sense and what do you, dear Signor Eco, think of our idea?

UE: "Here we have the case of a reader who is educated, but who, first, does not know how to read a novel as a whole, but takes the various parts one at a time; second, has no sense of irony; and third, does not distinguish between the author's opinion and his own" (Eco, 2016, p. 189).

WF/IF: Oh, your novel *the Foucault pendulum* has not only been praised beyond all measure. It has been read as a witty and sophisticated parody of conspiracy theorists, but it has also been called esoteric writing and an outmoded critique of the humanities. Personal and unsympathetic attacks on the author, i.e. you, could also be found in the vastness of the internet

(continued)

Reminder: All quotes from Umberto Eco that we use in this book were not taken from original Italian publications, but from German translations of Eco's works.

(continued)

UE:	"I have suffered so often from the accusation that I want to appear likeable at all costs that it now fills me with pride and virtuous satisfaction to discover myself to be unlikeable" (Eco, 2012, p. 14).
WF/IF:	But, dear Signor Eco, once again to our impertinence, to take *the Foucault pendulum* as the thematic anchor, so to speak, for our own literary enterprise: In more than 750 pages, you unfold a crime satire about conspiracy theories, esotericism, and philosophical chaos. Every detail in the book, as in a mosaic, leads to a new track, is charged with meaning and acquires new significance by being linked to other details. I guess that's what you call intertextuality in your circles. Have we read your novel according to your intentions?
UE:	"You were quite right. Every opportunity becomes significant when you connect it to another. The connection changes one's perspective. It makes one think that all appearances in the world, every voice, every word written or spoken, do not mean what they seem to mean, but speak of a mystery. The criterion is simple: one must suspect, always suspect. Secret messages can also be read out of a one-way sign" (Eco, 1991, p. 442).
WF/IF:	It will probably be the same with the search for fixed points in our life. Sometimes we find a fixed point and this leads us to another, this again to another and so on; a one-way sign can be a fixed point, but it can also be experienced as a threat by free citizens with their demands for free travel.
UE:	"The false is precisely the notion of 'this point', my friend" (Eco, 1990, p. 243).
WF/IF:	Instead of fixed points, one could speak of the search for sense. What would be the sense of life then?
UE:	"In the attempt to grasp an ultimate, unattainable sense, one accepts an inexorable slipping away of sense" (Eco, 1991, p. 15).
WF/IF:	That we humans are looking for support and security in a time and a world that seem to be threatened in many ways cannot be denied. Xenophobia, fear of refugees, right-wing populism, fake news, climate change, the threat of large and small wars and much more are among the signs with which we try to describe the threats. Speaking of xenophobia, in one of your occasional writings you write, we'll allow ourselves a quote, "Obviously, one cannot do without the enemy. The figure of the enemy cannot be abolished by processes of civilization. The need for it is innate even in gentle and peaceful man" (Eco, 2014, p. 27).
UE:	"Whether meant as a joke or seriously, these remarks were by no means plucked out of the air. That we were moving in reverse had, after all, already become clear after the fall of the Berlin Wall, when the political geography of Europe and Asia changed radically" (Eco, 2012, p. 11). "This, however, is not the end of the story of regressions, and the beginning of the third millennium was particularly fruitful. To take just a few examples: After the 50 years of the Cold War, we had the triumphant return of the hot shooting war with Afghanistan and Iraq […]. Resurgent have been the Christian fundamentalists […]. Triumphantly returned has been anti-Semitism […]" (ibid., p. 12). "It almost seems as if history, fatigued by the leaps it has made over the last two millennia, is rewinding in on itself to return to the comfortable glories of TRADITION" (ibid., p. 13; emphasis in original).

(continued)

(continued)

WF/IF:	"Celebrations of the glories of tradition" – The new nationalist and right-wing populist movements and aspirations come immediately to mind, whether in Italy, in Germany, Poland, the UK, Hungary or the US, fueled and staged in loud and angry voices by the respective populists-in-chief and many others.
UE:	"But one knows that the more frustrated one feels, the more he is seized by a delusion of omnipotence and a desire for revenge" (Eco, 1991, p. 19). "The populist invokes the popular will, but the 'people' as the expression of a single will and unified sentiments, as a quasi-natural force embodying morality and history, does not exist" (Eco, 2012, p. 115).
WF/IF:	To address another issue: Conspiracy theories are back in vogue. We wouldn't have thought so. Viktor Orbán believes, at least that's what he's shouting to the masses, that Hungarian-born US philanthropist and billionaire *George Soros* intends to destroy the ethnic homogeneity (whatever that is) of the Magyars. Donald Trump thinks twitter, controlled by the democrats, is censoring his tweets. Members of the AfD see conspiracy theorists at work behind the accusations that the AfD has received dubious donations, etc. etc.
UE:	"The plot syndrome is as old as the world […]. The psychology of the plot arises from the fact that the most obvious explanations of many worrying things do not satisfy us, and not infrequently because it hurts us to accept them […]. In a sense, the suspicion-led interpretation frees us from our own accountability, because it makes us believe that there is a secret behind what worries us, and that hiding this secret is a plot to our detriment. Believing in the plot is a bit like believing in a miraculous cure, except that with the latter one tries to explain not a threat but an inexplicable stroke of luck" (Eco, 2016, p. 79 f.).
WF/IF:	In our book we have used, among other things, the Marxian metaphor of the *extended body* to refer to relevant environments in which we humans search for support. The social media that we use every day, we have also en passant attributed to this extended body. What do you think about this?
UE:	"The cell phone is the natural extension of his corporeality, the extension of his ears, his eyes, and often his penis" (Eco, 2016, p. 59).
WF/IF:	Yes, then we would be on the subject of medial realities and medial communities, which, we suppose, may well be among the fixed points to which we try to cling.
UE:	"You can have thousands of contacts on Facebook, but in the end, if you're not completely full of it, you realize you're not really in touch with flesh-and-blood people, and then you look for opportunities to hang out and share experiences with people who think like you do. And as Woody Allen recommended, I can't remember where: If you want to meet girls, you have to go to piano concerts. Not rock concerts where you're yelling toward the stage and you don't know who's next to you, but the concerts with symphonies and chamber music where you can socialize during the intermission" (Eco, 2016, p. 157).
WF/IF:	Our book is a collage. For this we have also drawn on our own earlier works and, so to speak, quoted or copied ourselves. What do you think, dear Signor Eco, of such methods?

(continued)

(continued)

UE:	"… in the end, a good lecturer always notices when a text has been copied indiscriminately, and smells the forgery – while, I repeat, a well-chosen copy is well worthy of praise" (Eco, 2016, p. 48).
WF/IF:	This naturally raises the question of the ethics of human interaction and of your own ethical principles.
UE:	"It is obvious that the appeal to human dignity is a principle that establishes a common way of thinking and acting: never to use the other as a means to an end, to respect his inviolability in all circumstances and always, to see in every person at all times an unavailable and inviolable being" (Eco, in: Martini & Eco, 1999, p. 79 f.).
WF/IF:	At the end of our virtual meeting, allow us to ask you about the motives that drove you to write all these inspiring and exciting things.
UE:	"… to leave a message in a bottle, so that what you believed in or what you found beautiful is also believed or found beautiful by those born after you" (Eco, in: Martini & Eco, 1999, p. 89).
WF/IF:	Dear Signor Eco, we thank you from the bottom of our hearts for the stimulating virtuality and wish you, well, rest, due honor and peace.
UE:	"But the whole thing is obviously not my problem" (Eco, in: Martini & Eco, 1999, p. 63). "So I might as well stay here, wait, and look at the hill. It is so beautiful" (Eco, 1990, p. 754).

References

Eco, U. (1990). *Das Foucaultsche Pendel*. Berlin: Verlag Volk und Welt.

Eco, U. (1991). *Über Spiegel und andere Phänomen*. München: Deutscher Taschenbuch Verlag.

Eco, U. (1999). Wenn der andere ins Spiel kommt, beginnt die Ethik. In C. M. Martini & U. Eco (Eds.), *Woran glaubt, wer nicht glaubt* (pp. 82–93). München: Deutscher Taschenbuch Verlag.

Eco, U. (2012). *Im Krebsgang voran*. München: Deutscher Taschenbuch Verlag.

Eco, U. (2014). *Die Fabrikation des Feindes*. München: Hanser.

Eco, U. (2016). *Pape Satàn*. München: Hanser.

Further Reading

Becker, J. (1969). *Jakob der Lügner*. Berlin: Aufbau Verlag.

Berliner Zeitung.de. (2017). Bundeszentrale für politische Bildung. Krüger vor Wahl besorgt über Stimmung im Osten.https://www.berliner-zeitung.de/politik/bundeszentrale-fuer-politische-bildung-krueger-vor-wahl-besorgt-ueber-stimmung-im-osten-28461828. Accessed: 24. Okt. 2018.

Bpb (2016).*Arbeitslose und Arbeitslosenquote*. Bundeszentrale für politische Bildung.http://www.bpb.de/nachschlagen/zahlen-und-fakten/soziale-situation-in-deutschland/61718/arbeitslose-und-arbeitslosenquote. Accessed: 6. Dez. 2016.

Esch, T. (2014). Die neuronale Basis von Meditation und Achtsamkeit. *Sucht, 60*(1), 21–28.

Fletcher, G. J. (2015). Accuracy and bias of judgments in romantic relationships.*Current Directions in. Psychological Science, 24*(4), 292–297.

Frindte, W. (1990). Neonazis hausgemacht- sozialpsychologische Anmerkungen zum gesellschaftlichen Wandel in der DDR – Am Beispiel des Umgangs mit jugendlichen Subkulturen und Neofaschismus. *Päd-Extra & Demokratische Erziehung, 3*(6), 29–33.

Jonas, H. (1979). *Das Prinzip Verantwortung. Frankfurt a. M.: Insel Verlag (English version 1984: The Imperative of Responsibility)*. The University of Chicago Press.

Kuhn, T. (1962). *The Structure of Scientific Revolutions*. Chicago: The University of Chicago Press.

Lamberty, P. (2017). Don't trust anyone: Verschwörungsdenken als Radikalisierungs beschleuiniger?*Journal Exit-Deutschland. Zeitschrift für Deradikalisierung und demokratische Kultur, 5*, 73–80.

© The Author(s), under exclusive license to Springer Fachmedien Wiesbaden GmbH, part of Springer Nature 2022
W. Frindte, I. Frindte, *Support in Times of No Support*,
https://doi.org/10.1007/978-3-658-38637-5

Luhmann, N. (1984).*Soziale Systeme*. Frankfurt a. M.: Suhrkamp Taschenbuch. English version: Social Systems. Stanford: Stanford University Press (1996).

The Guardian. (2017). Trump hails 'most successful first 100 days in history.https:// www.theguardian.com/us-news/video/2017/apr/29/donald-trump-hails-most-successful-first-100-days-in-history-video. Accessed: 18. März 2019.

Welt.de. (2018). Darum will Nahles die Autoindustrie zur Chefsache machen.https:// www.welt.de/politik/deutschland/article186321180/Automobilindustrie-Bundesregierung-prueft-Nahles-Vorschlag-einer-Industriepartnerschaft.html. Accessed: 20. Mai 2019.

Zeit Online. (1998). Hass, nur Hass. Im Osten gehört die Gewalt von rechts zum Alltag.https://www.zeit.de/1998/38/199838.rechtsextremismu.xml.   Accessed: 10. März 2019.

Zeit Online. (1999). Die importierte Moral.https://www.zeit.de/1999/15/199915. ostmoral_.xml. Accessed: 10. März 2019.

Author Index

Subject Index

© The Author(s), under exclusive license to Springer Fachmedien Wiesbaden GmbH, part of Springer Nature 2022
W. Frindte, I. Frindte, *Support in Times of No Support*,
https://doi.org/10.1007/978-3-658-38637-5

Printed by Printforce, the Netherlands